Dedication

*With love and admiration for
my wonderful wife
and best friend
Sandy*

and

the monuments of our lives

*Son: Richard Frederick Dauch
Son: David Charles Dauch
Daughter: Teri Ellen (Dauch) Gigot
Daughter: Jane Ellen (Dauch) Harvey*

*in recognition of their devotion, love, support, and
Dauch determination!*

FOREWORD

In my northwest Detroit home hangs a plaque recognizing my work in establishing Chrysler's new Jefferson North assembly plant. The award holds half a brick from the old plant that served Chrysler for 65 years. The other half hangs 20 miles away in Dick Dauch's home. His plaque, like mine, was a gift from the United Auto Workers and plant management. Like mine, it bears only two names, his and mine.

Unionized workers don't present awards to management very often, but Dick is an unusual manager. He bit into the concepts of teamwork, worker communication, industrial democracy, and commitment to excellence like a bulldog and would not turn them loose. At the same time he believes manufacturers must think globally, must examine themselves constantly, and must expect manufacturing to be tough—a two-fisted battle, he calls it.

Dick operates at only one speed: flat out. I know. For years, my job was to keep up. His book moves at the same pace. In it, manufacturing people around the world will find a wealth of management tips and insights about product development, production, and quality. The chronicle of Chrysler's manufacturing renaissance is really just a bonus.

I met Dick Dauch in 1980, right after Chrysler's loan guarantee was approved. We in the UAW played a major role in securing that guarantee and the company's survival. In the process, many UAW members made concessions, and, like management's, our commitment was enormous.

When a small group that included me met in Lee Iacocca's office to discuss the next steps, three serious questions emerged. What do we do next? How do we move toward profitability? How do we thank the American people? We agreed product quality was the one answer to these questions, and the company's union-management joint quality product improvement program was born.

Top management, along with the top union leaders, articulated and directed the program. Union and management leaders toured Chrysler plants and offices to deliver the quality message directly to the troops.

They listened, and they were impressed. Along with Dick and other Chrysler top executives, I preached to managers and workers together that no quality means no sales; no sales means no jobs. Never before had our workers seen management and labor saying the same thing in the same room at the same time. Some long-time union members could not believe it. I asked them to "lend us your hand to produce quality products. If you will not do that, then give us your goodwill. If you can't do that, then get the hell out of the way so we can take care of business." It sounded like Chrysler's new slogan, "Lead, follow, or get out of the way."

About 160 meetings like this were held across the U.S. and Canada, and Dick Dauch missed but half a dozen. I could tell he and I shared the goal of saving Chrysler, jobs, and worker dignity. His passionate commitment to quality and the worker was inspiring. But leadership, whether management or union, could not do all the thinking, as we both realized. Worker feedback was a critical piece in the profitability puzzle.

Workers began letting management know when trouble was coming, where the problems were, and how to fix them. The self-directed teams and modern operating agreements jointly developed by management and the union chipped away at the attitude that the foreman's job was to crack the whip over workers who did what they were told, and only what they were told. We formed teams of 10 to 15 people to ask for ideas, and the ideas came fast and furious. Quality improved, productivity increased, flexibility developed, profits reappeared.

Dick went into the plants, walking the line and talking to people. He wanted to see for himself why a part wouldn't fit or why paint was a problem in an operation. He was my problem-solver, as I was his. Trading favors helps. Common goals are critical. The level of communication and cooperation he and I enjoyed could be a model for other managers and union leaders. Letting your management counterpart know when trouble is heading his way can keep costs down, production rolling, quality up, and gray hairs off both your heads. Dick also helped re-establish the critical employee training and skill development vital to Chrysler's resurgence.

Since my retirement, I tell my students at the University of Detroit/ Mercy College, where I lecture, that practical knowledge is what faces and conquers the challenge of day-to-day production. Those who confronted the struggle, made the mistakes, fought the battles, and gathered the rewards of the marketplace have that knowledge. Members of this small, elite group don't pass along their secrets very often, but Dick's manufacturing knowledge and passion is all set forth here, in these pages.

Marc Stepp
International Vice President (Retired)
United Auto Workers, Chrysler Department
Detroit, Michigan

ACKNOWLEDGMENTS

I am deeply indebted to many people for their assistance in preparing this book. Tom Drozda, Bob King, and their staff at SME were of immense help in providing professional support. Others jumped in to help get the information needed to finish the manuscript. B.G. ("Bob") Mathis, Rick Rossman, George Dellas, Dennis Langlois, Jack Fallon, and Marion Cumo provided significant contributions.

I am especially grateful to Dr. Jack Troyanovich for his encouragement, ideas, energy, and skill in translating my experiences and strong feelings into coherent English.

A special thank you to the four outstanding professionals who assisted me as executive secretaries during my corporate officer-ship years from 1976 to 1991: Patricia Twyman, Bonnie Gatewood, Ginger Jeffrey, and Mary Ann (Simek) Demski. They are "Top Drawer" people who ran efficient, caring, responsible schedules for me. Thank you, Pat, Bonnie, Ginger, and Mary Ann.

I also must acknowledge all those whose influence, intelligence, experience, and efforts supported and guided me in my automotive manufacturing and sales career. This includes the tens of thousands of dedicated salaried and hourly men and women working together in scores of factories in several countries and union organizations. It also includes thousands of automotive dealers, suppliers, and transportation firms who contributed to my vision of teamwork and participation. This massive personnel resource greatly assisted our success in championing world-class manufacturing.

During the rebuilding of Chrysler Manufacturing, I surrounded myself with managers I could trust. I want to thank them here: Dick Acosta, Don Anderson, Fred Bartz, Jake Bass, Richard Bates, Tom Breneiser, Marion Cumo, Tom Delanoy, Leroy DeLisle, George Dellas, Tony Diggs, Dick Donaldson, Bernie Dukat, Jack Fallon, Forest Farmer, Tom Fidoe, Buck Hendrickson, Bill Hicks, Tim Hiller, John Hinckley, Felicia Howell,

Bob Karban, Jr., Dan Keenan, George Knapp, Chub Krug, Frank LaManna, Dennis Langlois, Ray Lash, Howard Lewis, Jerry Mathis, Jim McCaslin, Jack McCleary, Michael Medlock, Andy Niflis, Jim Partlow, Roger Patel, Stan Paurazas, Jim Penrod, Rod Peters, Bob Piccirilli, Jr., Bob Potter, Brian Prucher, Yogen Rahangdale, Durward Roller, Sham Rushwin, Al Schell, Ron Stewart, Dr. Jack Troyanovich, Joe Tucker, Joe Tvrdovsky, Jack Wagner, Jim Wagner, Jackie Washburn, Allen Willey, Bruce Woodward, and Rick Zella. If I've forgotten or overlooked others, I sincerely apologize.

Compassionate and effective mentors over my 27 years of manufacturing were Elmer Sykes, Fred Caffrey, John "Dutch" Gembel, Cliff Vaughn, Charles Delanoy, George H. Johnson, and Norm Ellis of General Motors; Jim McLernon and Toni Schmuecker of Volkswagen; and Steve Sharf, Gerald Greenwald, and Lee Iacocca of Chrysler. These hourly and salaried veterans also guided me: Donald Fries, Grant Carradine, Ron Batterby, Tom Czerniak, Fred Meissinger, Jim Dawkins, Ed Piesko, Larry Adderly, Leonard Alexander, Jim Dantzler, Bill LaRowe, Leonard Wakefield, John Sorrels, Bill Wright, Jerry Easterwood, and Marvin G. McFadden.

During the time we were busy building Chrysler's products, the company's image was being upgraded by Jim Tolley, Baron Bates, and later Bud Liebler.

Finally, my thanks go to my parents; my brothers Gale, Bill, Jack, George, and David, as well as my sister, Nancy; my eighth-grade mathematics teacher and coach, Earl Bowersox; my professor and friend, Dr. Mart Fowler; Purdue coach Jack Mollenkopf; and above all, my best friend, wife, and partner of 33 years, Sandy, for providing her usual positive spark, patience, encouragement, and love as I immersed in sculpting my *Passion for Manufacturing*.

TABLE OF CONTENTS

INTRODUCTION

My purpose in writing *Passion for Manufacturing* is to pass along my manufacturing and management experiences. My hope is that this information will be used by manufacturing professionals to enhance their skills and make them more competitive on a global scale.

This book includes many references to the career steps I took since I entered manufacturing in 1964. For better understanding, and some perspective, a chronology follows.

1964	1964	1965	1967	1968	1970	1971	1973	1974	1975	1976
Bachelor of Science, Industrial Management Purdue University	College Graduate in Training Flint Assembly, General Motors	Production Foreman Flint Assembly, General Motors	Production General Foreman Flint Assembly, General Motors	Superintendent of Production Flint Assembly, General Motors	Chief Inspector Flint Assembly, General Motors	General Superintendent of Production Flint Assembly, General Motors	Plant Manager Livonia Spring and Bumper, General Motors	Assistant Detroit Sales Zone Manager General Motors	Plant Manager Detroit Gear and Axle, General Motors	Vice President of Manufacturing Operations Volkswagen Manufacturing Company of America (VWMoA)

1978	1980	1981	1985	1985	1987	1988	1988	1989	1991½
Group Vice President - Manufacturing Operations Volkswagen of America (VWoA)	Executive Vice President of Diversified Operations Chrysler	Executive Vice President of Stamping, Assembly, and Diversified Operations Chrysler	Dean's Advisory Council Member Krannert School of Management Purdue University	Executive Vice President of Manufacturing Chrysler	Member - Board of Trustees Ashland University (Ohio)	Governing Board for the Leaders For Manufacturing Program Massachusetts Institute of Technology	Executive in Residence at the L.A. Iacocca Institute of American Competitiveness Lehigh University	Executive Vice President of Worldwide Manufacturing Chrysler	Retired

I have made many references to Chrysler facilities in this book. Appendix A lists the plants, their functions, and a comment.

I trust you will find the comments, tips, and case studies useful in your efforts toward global competitiveness.

Richard E. Dauch

Chapter 1

BORN FROM BANKRUPTCY'S BRINK

My passion for manufacturing began early. I know this is hard to believe, but of all the career choices to a boy of 10, mine converged quickly on car building. I loved trucks, I loved cars, and I knew I wanted to build them when I grew up.

I was the youngest of seven children, six of whom were boys. We operated a 127-acre dairy farm near Norwalk, Ohio. My parents, W.G. Albert and Helen Dauch, were stalwart managers, running the family and running the farm. It took leadership to decide how the farm was to be managed and my father provided it. The humaneness and compassion came from my mother. Their seven offspring soon learned the work ethic, standards of quality, and how to divvy up the work so the farm could function independently. We shared those wonderful values that rural families exhibit: pride, strength, unity of purpose, and growth.

Farming is a seven-day-a-week job: Cows must be milked, pigs slopped, and chickens fed—every day, whether you feel up to it or not. Milking is a twice-a-day chore, at five in the morning and five in the evening. My parents allowed us to play, they encouraged our interest in sports, and they wanted us to participate in school activities, but they had no sense of humor whatsoever about missing our daily chores.

The most important thing my parents and family taught me was a sincere compassion for people. I have always tried to have sensitivity and understanding and show warmth for those with whom I was dealing—to listen and let them know I cared about them as individuals.

My parents taught us first how to work and then to respect the fact that work is good; it's not bad or something to avoid. I learned how to work with others and appreciate what can be derived from working together.

To teach us the value of farm products, my parents let each of us choose whether to raise our own calf or horse. All but my brother David chose a calf. He picked an unbroken Indian pony. He had more fun but we made more money.

The rest of us each fed, groomed, and nurtured a scrawny, awkward, frightened little animal into a magnificent milk cow or bull. I was thrilled as I watched my bull, ''Bones,'' grow large, strong, and, to me, very beautiful. When I sold him at auction, he weighed over a ton. It always amazed me how much money these huge animals brought at breeding time. It seemed like a lot of dollars, but they represented a lot of hours of hard work. It was my first job, and it hardly paid 20 cents an hour!

Drawn to Industry

Our Holstein dairy farm was about 45 miles from Cleveland, and our milk was trucked there by my cousin Floyd Garner. During the summer months when I wasn't in school, he would let me ride with him. We stopped at every farm and picked up milk. We drove past miles of corn, cabbages, and cattle to the big city and its contrasting hustling industry. Most of the details of those days are gone now, but the images of what I saw then when I was 10 years old, are still fresh. On the outskirts of Cleveland is Lorain, a steel-mill and auto-factory town, and I was excited about the streams of new cars and trucks pouring from the factories and which we saw on carriers and railroad cars as we passed by.

From within those sprawling industrial complexes, with the monstrous smokestacks typical of 1950 America, trucks came and went, fork lifts shuffled pallets of various sizes and shapes, and multitudes of people scurried in every direction—all of this driven by a purpose I wanted to understand. The contours, colors, bright trim, and red tail lights of those fancy new cars on carriers sparked my imagination. ''Wouldn't it be great to work with these every day?'' I thought. I couldn't tear my eyes away as these images disappeared past the back window of our truck.

It was then I decided to be a builder of cars and trucks.

At that time, I first focused on manufacturing. I knew it was for me because of my love for everything on wheels that went fast or did useful work. Later, I would beg my older brothers, uncles, and friends to take me through factories. All through high school, I made it a point to go on every plant tour I could, from my first—that Fairmont dairy-processing plant in Cleveland—to foundries to stamping plants to machine shops and all forms of manufacturing. We moved to Ashland, Ohio, when I was 12, and I toured the Myers Pump factory every year I was there because it was the biggest and best plant in the area. I saw sand casting, machining, painting, and assembly. I even toured a candy factory once, but somehow that didn't have the appeal of transforming steel into a car that can zoom down the road at 100 miles an hour.

Clearly, I had a greater passion for cars and trucks than my brothers. They got a kick out of my ability to close my eyes and identify nearly every truck passing our house on the main highway. I knew whether it was a Reo Crossfire V-8 or a Mack diesel just from the sound of its engines. I could tell you just about anything you might want to know about a '53 Chevy, Ford, Plymouth, or Caddy.

I also knew I never wanted to work for Studebaker. My dad bought a Studebaker pickup. I thought it was a real dog and made the mistake of telling him so. That was the last time I severely criticized his judgment! I thought our 1948 DeSoto was a fine-looking automobile, although the hood was way too long. It was a beautiful car but clearly not designed for women. My poor mother had to put two pillows under her fanny just to see over the steering wheel.

My favorite of the Big Three then was General Motors, followed closely by Chrysler. Ford finished last. At that time, I did not like Fords primarily because two of my brothers loved them. It was pure sibling rivalry, and I was just reacting to their taunts. They called my GMCs "General Mess of Crap" and the best I could malign their favored Fords with was "Future Of Reckless Drivers." American Motors meant nothing to me then, and I was completely turned off by Studebaker's products and vowed I'd never work there. My other brothers didn't really care about cars and trucks, other than as tools to get the job done.

The Dauchs are natural entrepreneurs—strong-willed, independent, intelligent, and very capable of going out on their own. My oldest brother, Gale, went into the steel-fabrication business. He built, among other things, several roller coasters for Cedar Point, a major amusement park on Lake Erie. I'm very proud of that because it parallels the car business with its steel structures, precision engineering, and manufacturing for maximum people-handling safety. My sister, Nancy Smith, and her husband, Bart, owned and operated restaurants. My brother, Bill, and his wife, Mona, own a concrete company, a trucking company, and a builders' supply company. They have all been successful.

My brother, Jack, tested out of a portion of his Master's Degree which he acquired at Harvard. My sister was salutatorian in her high school class, showing it wasn't just Dauch intensity, but that intelligence was also involved. Jack worked at NASA for the Teledyne Corporation for 10 years as a Radiation Safety Manager. He received a Master's at Harvard, and started his own occupational-health service business. My brother, George, is a long-term employee of United Parcel Service. My brother, David, followed my father's example and went into insurance and sales. My dad was a sales and insurance executive as well as a farmer.

Pigskin Previews

Football has always been a big part of my life because it challenged the competitiveness in me. My oldest brother, Gale, played end for the New London Wildcats. The next oldest, Bill, was team captain and an outstanding fullback on the Wakeman Western Reserve Rough Riders. Brothers Jack and David (team captain) played for the Ashland Arrows. I obviously looked up to them as genuine heroes. I was born with God-given athleticism: speed, quickness, size, and jumping ability, and took to athletics like a duck to water. I learned through getting roughed up by the older boys every day that I enjoyed competition and physical contact.

I didn't get a chance to play football formally until the seventh grade because our country school—grades one through six—couldn't afford athletic programs. So, I played baseball and softball there, and a lot of rough-house football out in the school yard. Baseball is too slow for me. I love to play it but hate to watch it. I always wanted to be a participant, active and involved.

Football was ideal for me. It requires teamwork, tremendous skill, intensity, great stamina, and courage because it's a violent game. If you really love to compete, I don't know of anything better to express that desire.

Many of the lessons I learned on the playing field translate to the industrial environment. As I once said in an American Profile interview for public television, when asked what's it like working for Lee Iacocca, "It's great, as long as you can take the beating." Had I not played against Dick Butkus, Carl Eller, Bobby Bell, Roger Staubach, and other Football

Hall of Famers, I'm not sure I could have endured the management style Chrysler had in those Marine-commando days of the early '80s, and taken the pressure and stress that went with losing $7 million a day and scrambling for our very lives—every day.

That athletic experience and the fundamental family values I acquired back on those Ohio farms sustained me through those challenging years at Chrysler. Frankly, I thrived on it. Whether it's a family team, football team, or industrial team—the key is to have compassion for everyone in the group. They're the ones who will help you do what must be done. You must respect the team, its individual members, and its task.

My first team was that nine-member family unit running a farm. My next teams were more formal athletic ones that had to be highly disciplined. Nobody speaks in the huddle but the squad leader, the quarterback, and he takes orders from the field general, the head coach. From my first coaches in seventh grade up to Jack Mollenkopf in college, I found coaches to be demanding, direct, and ill-tempered at times. You had to be prepared to handle some very tough situations they put you in, and that experience helped me become the right type of person to fit well into an Iacocca management team. This wasn't just another football game, it was economic war. We needed a Herculean effort from everyone to save this once-proud company from the scrap heap after decades of neglect.

Football develops character, courage, stamina, and quick thinking. So does military combat. I've been asked whom I respect more, Vince Lombardi or George Patton. I can't answer that because I hold them both in high regard. I always respected military history and had a great fondness for athleticism. I treasure a personal letter from Vince Lombardi inviting me to be part of the Green Bay Packers. I declined because I had hurt my knee one time too many and was married with two kids after just graduating from Purdue. I decided to go directly into industry, which was the right decision, but a tough, emotional choice at the time.

I never met General Patton, but I did meet his son—who was also a general—when I was chairman of Chrysler Defense. We were in the process of building and launching the Abrams battle tank, and he was so pleased with the tank, that he called and asked to get together. We had a nice lunch in my office, and I still have a picture of us taken on that day. Thus, I have a fondness for the Patton family and for what they've done for our country, just as I am fond of what Lombardi did for football and our national competitive spirit.

Ticket to College

Football was the key to my getting a college education. Most of my family took their high-school diplomas, put them in a drawer, and went straight to work as we were not well-to-do. My brother, Gale, did have a chance to play one year at Ohio State under their football program but chose not to continue. Jack and I were the only ones to go beyond a year or two of college. Football was a way up and out for me. It gave me both a formal education at a prestigious university, and the opportunity to play, at a high competitive level, the sport I love.

There were several GM executives at a very critical game in the fall of 1963 when I was a senior at Purdue, and we gave a good whipping to The University of Michigan at Ann Arbor. Purdue football teams had beaten Michigan at West Lafayette but never at Ann Arbor. We were the first!

I remembered the 16–14 beating the Wolverines gave us two years earlier when I was a sophomore, and I vowed with my buddies, Bob Lake and Ron DiGravio, that it would not happen to us again. In '63, we got our chance on national TV. After knocking the home team on their butts on the first play from scrimmage and causing a fumble, we put the ball in the end zone three plays later. Michigan never recovered.

That game had an impact on my life. Sometime later, I met with those GM executives who had been rooting for Michigan that day, and after I graduated, they thought it might be wise if I shared some of my friskiness and competitive juices with them at General Motors. They made me an offer. I accepted, starting my manufacturing career in GM management's lowest entry-level salaried position—CGIT, College-Graduate-In-Training.

Making the First Team

On August 24, 1964, 22 years old and armed with a degree in Industrial Management and Science from Purdue University and the strain, pain, and glory of 10 years of football, I joined what I felt was General Motors' Number 1 team: the Chevrolet Motor Division. My first job was at GM's Flint, Michigan, car and truck assembly plant.

I had a crucial decision to make my first day at GM. The plant manager, Tom Schooley, asked me a simple question, "Would you like to work on the car line or the truck line?" After some thought, I answered, "Mr. Schooley, I'd be honored to work on your truck line."

There were several college graduates in training at the plant that year, and I was the only CGIT who chose the truck line. Schooley was surprised and asked, "What in the hell are you doing that for?" I said, "Well, I grew up on a farm and was always around trucks. I know trucks mean work, and work means schedules and discipline. I like work, schedules, and discipline and the challenge all this will bring me."

I was lucky. I got into trucks just before truck volume in this country began surging upward. By 1973, when I was 30, I had the privilege of being appointed the youngest plant manager in the history of the Chevrolet Motor Division, an accomplishment I am very proud of, and a record that still stands today.

I became plant manager of a Class A, 3000-plus employee plant, and I achieved this by working my way up through the intermediate positions of foreman, general foreman, shift superintendent, chief inspector (head of quality at the plant), production general superintendent (both shifts) and finally, plant manager.

After I served as plant manager, GM offered me an opportunity in sales. The offer was another crucial decision for me because it was professionally a step backward to a lower grade level, but it could be important strategically. I accepted because I felt it would broaden my base, give me a better understanding of the auto industry, and help me advance later.

I had never worked in sales in my life. The closest I had come was the second-hand experience received by observing my father spending nearly 30 years in a successful career in the insurance business. The opportunity was to exchange jobs with another fellow—I would go from manufacturing to sales for a year, and he from sales to manufacturing.

This experience as assistant sales manager in the Chevrolet Detroit zone, working with 156 area dealers, taught me how the retail merchant handles wholesale and retail duties, and how factory sales handles wholesale responsibilities to the dealer. It helped me better appreciate the linkage from customer to dealer to order processing to factory to supplier to production. It also taught me how slumping dealer sales can shut down plants and ultimately close them for good. I received excellent guidance from Zone Manager, Robert Porter. It was an excellent year for me.

When I returned to manufacturing, I was rewarded by being put in charge of the biggest GM plant in North America, an inner-city plant, Chevrolet Detroit Gear and Axle. I was now plant-complex manager. Instead of having 3000 people, I had over 7000.

This inner-city work force was a big demographic change from the suburban plant I had worked in previously, which turned out to be remarkably important to my future challenges in running Chrysler manufacturing. With most of its facilities in the Detroit area, Chrysler primarily has an inner-city work force. Running GM's Detroit Gear and Axle complex prepared me for what to expect in those kinds of plants later on.

Moving Up Internationally

In 1976, the general manufacturing manager at Chevrolet, James W. "Jim" McLernon, unexpectedly left GM to become the new president of Volkswagen Manufacturing of America. I never thought I would leave GM, and I still have great respect for the company and its people, but McLernon was very persistent in recruiting me to be VWMoA's vice president of manufacturing. I signed a multi-year contract and started work there in 1976.

I'd have been foolish to turn down this opportunity although there was significant risk. I've always been willing to take risks but, hopefully, only measured risks. There were times when my father said he wasn't sure of my sanity. When I later went to Chrysler, for example, he thought I'd gone completely overboard, and he had good reason to believe that because all the data then made Chrysler look like a dead duck.

The risks at VW of America were huge. There had not been a foreign-owned volume transplant in this country for generations. I felt good about developing a working relationship between the German and American people, and I wanted to learn international trade. I felt we would finally prove that American workers were not the source of the quality problems in this country. I strongly felt it was management and its system that was causing these problems.

In less than four years, under McLernon's leadership, we built a self-sufficient manufacturing organization. Our planners imported jigs, fixtures, tools, and dies from Germany. They designed and purchased others in the United States, Brazil, and Japan. The industrial engineers reviewed and modified German time-study practices. Our transportation people shipped machinery into the plant and organized the movement of parts in and cars and trucks out. We trained production supervisors by having them disassemble and reassemble German-built Rabbits until they could do it blindfolded.

We needed to write procedures for everything we did because none existed. We hired more than 4500 employees, from plant manager to assembler, writing the book on the fly, and relocating many of our key people, some of them several times. In addition to building and equipping

The first VW Rabbit from the Westmoreland, Pennsylvania, plant. Watching the roll-off are (l to r): VW-AG World Chairman Toni Schmuecker, Group Vice President of Manufacturing Operations Dauch, and Jim McLernon, President of Volkswagen Manufacturing of America.

a two-million-plus-square-foot (more than three dozen football fields) modern assembly plant, we also were aggressively acquiring other manufacturing facilities. We purchased and refurbished a former American Motors stamping plant in South Charleston, West Virginia; built a new, green grass factory in Fort Worth, Texas, to supply VW air conditioning and heating systems; bought an additional plant in Sterling Heights, Michigan, from the U.S. government; and got plans under way for a second assembly plant, if needed, at that location.

In less than two years, we were building good quality automobiles at Westmoreland—quality that, as measured by the Wolfsburg home auditors, was superior to any other factory producing Golf or Rabbit cars in seven other locations around the world. It showed that American workers were equal to—or better than—any in Germany, South Africa, Belgium, Mexico, or wherever.

By 1979, I was in the middle of the action—a group vice president of manufacturing for Volkswagen of America. The assembly plant in Westmoreland County, Pennsylvania, built in record time, was churning out 1000 sturdy little Rabbits every day. We scheduled overtime occasionally, even though the harbinger of economic recession was everywhere. General Motors was holding its own. Ford would be in serious financial difficulty were it not for its European operations. Chrysler was a basket case.

Lee Iacocca and Lars Larsen, a key officer, already had made several trips to plead for $1.5 billion in loan guarantees from Washington—funds desperately needed to keep Chrysler in business long enough for Lee to reorganize it, heal it, make it viable. I felt sorry for him then. Our political system was putting that proud man through the paces of petitioning for aid as a circus clown teases a terrier to jump through the hoop.

Success was in the air at Volkswagen of America, however. We had fun getting Westmoreland going, I had learned quite a few things, but I knew I didn't want to spend the rest of my career working for a foreign-owned company. I should have been satisfied with my life. After all, I wasn't yet 40 and was already a group vice president. The company I was helping build was thriving. I felt something gnawing at me, however, at a time when I should have been sitting back and enjoying the fruits of our company's and my own considerable labors.

Crisis at Chrysler

In 1979, every newspaper and magazine carried blazing headlines and tart editorials casting Lee Iacocca in the role of a con man attempting to swindle taxpayers out of their hard-earned money. Journalists everywhere portrayed Chrysler as a doomed company. America seemed prepared, even eager, to desert one of its own in an hour of need.

The Wall Street Journal was particularly vicious of its treatment of Chrysler. On August 3, 1979, its editors took a first bite:

> Chrysler Corp.'s request for $1 billion in advance federal tax "credits" to bail it out of its serious financial difficulties is not something we can support. As England and any number of other countries have learned, government subsidies to sick corporations become a never-ending business, eventually applying a crushing burden on taxpayers and economic efficiency. To maintain a healthy economy government must simply let companies adapt to their

changing fortunes, cutting losses before they become unmanageable.[1]

In a September 4 *WSJ* article, entitled "Chrysler Bailout: Rewarding Failure?" David Stockman, a congressman from southwestern Michigan who later became President Reagan's budget director, wrote:

> For more than a decade, Chrysler bled its balance sheet with foreign acquisitions that produced more losses than new markets. Its domestic diversification efforts yielded a similarly large crop of lemons. Meanwhile, its domestic auto market share plummeted by 37%, as it consistently got to the showroom with too little too late.
>
> By the close of 1978, Chrysler's lone remaining competitive strength was in the non-passenger vehicle market—vans, pickups, and recreational vehicles. It had captured over 30% of the van market in recent years, compared to just over 10% of passenger auto sales. But vans share a common trait with tourist areas distant from the major cities: Sales plummet spectacularly during periods of temporary gasoline unavailability. Chrysler's July van sales were off 65% from the previous year, compared to a 9.6% decline in total U.S. auto industry sales.[2]

In a November 13 editorial, entitled "The Chrysler Non-Solution," the *Journal* offered some dire predictions:

> What will have been achieved if Chrysler does manage to wobble on? In the face of Japanese, European and U.S. competition, Chrysler still will have trouble selling cars. Workers' jobs still will be in jeopardy. Meanwhile capital will be diverted from other enterprises that are more likely to succeed competitively, and the jobs at those firms won't be available.
>
> What's more, the politics accompanying a Chrysler guarantee will make it almost impossible for the company to take the necessary steps to survive. For the company to be able to produce at all competitively, most analysts argue it will have to abandon many of its old plants, streamline many of its operations, and perhaps even give up trying to be a full-line producer. Widespread layoffs may therefore be crucial to a genuine Chrysler turnaround.[3]

A November 26 *WSJ* editorial deftly delivered this blow:

> Chrysler . . . is suffering from more than a temporary squeeze on cash flow. Its main lines of business are in trouble: even in America the company can't sell enough cars, vans and trucks, and export opportunities are limited. As a full-line producer, Chrysler may not

11

have sufficient market share to survive in an industry where economies of scale are enormous, and ferocious international competition puts strong pressure on prices. And government regulations, such as fleetwide mileage requirements, restrict the company's ability to specialize.[4]

On December 19, 1979, in "Laetrile for Chrysler" (referring to a drug once touted as a miracle cancer cure), the *Journal* espoused another miracle cure:

> Bankruptcy is not a happy fate, but if Chrysler really cannot fend it off on its own for even a few more weeks, then clearly the time is past for less drastic treatment. Bankruptcy is painful surgery, but it is infinitely better than laetrile.[5]

A year and a half later, the *Journal* wrote this in "Chrysler's Dance":

> Chrysler has recently been proposing to sell itself to Ford. This is a splendid idea. Back when the bailout was proposed, we ourselves wrote that if Ford were allowed to buy up the viable parts of Chrysler, the nation would get the advantage of at least one domestic competitor for GM.
>
> But no one wants to dance, Chrysler Chairman Lee Iacocca complains, after being bluntly rejected by Ford, and also after surveying potential foreign purchasers. Well, who would if the prospective partner is wearing $1.2 billion in debt and $1.28 billion of unfunded pension liabilities? If Chrysler stepped on your toe, it'd mean a wheelchair for life.
>
> Back when we proposed selling parts of Chrysler to Ford, we had a plan to handle this part of the problem. When the architects of the modern corporation were inventing limited liability, there was another wonderful device called bankruptcy. This would allow you to sell Chrysler's assets for whatever they are worth, and apply the proceeds to its liabilities. For precisely this reason, bankruptcy is even now an attractive alternative.[6]

A Widow's Woes

Such media abuse heaped on a company I viewed as an American institution made my hackles rise. As a family-centered, country boy from Ohio, an ex-Purdue fullback and linebacker, my competitiveness is made in America and sanforized: it won't wash out. I love a good scrap, and this Chrysler battle sounded like it was right up my alley.

What really touched me, however, was a Florida visit with my wife,

Sandy, to see her parents, Cass and Fred Rule. Among the Rule's many friends was Mary Shea, a widow in her 70s. Her husband devoted his entire career to Chrysler, and Mary depended upon the company for her income. Chrysler's troubles were on her mind every time I talked to her during that brief vacation. She equated her own survival with that of the company. It obsessed her. Back in Detroit, I began to wonder how many Mary Sheas there were in the country; how many innocent people would be hurt by Chrysler's impending collapse.

Roger and Me

One of my good friends is Roger Penske, former race car driver and highly successful businessman. Roger and I met when I was on my assignment as assistant zone manager for Chevrolet Detroit. One of 156 dealers I was servicing then was Penske Chevrolet in Southfield, Michigan. I was forced to become somewhat of a number cruncher then (something I have never enjoyed), and I got together with Penske to discuss his dealership's performance. Frankly, the numbers at that time were disturbing to us at GM, and in challenging him to improve on them, I helped set off the thought process that led him to acquire a Detroit Diesel distributorship. We worked out an arrangement to have his "nominee"—Walter Czarnecki—become the dealer principal at the Chevrolet dealership, while keeping the magical "PENSKE" name on the building.

He felt it was pretty gutsy for a greenhorn assistant zone manager on a one-year sabbatical to talk that tough and direct to the principal of a major dealership, but he had to admit I was right—he had been functioning somewhat as an absentee owner, and the numbers proved it. I was always taught to be honest, candid, and get results, and that was what I was trying to do here.

He told me later that I was the toughest, no-nonsense executive he had ever sat across a desk from, and I had clearly captured his attention. From there, I worked with him, helping him pursue his expansion from cars to engines, and we've been good friends ever since. Roger followed my career closely after that, and our relationship is one of the major benefits I derived from that single year in sales. Had I not chosen that path in my career, I never would have met him.

Roger and Lee

Lee Iacocca and Roger Penske both graduated from Lehigh University with engineering degrees. By the time Roger and I got to know each other, he and Lee were close friends, and by the time I was working for VW, both were on the board of trustees for Lehigh.

One day when Iacocca was with Penske at a Lehigh board meeting, after Lee had been at Chrysler for a few months, Penske suggested that Lee approach me about joining the Chrysler team.

Later when I was at a VW board meeting in Wolfsburg, Germany, I got a call from Penske's office asking if I might stop at his home in Piscataway, New Jersey, on the way back. After my arrival at JFK, I was flown there by Penske's personal helicopter.

That night, after dinner with Roger and his wife, Kathy, he and I went for a short walk around his estate. He told me: "Dick, I don't think Chrysler will make it unless they fix their factories and straighten out their union situation. It's a matter of whether you, who have a good job and good career going, want to take another gutsy risk."

I replied, "Risk has never scared me, Roger, but I must be able to measure it, and I can't do that unless I meet with Iacocca eyeball to eyeball and have a long, hard discussion on the issues."

Negotiating with Lee

Lee Iacocca called me in May 1979. I met him at his home, and we went down into his private office, which he called Lido's Lounge. He was emphatic that Chrysler would make it, and he felt I could help him in sales as a possible vice president.

I was surprised but thought it best for him to set the tone. He needed leadership. I didn't. His company was in trouble. Mine wasn't.

"Why should I go to work as a vice president when I'm already a group vice president?" I asked. "I'm not stepping back."

Iacocca laughed in his own inimitable way, and said "Hey, we're talking major league ball here, compared to minor league ball."

"Yeah," I said, "but my minor league is making good money, and your major league is losing it by the bundle."

"You know," he laughed again, "you've got a lot of feistiness in you."

Although it was a cordial exchange, I could see we were getting nowhere. "Sir," I said, "I was honored and privileged when my son, David, took the call and said you would like to meet with me. Here I am at 11 o'clock at night, out of respect for you because you're an automobile man. If you've got a problem, and I can help, we might work something out. Right now, however, we're on the wrong path."

14

I told him I felt Chrysler's real focus and need was in my strength—manufacturing. "I've spent only one year in sales," I said. "I'm the wrong guy for that role, and besides, I would not want to sell that stuff you're building right now. Your factories need fixing. Your people need care. Your whole system must change. I know how to do it, but I won't unless you give me your full support."

Today, I feel very good about taking that position with him then because, 14 years later, manufacturing is one of the major strengths of Chrysler. Back then, however, I told Iacocca, "We Americans are so far behind on technology, process flexibility, people training, teamwork, and supplier materials management that it will make your head spin."

He asked "Why do you say that?"

"VW is an international-thinking company," I explained, "and I have been intimately involved with the Germans, Swedes, Mexicans, Belgians, and Japanese. I don't even have to see what you have at Chrysler because I know it's worse than what we had at GM. What I saw there was good, but it wasn't world class. What I see today at VW, Audi, and Porsche is approaching world class in some areas and behind GM in others. If Chrysler wants to compete, you must do world reviews and learn what first-class manufacturing is all about!"

But he was stuck on the idea of me for sales, not manufacturing. He was president at this time, not chairman. "Sir," I told him, "you're the president, you don't set policy."

"Well," he said, "I'm going to be chairman."

"When you are, call me," I said. I suppose that was a bit brash, but it was just an honest statement. Despite this impasse, I could tell Lee and I had good chemistry because I had arrived there at 10:30 that night, thinking we would have an hour meeting but didn't leave until well after 2:00 in the morning.

So, we cooled it for about a month and then had another series of meetings until we reached an agreement that I would start to work for him in manufacturing on April 1, 1980. Part of the delay was because I was under contract to VW until that date, and I'm not one to break a contract. I showed up at Chrysler the day my VW contract expired and became executive vice president of diversified operations.

Iacocca met my needs, I met his, and we had a great 11-year relationship. He was a person I enjoyed helping and from whom I enjoyed learning. The two smartest, sharpest businessmen I've ever dealt with are Lee Iacocca and Roger Penske. I was very fortunate to meet them both.

Desperate Measures

Although I had read about Chrysler and talked to many people in the know, once on board I discovered the company was in worse shape than I had ever imagined.

The *Wall Street Journal* was right about one thing: Chrysler was on the verge of bankruptcy. The organization was fat and lazy, with a balance sheet and stock price reflecting a horrendous $350–$450-million hemorrhage per quarter—$6–$7 million each working day! In his best-seller about the auto industry, *The Reckoning*, David Halberstam describes the company as "the embodiment of what had gone wrong with American heavy industry in the last twenty years."[7] I began to see what he meant.

The plants I inherited were like industrial museums, old, dangerous, dark, gloomy, inefficient, rat-infested, and obsolete. The work force was demoralized. Interactions among workers—including their union representatives—and managers were inflexible and confrontational.

I would routinely get calls from our financial people like this: "Dick, we must build and ship 4200 cars and trucks by the end of the second shift tonight to make payroll." Once those 4200 vehicles passed to the ownership of the dealers, we could draw on their accounts to pay our workers and critical suppliers. Shipping those cars kept the company alive for another day, or sometimes, when we were lucky, kept us a whole week ahead of bankruptcy and the final nail in the coffin.

When Iacocca asked me what was needed to fix manufacturing, I answered bluntly: "It's not a matter of changing the bath water. We must throw out the baby." We were not too proud to learn from competitors. We acquired technical know-how from around the world, sending study groups to Australia, Brazil, Canada, France, Germany, Italy, Japan, Korea, Mexico, Spain, and Sweden, as well as throughout the United States. Even before we addressed the technical problems, though, we began sorting out the most important ingredient in any turnaround—our people.

People First

My instinct is to address people problems first. Whenever I can get people to work together, problems eventually get solved. I learned this as a boy, working on our farm. Everyone in our family pulled together to keep it going. We joined with our neighbors and friends to plant and harvest, rebuild a barn, or string miles of fence. My football years at

Members of union and management gathered together to celebrate the eighth anniversary of the Joint Product Quality Improvement Partnership. Bringing together union and management for the common goal of improved quality was one of the keys to Chrysler's success. Seen here are (l to r): Joan Patterson, co-director of joint skill development, UAW-Chrysler Department; Gino Gio-condi, Chrysler vice president-quality and productivity; Marc Stepp, vice president, UAW-Chrysler Department; Homer Jolly, administrative assistant to the vice president, UAW-Chrysler Department, and Dauch.

Purdue reinforced these childhood experiences. If our team didn't pull together against the opposition, the Boilermakers could not win, no matter who we were individually.

I began the task of rebuilding Chrysler Manufacturing by gathering a cadre of trusted managers. I knew or worked with each of them during my previous 16 years at General Motors and Volkswagen and knew I could rely on them to keep their fingers on the pulse of events in the organization and react accordingly. I knew they would be frank in advising me of conditions and events about which I needed to know in order to effectively manage.

The next step was to get to know key long-time Chrysler employees. Their help was essential for me to adjust to the Chrysler culture and eventually modify it. As soon as we felt fairly comfortable with our roles on this new team, I began establishing a positive relationship with the United Auto Workers (UAW). As luck would have it, I was paired with Marc Stepp, my UAW counterpart. Marc and I were one odd couple. He was in his late 50s; I was in my late 30s. He is black. I am white. He lived and worked in the inner city. I came from the country to suburbia. He rose through the union and I through management. Nevertheless, we shared a common concern: saving Chrysler and the jobs and dignity of its people. Chrysler's troubles were so bad that we had to be straightforward with each other from the first moment. And we were.

Next, Quality

One of the most positive elements of Chrysler's loan guarantee was a program to improve the substandard quality of the vehicles. When the loan guarantee act was approved by Congress and the President, it mandated that Chrysler and its key union, the UAW, work out a quality-improvement program outside any contractual agreements. It became formally known as Product Quality Improvement or PQI. Marc spearheaded the U.S. effort from the union side. Dick Vining, then executive vice president of manufacturing, headed up management's efforts. They became the co-leaders of PQI.

I was in a support role then because I was executive vice president of diversified operations and had 16 Chrysler factories building components. Later, after Vining retired, Steve Sharf replaced him, and then I replaced Sharf, so eventually, I became co-leader of PQI along with Stepp, who remained head of the union at Chrysler.

Although the initial PQI program was formulated before I joined Chrysler, we adapted and matured it. It eventually became PQIP—Product Quality Improvement Partnership—and I was part of that improvement. Marc and I wanted it to be a formal partnership—a critical point to us both.

To dispel the deep suspicion—even antagonism—existing between union and management, Marc and I attended more than 150 plant meetings, appearing before every one of Chrysler's 60,000 American workers and most of their managers to demonstrate mutual trust and respect. "No quality, no sales . . . no sales, no jobs!" was Marc's favorite opening line. The audience may not have liked the messengers, but they eventually accepted the message: Cooperation was the only way to improve the quality of the vehicles that put bread on all our tables.

Marc's counterpart in Canada was Ken Gerard, a giant of a man—strong, proud, outspoken, tough, and, at times, bitter. I made my first major move on Gerard's turf by advocating replacing the rear-wheel drive M-body, J-body, and Y-body vehicles at the Windsor, Ontario, assembly

Marc Stepp lays it on the line for a group of Chrysler workers. "No quality, no sales . . . no sales, no jobs," was Stepp's favorite line to Chrysler workers. Stepp and Dauch attended more than 150 plant meetings, appearing before every one of Chrysler's 60,000 American workers and many management groups. (United Auto Workers photo)

plant with the then-unproven minivan. Ken fought me tooth and nail on a plan that he claimed was madness. After many difficult meetings, however, we eventually came to trust and respect one another. Years later, we jointly performed the dedication ceremony for the one-millionth minivan produced at Windsor Assembly. I felt very honored when Ken's family seated me immediately behind them at the memorial service in the union hall after he passed away.

Unionization of the U.S. work force declined, from a high of 32% 20 years ago, to 13–15% today. A dizzying pace of technological innovation, global competition, and a relentless shift from an industrial to a service economy hastened this change. In the domestic automobile industry, however, working with people still means working with unions.

When I came to Chrysler, motor vehicle manufacturing was labor-intensive and low-tech. For example, in 1980, Chrysler had less than 200 robots; in 1991, when I left the company, it had more than 2500 robots, some with third-generation technology. We had to accompany this aggressive transition to modern, reliable, flexible technology with an education and training effort of equal vigor. You cannot expect high-tech work from low-tech workers.

Coaching Suppliers

Embracing new technology and improving the reliability and repeatability of our in-house manufacturing served no purpose if we continued using low-quality purchased parts. For this reason, we initiated efforts to improve our relationships with suppliers and then pull their manufacturing processes, practices, quality, and delivery systems into the modern world.

I asked Dave Platt, Chrysler's vice president of procurement and supply, if we could meet jointly with the suppliers. He agreed, and we met with them annually from then on. Our working relationship changed dramatically as together we developed and met quality, cost, design, and delivery objectives. When we sent our purchased-parts quality engineers out to help suppliers, they responded by improving so much we could virtually eliminate inspection of parts coming into the plants.

Building a New Image

An important part of this story is image. Chrysler's image was one of stodgy, conservative cars for blue-collar workers and people over 50. Hal Sperlich (president), and Jack Withrow, (executive vice president, product development), and the engineering staff began the change with the K-car. I was amazed at how quickly the K-car convertible came off the drawing boards—that is, until we had to build it. The need for speed and economy compelled Chrysler Engineering to design and develop a convertible very simply. At a station on the trim line at our Number 1 St. Louis facility, a hulk of a guy stood with a power hacksaw. He cut the roofs off as many two-door K-cars as the daily build schedule required. Those convertibles sometimes squeaked, leaked, and rattled like a mariachi band, but they were the only game in town to rekindle the flames of the rag-top buffs and were a big help in changing public perceptions about the company. Today, of course, Chrysler convertibles are designed, engineered, and manufactured to be convertibles, and they have lost any rattles, squeaks, and leaks. The leadership of John Felice, Rod Peters, and Paul Snyder was instrumental in our ultra-successful convertible program.

Then came the minivan and a real shakeup in the Chrysler image. Launched October 7, 1983, as North America's first front-wheel-drive,

The convertible is the car that changed the image of Chrysler. Shown here are LeBarons and Dodge 400s in the build-up area at Chrysler's St. Louis Assembly Plant. During this operation, the car was fitted with a convertible top, and the hydraulic cylinders for raising and lowering the roof were attached. The car also received a rear closure assembly for rear seat attachment and soft top storage, and shoulder bolt brackets. (Chrysler photo)

fuel-efficient "van-wagon," this high-risk adventure created an entirely new class of vehicle—a hybrid of a truck and a family sedan. Not only was it different, the minivan was built in a completely new way. In manufacturing, Steve Sharf and I shared the risks with other top managers, including Iacocca; Gerald Greenwald, vice chairman; Sperlich; Ben Bidwell, executive vice president, sales and marketing; Don DeLaRossa, vice president, product design; Platt, and Withrow. We gutted and refurbished the vintage-1928 Windsor assembly plant and installed robots on a large scale for the first time in the paint and body shops. A scheduling concept called in-line sequencing abolished the large buffers of parts that were the hallmarks of auto assembly plants, and this discipline allowed Just-In-Time materials management to become a reality. The revolution had begun!

All these risks paid off. Chrysler's image soared and the company established itself at the cutting edge of manufacturing technology and methods. Three plants in three countries now produce the minivan, Chrysler's highest profit mass-production vehicle. A key manufacturing executive, Michael Lutsch, helped launch all three of these plants.

We financed our renaissance with $1.2 billion of the $1.5 billion in federal loan guarantees. By 1981, we had reduced our break-even point from 2.3 million units three years earlier to a manageable 1.1 million

Iacocca and Dauch with the first minivan to roll off Windsor Assembly—a grand slam in the marketplace.

units. Iacocca gave a symbolic bottle of black ink to our key people the first day we made a ham sandwich of profit in the fourth quarter of '81.

The operating profit for 1983, the year of the minivan launch, was $925 million, the best in Chrysler's 58-year history. At the National Press Club on July 13, 1983, Iacocca announced the payoff of the debt to the banks seven years early and at interest rates as high as 15.9%. We had regained our independence!

Turning Technology Around

We played manufacturing-technology catch-up ball with the rest of the industry during my first five years at Chrysler, but eventually we leapfrogged everyone in paint systems, body-shop automation, materials management, corrosion protection, power train warranty protection, and specialty robotic applications. Accomplishing this in so short a period meant running flat out. In other words, we ran a marathon of 100-yard sprints, and by 1990, Chrysler was a leader in manufacturing competitiveness.

	1980	1989	1992
Computers	1000	10,000	15,000
Industrial Robots	100	1700	2500

The use of robots and computers within Chrysler dramatically increased between 1980 and 1992.

In 1980, we had 1000 computers in manufacturing; by 1992 we were using 15,000. In 1980, we had no transfer presses in our stamping operations. By 1991, we were operating six high-efficiency transfer presses and had firm budget plans for 10 more. In 1980, we were using two computer numerically controlled machining units; by 1991, we had more than 600 at work! Following the acquisition of American Motors Corporation, Chrysler improved the build quality at the AMC Toledo assembly plant and increased Jeep production 50%.

The Chrysler Manufacturing Technical Center on Outer Drive in Detroit was established in 1982. The Chrysler concurrent engineering organization at the Liberty Center in Auburn Hills, Michigan, was founded in 1986 to design a new generation of processes and products, the key one being the all-new four-door family of LH cars for the '90s.

In 1988, we opened the New Mack Process Development Center to prove out new processes in partnership with vendors and to prepare for our new inner-city Jefferson North assembly plant in Detroit. The Chrysler Technology Center in Auburn Hills was dedicated in October 1991, putting most of the company's design, engineering, procurement, corporate training, and manufacturing processing, pilot plant, and paint talent under one roof.

In the assembly plants, plant-wide factory information systems custom-designed in the Manufacturing Technical Center, monitor all robots, automated systems, computer-controlled machines, and conveyors. These FISs use color graphics to identify and diagnose malfunctions, maximizing equipment uptime. Prior to 1983, Chrysler had no commodities on Just-In-Time delivery schedules; by 1991, the assembly plants received almost 80% of their daily dollar inventory value JIT. This step alone improved Chrysler's production inventory turn rate more than 400% over 1980 and eliminated $1.7 billion in inventory. More than 28,000 manufacturing employees have been trained in statistical methods. Productivity almost doubled from 1980 to 1991, and customer-reported warranty claims during the first year of service dropped 65% from 1980 levels.

We completely rebuilt our paint systems, and today Chrysler is com-

Communication is a key to a successful work force. In the paint shop, Dauch explains some quality-related issues to the staff. The location is the control room. Note the staff is dressed in white for cleanliness and to establish an image of hospital clean environment. Looking on is Yogen Rahangdale (Chrysler photo)

petitive with anyone in the world on finish quality. You must have good metal to have a good finish, so we upgraded every exterior body panel (except the roof) from cold-rolled steel to low-carbon, galvanized, pre-coated, and specialty steels. We pioneered this concept for the industry. Every external body die and body welding machine had to be reworked but it was worth it.

Chrysler has been the recognized leader in corrosion protection since 1985. Hundreds of millions of dollars in paint system costs have been saved since 1985, and reductions in paint use now save more than $100 million annually.

Almost 6000 people labored in the old 3.6-million square foot Jefferson assembly plant, nicknamed "Fort Courage," to produce 1000 K-cars per day. The Jefferson North plant (opened in January 1992) with 60% less floor space than the old plant produces 720 Jeep Grand Cherokees daily, a vehicle 25% more complex, with approximately 2200 workers.

The Chrysler Trenton (Michigan) engine plant evolved from a single-product facility in 1980 to one that in 1992 produced eight distinct products, including four-cylinder, six-cylinder, turbo, and nonturbocharged engines.

Conveyor technology now brings manufacturing operations to an optimum height for workers, freeing them from dark, confining, greasy pits. In the stamping and power train divisions, installing cleaner, safer welding operations, as well as machining processes using synthetic coolants, has dissipated the smoke, mist, and fog of traditional manufacturing. Since 1984, lead-based solder has been eliminated in the stamping and body-building of all new products. Materials discipline—together with replacing disposable cardboard and wood packaging with lightweight, collapsible, returnable containers—has made plants cleaner, brighter, safer, and more efficient.

Plant communities benefit greatly from these cleanup efforts. The transfer efficiency of paint systems, for example, increased from 35% in 1980 to nearly 85% in 1992, reducing volatile organic compound emissions. Chrysler leads the industry in waste-product recycling and is the only auto company recycling paint sludge to 100% reusable powder.

Our Turnaround Technique

When I came to Chrysler, its costs were higher than those of any other domestic automobile producer except AMC, and it lost nearly $4 billion between 1978 and 1981. From 1982 to 1990, pretax earnings were $12.5 billion and after-tax profits were over $9 billion. In 1990, despite dramatic volume reductions, Chrysler was the only domestic auto producer to post a profit. We took a $7 million-a-day loser and turned it into a $7 million-a-day winner, averaging over $1 billion per year in profits from 1983 to 1989. How did we do it?

We did it by dramatically improving product designs. Chrysler designers and engineers now respect the realities of manufacturing processes.

We did it by modernizing antiquated plants and introducing JIT materials management, by intensifying process control with statistical methods, and by working with suppliers to improve their products.

We did it by introducing aggressive quality assurance and reliability programs.

We did it by cultivating constructive relationships with suppliers, joint-venture partners, workers, unions, and state and federal governments. And we did it by creating far-reaching worker participation programs.

Ergonomics played an important role in the new Jefferson North Assembly Plant in Detroit. The underbody of the 1993 Jeep Grand Cherokee is set on a 37-degree angle to reduce worker stress and fatigue. I learned this technique from Volkswagen. (Chrysler photo)

Back from the Brink

Yes, Chrysler had been on the brink. We were not only on the edge, our fanny was hanging over, with only our fingernails holding us to that ledge. Once we had crawled back up, we vowed we would never let that happen to us again.

We were able to do all this because Lee Iacocca had the courage to take on a hostile press and an indifferent government bureaucracy and to unconditionally endorse Chrysler manufacturing. Working with Iacocca

A corporate call to arms, this poster appeared throughout Chrysler Manufacturing facilities. Vice president, marketing, Joseph Campana and I worked on this project.

was exciting. He is a brilliant product and marketing strategist. His high energy is complemented by a keen intelligence expressed in direct, incisive language. His dedication to the American automobile industry is legendary.

Iacocca loves sports and other performances that exhibit discipline, preparation, and precision. He is moved by Vince Lombardi's raw, tough, team-oriented, no-nonsense competitiveness. Had he chosen a different career path, Coach Iacocca's oratory would have rivaled that of Lombardi, Knute Rockne, Bear Bryant, and Woody Hayes. We know this from his impassioned lectures and motivational speeches. He is a decisive manager who can handle multiple stimuli simultaneously, shifting from one idea to another—and from the private to the public tone—quickly, and usually with flawless timing. He knows when to initiate, when to energize, and when to follow up. Above all, he never confuses effort with results.

His encouragement and support enabled manufacturing to achieve massive improvements in modernization, product quality, unit cost, process flexibility, and employee training. I had planned to serve for five years under his leadership to rebuild Chrysler manufacturing. That task took 10 years. In this business, it was the opportunity of a lifetime.

References

1. "Chrysler as Victim," *The Wall Street Journal*. Aug. 3, 1979, p. 8.
2. Stockman, David A. "Chrysler Bailout: Rewarding Failure?" *The Wall Street Journal*. Sept. 4, 1979, p. 18.
3. "The Chrysler Non-solution," *The Wall Street Journal*. Nov. 13, 1979, p. 22.
4. "No Lockheed Parallel," *The Wall Street Journal*. Nov. 26, 1979, p. 24.
5. "Laetrile for Chrysler," *The Wall Street Journal*. Dec. 19, 1979, p. 18.
6. "Chrysler's Dance," *The Wall Street Journal*. April 15, 1981, p. 28.
7. Halberstam, David. *The Reckoning*. New York: William Morrow and Company, Inc., 1986, p. 549.

Chapter 2

MENTORS AND METRICS

As the twig is bent, so grows the tree. When I first got to Chevrolet Flint Assembly and was assigned to the truck line, the superintendent of that line was Elmer Sykes. He was a wonderful man and an excellent mentor, but I didn't work directly for him. A general foreman, John "Dutch" Gembel, worked for Sykes. I was assigned by Sykes to work for Gembel.

Dutch was one of those self-taught people. He didn't have the privilege of going to college or getting much formal education. He first worked in the coal mines and steel mills of Pennsylvania. He saw then that the auto industry in Detroit was growing and risked the move from Pennsylvania to Michigan, settling with General Motors in Flint. He worked the truck line as a blue-collar worker for 11 years before becoming foreman. He remained with trucks, supervising the building of frames, chassis, engine-dress, final assembly, and rework, until he was eventually promoted to general foreman.

Dutch Gembel knew the working man first-hand. He saw an opportunity to do something for a guy like me who was rugged, young, healthy, well-educated, competitive, and had a good feeling toward people. He didn't know me from Adam, yet a month later, we had this very private discussion. Dutch told me, "Young man, I want to help you. I'm going to teach you everything I've learned, and I want you to move ahead and make it big because, with my lack of education, I could never get past general foreman.''

This showed me Dutch had a very big, warm heart. He taught me how to think like the working man on the line. I never had worked on the line. The last time I worked with my hands was on the farm. ''I've worked the line for over a decade,'' he said. ''Those men and women have tremendous ingenuity, intelligence, and skill, but they will not give it to you unless they know you care about them.''

He taught me to never let a day go by that I didn't say good morning or have a discussion with every employee on my payroll. I did that every day I was a CGIT, a foreman, or general foreman. As my jobs got bigger, I obviously couldn't continue doing that. As a superintendent I had 700 people, then 3000 as plant manager, but I made sure the first thing I did in those roles was be people-sensitive. John Gembel, as well as my mother, were the two people who taught me that sensitivity.

Dutch taught from the *Chevrolet Foreman's Handbook* which contained all the basics a player would ever need to play the game. To me it was akin to a Big Ten football playbook. The lessons were timeless: ''A foreman must accept responsibility for doing work that must be done by, with, and through people. The objective of the job is to use the knowledge and abilities of employees and to encourage and develop employees.''[1]

As I moved up in that same plant, my next mentor was Fred Caffrey. Fred was very well educated, an East Coast guy from New York. He earned his engineering degree from The University of Michigan, and he was powerfully focused on technology, taking risks, and being very gutsy.

Fred Caffrey was a marvelous mentor, wonderfully intelligent, tough, and innovative. For example, the Flint plant got their car bodies from an attached plant called Fisher II—known for being a rebel house that went on strike about every year. General Motors corporate got fed up one year when Fisher II went out once again. We had to shut our passenger car line down. GM made a major decision—with a lot of help from Fred—to convert both facilities to an all-truck complex, operated by Chevrolet.

Fred picked me as his right arm to be the production boss. From this hardened 10,000-person work force, we had to pick the best 6000. The result was, instead of having rabble-rousers and much labor distress, we had three years with no labor problems and frequently the highest quality of the eight GM truck-producing plants in North America. For this accomplishment, I was rewarded with a promotion to plant manager.

A third mentor was Jim McLernon who had the guts and courage to leave GM after 27 years where he obviously had a highly successful career. But Jim wanted to do his own thing as the president of a major arm of a foreign-based company, Volkswagen.

McLernon was one of those very bright, positive-thinking people with a disarming, contagious smile. If you were around him, you simply felt good, and that, I suppose, was how he recruited me from GM. I enjoyed working with him, and we both were interested in learning international commerce since our focus at GM was on domestic operations.

VW was a growth curve for both of us and, after four years, Jim decided he wanted to continue his career there. I decided to go with Lee Iacocca and Chrysler and help an American car company turn around.

At Chrysler, a key mentor was Steve Sharf, who preceded me as head of manufacturing. Steve is one of the brightest men I've met. He worked at Ford for many years before coming to Chrysler. He saw Chrysler as one final chance in his career to get the fulfillment and satisfaction that everyone seeks.

When I first met with Steve, Iacocca told us, "Dick, I'd like you to work in an understudy capacity to Steve Sharf." "Fine," I said, "I came to work for you and Chrysler, and whatever you assign me, that's what I'll do." It was a solid relationship, working four years directly for Sharf. They were rewarding years for both of us and the company. We are good friends to this day and continue to counsel each other. He's a fine human being who found that fulfillment he was seeking at Chrysler, and justly so because Chrysler, in turn, was rewarded by his leadership, loyalty, and dedicated service.

Seven Metrics

I learned from Dutch Gembel and these other mentors the seven metrics of global manufacturing competition.

Feasibility is first. Product, process, and people must come together with precision of execution. Each must be capable and perform predictably.

Timing is a critical issue in terms of product development, changeover, and conversion of facilities. To survive, automakers (or any manufacturer for that matter) must continue making dramatic reductions in the elapsed time from product concept to production. Moreover, they must reduce the traditional 10–15-year product life cycles to four to eight years or less.

Technology and its continual development is a third essential element of global competitiveness. It must be proven, efficient, reliable, cost-effective, and flexible.

Flexibility is critical. Flexibility in facilities, processes, suppliers, and personnel is mandatory to respond quickly and effectively to global market demands.

Product quality is the fifth metric. Customer satisfaction is the price of admission to the market. Continuous improvements, measurable in reduced warranty claims, are the yardsticks of quality and customer satisfaction.

Product cost goes hand in hand with this. The relentless pursuit of the title of "low-cost producer" is imperative in achieving a competitive advantage. As a percent of sales, Chrysler's total labor cost is now lower than that of General Motors, Ford, Honda, Toyota, Nissan, and Volvo. Ultimately, low-cost, quality producers win the market.

Human capability is the most important metric. Today it's called empowerment. Rapidly developing technology is transforming manufacturing, which was once labor and experience-based, into enterprises driven by knowledge and technology. America's place in the new world economic order depends on full commitment to investment in training and education to give our people the tools and skills to compete.

Global competition has hit not only automotive but textiles, consumer electronics, computer hardware, steel, machine tools, tool and die, shipbuilding, mining, road building, and construction—all key industries America once dominated. Our nation must fight in these and other critical value-adding industries. We don't need miracles here. It must happen in thousands of small ways. Everything we do—be it major or minor—must be done right the first time, every time.

R.H. Hayes and Steven C. Wheelwright amplify this point in their book *Restoring Our Competitive Edge: Competing through Manufacturing*:

> The solution to improving one's manufacturing competitiveness does not . . . lie in the "last-quarter touchdowns," "technological fixes," or "strategic coups" that Americans love so much. Instead, if the United States is to withstand and prevail against the onslaught of its foreign competitors, it will have to use the same approach to competition they use: continually putting its best talent and resources

32

to work doing the basic things a little better, every day, over a long period of time. It is that simple—and that difficult.[2]

Three additional forces will complicate America's ability to compete in the future: automation, population, and attitude. By the year 2000, thanks to automation, unskilled and semi-skilled workers will be considered an intolerable excess. Low-skill white-collar jobs will be largely replaced by computers. Automation mandates labor flexibility and continuous training. A worker cannot learn a specific skill and expect it to remain in demand throughout a lifetime. All of us must update old skills and learn new ones in more frequent cycles.

The second complicating force is population. Today, the world has over five billion people. By the year 2020, less than 30 years from now, it will exceed eight billion. Nearly 95% of this growth will be in less-developed nations, pressuring Third World governments to create jobs. Expect these countries to restrict the import of American goods while exporting intensively to markets such as ours. Concurrently, slow population growth in this country will mean fewer young people entering the work force, placing more pressure on veteran workers to constantly develop new, more advanced skills. Will our work force be smart and flexible enough to compete with three billion more people worldwide?

A third, but most insidious force is attitude. I sense aimlessness in America. Portions of our society are losing the will to compete. There are powerful, seductive voices suggesting Americans give up the small car business, steel making, textile manufacturing, the electronics industry, etc. They promote the service sector and envision the United States as a servant nation. I disagree. We must *expand* our global manufacturing capability.

Success equals the drive and enthusiasm of the person running the business. Remember, there are three kinds of people:

- those who make things happen,
- those who watch things happen, and
- those who wonder what happened.

By nature, manufacturing is tough and unforgiving. To me, it's a two chin-strap game, where your head takes such a beating you have to replace the strap on your protective helmet at least once before the game is over. In such a game, winners and losers are often separated by attitude. The Japanese take full competitive advantage of the single-minded, fanatical attitudes of their employees. Our leaders must find ways to stimulate the competitive spirit in our employees or we will be unable to compete.

Developing a winning attitude for American industry requires leadership. Jack Welch—CEO of General Electric—has defined the challenge: "Good leaders create a vision, articulate the vision, passionately own the vision, and relentlessly drive it to completion."

Leadership and Timing

I saw a leadership challenge when we were starting a Volkswagen operation 4000 miles away from its parent and had only 18 months to do it. We had only a shell of a plant with a dirt floor. We had former coal miners, drugstore attendants, automobile salesmen—you name it—but they came together to manufacture a product that could compete in the marketplace. That startup was a huge success. It took much leadership from the plant manager, the employees, senior management, and our suppliers and dealers.

People with my leadership style are most effective when they are placed in three circumstances: The underdog, the startup situation, or a crisis turnaround. I've never enjoyed the more typical, mundane environments. I've always enjoyed trying to get a team of folks enthused to accomplish what others said couldn't be done. Part of that goes back in my German-American heritage to the saying *"Can't* never did nothin'." I never believed in the word, "Can't," and I don't believe in losing.

The only two places I know where leadership is taught is in sports and the military. I've seen leadership being taught to my son at the United States Military Academy, and I personally experienced it in football, basketball, baseball, and track. You win with good leaders; you lose with poor ones.

Leadership is easier to observe than to define. There are many maxims I keep close to me that give me direction. One is Teddy Roosevelt's "Do what you can with what you have, where you are." It takes a disciplined leader to support a statement like that.

Then there's Winston Churchill's "I didn't become prime minister to preside over the liquidation of the British Empire," and "I have nothing to offer but blood, toil, tears, and sweat."

Leadership will be most needed where there's most difficulty. Churchill was the leader of this century, yet his own people did not want his leadership for the seven years prior to the war (when he might have

34

discouraged it), and they rejected him six months after the war was won. Iacocca was a lot like Churchill. He provided the roar and the rest of us provided the support and precise execution.

Four Ms of Manufacturing

To manage the enormous complexity of manufacturing and to teach it to others, I reduce it to four basic categories.

- *Materials*, which must be scientifically verified as defect-free and delivered JIT.
- *Machinery*, which must be computer-controlled, reliable, and flexible.
- *Methods*, which must provide cost-effective, quality-driven solutions that are on time.
- *Manpower*, which must be retrained and redeployed with greater individual responsibility.

These clear, simple elements were displayed in Chrysler's plant managers' offices, on factory walls, and anyplace else where the people who would make it happen congregated.

Practice the four Ms and you produce a fifth: *manufacturing efficiency*.

Materials

Imagine this: a 1.5-million-square-foot building (that's 35 acres under one roof), 2000 to 3000 people working in it, three to five million parts from around the world arriving to be assembled into a new car or truck every 60 seconds. This is the modern automobile assembly plant.

Foreign trade zones are an important materials concept. Foreign trade zone status is important to a company's cost competitiveness. I brought this idea to Chrysler, in 1980, from our success at using it at VWoA.

It's not enough that these parts show up at the factory's receiving dock. They must be managed. Scientific materials management is a key tool in achieving cost and quality competitiveness since materials typically account for about 75% of total manufacturing costs. Measured by dollar value, in an efficient plant, about three-quarters of the parts should arrive JIT without stopping at warehouses between the vendor and the plant.

At Chrysler, we reduced the per-unit average inventory level at the assembly plants by more than 50% between 1980 and 1988. During that same period, we improved inventory turnover by 400%, from 15 turns per plant to over 60 in a given model year. We reduced the on-hand steel supply at our stamping plants from 33 days to about three! At the same time, we increased our annual raw steel purchase from 900,000 tons to 1.4 million tons.

JIT delivery forces schedule stability into the manufacturing processes—a big benefit. The plant must build the product right the first time down the line, with minimum repairs. In any manufacturing operation, whether it's roller bearings or roller skates, schedule stability and first-time-through capability are mandatory to achieve full productive potential.

We created a centralized scheduling system to do this at Chrysler. We took dealer orders from the sales department and sequenced them into a total plant and supplier schedule. One important byproduct was "block painting."

In the old days, painting one car red, the next one white, and the next blue, was commonplace. That's the way the dealer orders came in. We had no way to sequence the colors. With modern centralized scheduling, a plant can schedule entire blocks of vehicles of the same color. Consequently, the paint guns don't need purging as often. At today's paint costs, this means major savings. It also reduces overspray and environmental problems.

Getting inventory under control not only pushes costs down, it also pushes quality up. It forces both the factory and suppliers to find and correct quality problems rather than just hide them with excess inventory.

Another big advantage of modern materials management is it lets you see what you're doing. Before 1983, Chrysler's plants had cardboard boxes stacked to the trusses, full of parts for next week's production. The workers couldn't see or communicate with each other and felt like penned-in cattle. Low inventory levels enabled us to practice "visual management." By not permitting inventory to be stacked higher than 54 inches, a person of average height could stand at one end of the factory and see what was going on at the other end. It meant a neater, cleaner plant and did wonders for morale because people feel part of a team if they can see the other players.

In 1983–84 at Chrysler, we began reducing the use of cardboard, styrofoam, wood pallets, and steel banding in the plants. We required suppliers to ship parts and materials in lightweight, collapsible, returnable containers, many of them made of high-tech plastic. The Sterling Heights (Michigan) assembly plant led, in 1985, with over 90% of its containers being returnable and of collapsible design.

Machinery

Not too long ago, an assembly plant was staffed by hordes of people in greasy coveralls with many of them working in pits under the assembly line. The air was filled with the sounds of hammers banging on metal. Today robots do most of the welding, sealing, and painting. Conveyors bring the vehicle up or down, within easy reach of the assembler who no longer must bear the discomfort, confinement, and danger of a pit.

Between 1980 and 1988, we increased the number of computers in our plants eight-fold, to about 8000. They guide material delivery systems, monitor and control machinery, and simulate models that predict performance of future equipment and facilities. They also put robots through their paces. We slowly replaced most of our cumbersome hydraulic robots with lighter, more versatile, accurate, and reliable electric units.

With robots, we moved away from hard automation, such as press welders that can repeat only one function, to flexible automation. Robots are reprogrammable, which increases the scope of their tasks and thus productivity. When Chrysler began relying on robots, we immediately increased the pressure on our robot suppliers. It was they and the reprogrammability of their machines that greatly influenced our changeover time. Their machines had to deliver what was promised when purchased. To assure ourselves that they did, we required the suppliers to run the robots in their facility for 50 consecutive hours without malfunction before allowing installation. Suppliers of other equipment (such as conveyors) were required to run the machinery under production conditions for 20 continuous hours without failure. We called it our "50–20" procurement policy. If equipment failed, the supplier had to modify it and repeat the 50- or 20-hour cycles until it passed the test.

Advanced machinery also made a major difference in our paint shops. We had tremendous employee turnover there because of the heat, fumes, and actual paint inhaled when the worker crawled into the body to paint the roof, sides, instrument panel, and floor. Robots now do 100% of internal vehicle body spraying of minivans. We also made the paint shops as clean as a surgical ward. During painting, an electrical charge draws the paint to the vehicle body. This electrical attraction instantly bonds the paint to the vehicle, and this technology cleaned up the paint shop. Live potted plants now thrive next to the paint line. The days of solvent-sodden air are gone. The results show outside the plant as well. We achieved dramatic reduction of emissions into the air.

Methods

Methods are the processes used in a plant to solve the routine problems of manufacturing. They integrate people, materials, and machines into total coordinated systems. Perhaps the most innovative system developed during Chrysler's turnaround was in-line sequencing. It begins with plant layout, linking the sequential production steps like the cars of a train. In an assembly plant, it locks the vehicle into an unbreakable sequence through a two-day, 10-mile journey along a conveyor, monitored each step by computers and technicians. If a problem develops with any vehicle, it is pinpointed immediately and corrected so the vehicle can remain in sequence until completion.

In-line sequencing replaces uncertainty with predictability. This permits the assembly line supervisor to better manage the department and the plant manager to better run the facility. Before in-line sequencing, nearly seven of every 10 cars coming off the line needed repair or adjustment. In 1991, it was about one in 10. Quality comes from a proactively planned and balanced system.

Probably the most competitive issue in manufacturing today is flexibility. There are over 600 different vehicle models available to the American consumer. It's not enough today to have high quality and low cost. You must match or beat your competition in product introduction, innovation and availability.

Between 1986 and 1988, Chrysler introduced 12 new car and truck models, a record for the industry. General Motors brought out six new models, Ford unveiled four, and even mighty Toyota introduced just eight.

To accommodate our full-scale product assault, we came up with several flexible manufacturing techniques. When our salespeople said the demand ratio of one model to another (all built in a single plant) was changing, we simply reprogrammed the robot welders and painters, the computerized material-handling equipment, and the flexible assembly system. We then could easily build more of one style car or truck and less of another.

One manufacturing configuration that gave us this versatility was our simple flexible manufacturing system, called SIMFLEX. Traditionally, changing over subassemblies in a plant is anything but simple. For example, in the case of side-rail assemblies that support the weight of the engine, massive conventional tooling, often the size of a house, is set up to churn out endless runs of side rails. Changeover required days or weeks of downtime. With SIMFLEX, however, changeover often takes hours, sometimes minutes. At its core is a host of reprogrammable robots that can adjust to different subassemblies with ease. Such flexibility will help determine winners and losers in tomorrow's highly fragmented, fiercely cost-competitive market.

Manpower

The most important M is *Manpower*. Manufacturing needs our very best men and women, yet few Americans view manufacturing as an attractive career choice for our best and brightest. In Japan, top students pursue careers in manufacturing because it is regarded as the lifeblood of the nation. It should be here.

"Grow it, mine it, or make it—that's how we create wealth." Our economic progress is based on growing things in the good earth and mining things under it, and then making useful things from these raw materials. Our economic progress will be based on how well we sustain our agricultural, mining, and manufacturing industries. Yes, we will need services too, but we won't sustain them unless we make darned sure we're globally competitive in manufacturing!

Manufacturing is losing some of its best candidates because of the credence given to theories that our manufacturing base is collapsing and being replaced by a service economy. Some applaud this, but it is fool-hardy to think the U.S. can thrive on a service economy. Productivity growth in the service sector during the '80s was zero. American manu-facturing chalked up productivity gains of more than 4% per year throughout the decade and, in Chrysler's case, manufacturing productiv-ity grew over 7%! Our plan worked.

The service sector is presently 76% of the labor force. If there is no productivity growth in three-quarters of the economy, and manufacturing begins declining because of apathy, what will be the consequence for the United States as an economic power? Do we want to be a nation of servants? Who will we eventually serve? What will be the rewards? Who will determine our destiny? The only sensible answer is that we must compete with a vigorous *value-adding* sector of the economy; that means competing through manufacturing.

Competition, however, has increased exponentially during the last 15 years, largely due to massive foreign competition taking root in our own soil. These green field transplants are new-vehicle assembly and manu-facturing facilities staffed with young, well-educated, healthy work forces. Many have no union representation. Such plants have helped

My Schedule As Chrysler's Executive Vice President, Worldwide Manufacturing

5:30 am	Start your engine!
5:30–7:30	Exercise program, shave, shower, get dressed, breakfast, drive to work
7:30–8:15	Briefings on previous day's results and problems Discussions of issues of urgency
8:15–8:45	Discuss secretarial assignments, meeting schedule
8:45–9:00	Brief supervisors on any abnormal events or issues
9:00–Noon	Attend or host scheduled meetings or conduct a review of a corporate or supplier plant (average: two reviews per week) -Staff or strategy meetings -Operations management meetings -Quality reviews -Policy meetings -Product review meetings
12:00–12:45	Lunch and a brisk walk
12:45–4:45	Attend or host scheduled meetings or conduct a review of a corporate or supplier plant -Production planning -Production scheduling -Organizational planning -Budget planning and cost reviews -Capital reviews -Negotiation strategy
4:45–6:00	Private individual meetings
6:00–6:45	Private time; reflect on the day's events
6:45–8:30	Drive home, dinner
8:30–10:30	Telephone calls, correspondence, other ''homework''
10:30–11:00	Brisk walk
11:00–11:45	News Lights out!

create an over-capacity of five million units in North America alone. Imagine building five million cars and trucks every year for which there are no buyers! Maintaining our country's competitiveness will take nothing less than a concerted team effort of government, education, labor, and, above all, management.

Popular sentiment must change so manufacturing can attract the best. For me, "best" means you must have elements of toughness, intelligence, and competitiveness in your personality, yet matched with a willingness to listen and sacrifice for the greater good. Creating things is demanding, but no calling is more honorable. Manufacturing is a noble profession.

If you love manufacturing, you never watch the clock. I thoroughly enjoy being in the workplace, because that's where the action is. That's where the reality of whether our American economy can compete globally occurs. It's where minds and matter come together in a thing called work, and the results of that effort can be measured, quantified, and objectively evaluated.

Because quality characteristics are measurable, you must ask: What are the facts? What are the trends? What are the results? Are we improving or regressing? I'll guarantee that you will find that nothing is static or standing still. Too often when you review these facts, you find people coasting, and there's only one way to coast, the wrong way—downhill. In manufacturing, you must press to move uphill. This requires constant work. People may try to avoid it because they don't like work. I learned long ago that work is good; it's honest, and a good ethic to revere. When you have unity of purpose, work can become fun, and its result can bring you personal and professional satisfaction. I thoroughly enjoy it!

Murphy's Law rules manufacturing: whatever can go wrong, will. But therein lies the challenge and the reward. You have an opportunity to show the best that's in you when you rise to the occasion and master it. Manufacturing is not a nine-to-five job. Many operations never shut down. Someone must staff them 24 hours a day, seven days a week. A career in manufacturing means you work abnormal hours. It means you will definitely miss a few birthday parties, holidays, and Sunday afternoons.

The job compensates for this by giving you the opportunity to work with cutting-edge technology and people who are the salt of the earth. Moreover, you will be in one of the most powerful groups in the company—the one with the most people, the largest budget, and the most and largest facilities. You will be working in the activity that creates the most value.

Manufacturing takes guts, stamina, business acumen, and demands precision of execution. Only people with these qualities thrive in this game, and they are the most satisfying kinds of people to work with. The need to produce quantifiable results makes them reliable, trustworthy, and responsible. The inability to hide a lack of results makes them candid and honest. The many variables that can go awry in manufacturing make them agile problem-solvers. The inconveniences and discomforts of manufacturing make them patient, tough, and durable. The need for precision teamwork makes them cooperative, helpful, and sensitive. They are the best friends in the world. My greatest reward has been the privilege of working with these manufacturing and operations people.

Bill King, a colleague of mine from the purchasing group, had such qualities. Bill was one of those remarkably gifted long-time career men totally dedicated to Chrysler Corporation and just waiting for a fresh breath of new leadership and direction to come along. He was prepared to take the risk in the latter stages of his career to support these dangerous new directions we needed to take.

Bill had the courage to present them to Chrysler top management and demand to be supported in the days when everybody was betting 100:1 that we would go bankrupt. At that time, we were trying to get the machine, tooling, and equipment-supplying community to change their way of shipping their final goods to achieve better reliability in their component systems, whether robotic, mechanical equipment, or electrical systems. Bill gave remarkable support and leadership to a manufacturing group demanding these directional changes so our suppliers would not split the two crucial disciplines of manufacturing and purchasing.

Bill stuck it out with me until we turned the corner in our renaissance. I am convinced today that he is one of the leading reasons why we were so successful in the implementation of our 50–20 procurement policy for manufacturing equipment, tooling, and robots. I'll always have a warm spot in my heart for Bill King. He was a Chrysler executive who totally deserved his retirement reward.

Well, once you make a friend you have a friend for life. Coincidentally, Bill King retired in the city where I was born, Norwalk, Ohio. When he picked up *The Wall Street Journal* one day and read that I was leaving Chrysler, he was concerned for his old friend, so he called me at work. I had not heard from him since he retired. It was a wonderfully warm and sincere conversation, and he asked if I might have a half an hour yet that day to chat with him. I said, "Let's chat right now, Bill," and he said, "No, I want to come see you." I pointed out that it was a 300-mile round trip to Detroit, and said, "You don't need to do that," but he insisted.

Later that day, we met for 30 minutes. He had driven up just to give me a big hug and thank me for contributing to Chrysler's recovery in the decade of the '80s where he and I had a chance to align our career paths. It had to be face to face for Bill—a manufacturing professional—because a phone call just wouldn't do. We both had tears at our parting embrace.

Bill King represents the finest of manufacturing people. Our relationship demonstrates the quality of friendship bred by the rigorous glory of a life spent where the real action is.

References

1. *Foreman's Handbook.* Chevrolet Motor Division, General Motors Corp., Feb. 1960, p. 5.
2. Hayes, Robert H. and Wheelwright, Steven C. *Restoring Our Competitive Edge: Competing Through Manufacturing.* New York: John Wiley & Sons, 1984, p. 390.

Chapter 3

MAKING IT IN MANAGEMENT

For nearly 15 years, I was a company officer with two different premier automotive manufacturers. As group vice president of manufacturing operations at Volkswagen of America, I experienced a major startup when Chairman Toni Schmuecker convinced his organization that a manufacturing base in the United States was essential. This mammoth effort was severely complicated by its international flavor and time compression.

German was Volkswagen's language. There was not a single official document in English. Many stampings came from VW de Mexico where Spanish is the everyday language. We used engines from VW do Brasil where they speak Portuguese. In addition to the language problems, all VW specifications were in metric. As Americans, we were trained in the English system of measurement.

I quickly found that international business requires immense adjustment. The Volkswagen experience introduced me—in a dramatic manner—to the intricacies of global manufacturing at a time when most Americans were totally innocent of what the market would become a decade and a half later.

Mexico For Mexicans

In my first job at Chrysler, executive vice president of diversified operations, I was responsible for all of non-U.S. or Canadian car production, which included all of our Mexican, South African, and Australian operations. I also had 16 component plants producing radios, wire harnesses, starter motors, trim sets, etc., both in the U.S. and elsewhere, and I was chairman of Chrysler Defense and Chrysler Marine. So it was truly a diversified assignment.

When I got to Mexico and reviewed our Toluca Assembly, Toluca Engine, Toluca Condenser, Saltillo Engine, and Lago Alberto Assembly, I could see that we were in deep "banyo" (or however they spell it), 12 feet above our eyebrows.

This was the worst automobile operation I'd seen in my life! I decided there was little here worth saving, and we clearly needed a fresh start. I didn't like one thing I had seen. The plants required too much repair and used too much extra material. Parts and supplies and unfinished vehicles were sitting in open fields, under tents, or in leaky warehouses. "Fellows," I said, "we're not going to continue doing things this way. We need a new direction. We're going to change the course of this ship!"

Obviously, that scared this management team. That was not my intention. I wanted to get their attention. We were losing ground and were going to change our game plan. We had an American running our Mexican operations, Jack Parkinson; a plant manager had just quit at Toluca Assembly, and we had Mexican management at the other plants.

Continuing with my evaluation, I said, "I want this to become a Mexican nationalist-run subsidiary of the parent organization. But for a short time, I am going to put in six to eight hand-picked American executives, led by Tony Diggs for manufacturing and Michael Lutsch for quality." I told them the objective was to improve quality to a level equivalent to Chrysler's world quality standards. This was needed for our plants to be the first to deliver fully built up cars and trucks from Mexico to the demanding American market. They had to feel the sense of urgency because our parent was going bankrupt. Every day they were sitting down there in Mexico thinking things were okay, but we were dying in Detroit!

We changed every manufacturing system between 1980 and 1986. We ended up with Mexican nationals for all plant managers, including the managing director, Carlos Lobo. Clearly, there was a danger of bringing these management people on too fast. You can't prepare them in 12–24 months. Significant training was required to learn our technology, our philosophy, and how to install and support Chrysler's brand of infrastructure and support systems.

I did this at all our foreign plants, whether in Mexico, Canada, or Austria. I tried to let them know right away that I would be putting Americans in but only temporarily. "It all depends on how fast you can grasp our system and run with it," I told them, "but you must deliver results." We always tried to keep local leadership, with the rare exception of putting in particular persons for purposes of their development and exposure to international trade, as I had learned from my own years at VW.

We wanted to give every person in that organization a chance at career enhancement. If they felt there was a glass ceiling, then we wanted to prove to them that no such barrier existed. We wanted them to feel they could go right to the top. But first, they had to get qualified. "If you are short on job training," I told them, "we'll train you. If you're short on formal education, we will provide you with support, time, and money, but you must be the one to go do it."

On the other hand, if they didn't have the capability, we didn't want to apply the Peter Principle here—take people beyond what they are capable of doing. We had to balance these things, and it took six to eight years in some cases.

But we did it.

This may be diametrically opposed to the thinking of Nissan and others in their Mexican transplants, but that was our philosophy. It worked well then, and is working well today. The Chairman of Chrysler de Mexico, Vicente Ariztegui, gave us support.

Read This Before Signing

Heed the following if you are considering hiring into a manufacturing company as a member of management: You only have power once, and that is before you join. Once in the company, you will have a boss and be absorbed into the system. The players who are crucial to your new circumstances will be reluctant to bend for you after you have cut an initial deal. Therefore, negotiate the best conditions you can for yourself before you accept any offer. With that said, here are additional pre-employment points to remember.

Study the company carefully. Know its place and position in the market. Get to know the company's products. Study its customers. Tour its plants and facilities and get to know its people and process capabilities.

Look at the company's annual report and business trends of the past five years. Request information on the five-year business plan. Meet and talk privately with several employees and with suppliers and customers from different management levels and departments. Determine and evaluate the attitude and management philosophy of your potential teammates. Most important, study the corporate organization chart, paying special attention to the chief executive officer (CEO) and the top 10 executives. Note their system, substance, teamwork, style, track record, vision of the future, and personal desire to work with the leadership.

After researching the company, ask yourself if it really needs you. Are you a good fit? Does the chemistry of the organization motivate you professionally? Don't join unless you feel 100% committed to the organization's philosophy and future business plan because in manufacturing you will be asked to pay a steep personal price!

Surviving a Launch

If you join a company as a top manufacturing official, you will probably soon face the prospect of a major new product launch. I suggest a simple, systematic approach to survive, and hopefully thrive, during this process.

First, be sure your employees are fully trained to produce the new product before you begin the launch. Commitment to continual improvement is essential. This will greatly enhance the chances for a successful production startup.

Review relevant statistical process control data to be certain the processes are capable. Immediately fix those that aren't. In addition, schedule several pilot runs that approximate actual production conditions.

Have your suppliers certify the first 5000 parts (or a sufficient number) they ship to you for this launch.

For an all-new product, all-new facility, or all-new work force, launch only one shift at a time. Increase volume moderately until you reach planned full production. The learning curve and adjustment time are vital. Wait at least four to six weeks before launching a second shift. Launch successive shifts gradually, but faster than the first shift because you now have experience with the product, facility, work force, and supply base.

Phase in different configurations of the same family of products gradually. Keep product variety responsive to market needs. At Chrysler, we reduced color combinations across the corporation from 15–20 to 10–12. We still could produce different colors when required, however. At the same time, we changed to a higher technology base-coat clear-coat paint.

This provided much greater gloss, luster, and improved showroom appearance. We were always upgrading fit and finish.

The long-range product plan controls launches and what happens when. It is imperative that the manufacturing officer has a major input into this plan because it dictates the available budget, timing, and critical deadlines. Only the top manufacturing officials know how much time and how many resources a new product launch will need. They must know what kinds of designs will result in a quality product; after all, quality starts with design. They recommend which plant can accommodate the product at the appropriate time and what personnel can pull it off with the right quality, on time, to the expected volumes and mix, and within budget.

Top manufacturing officers will thrive or fail based on how much they influence the long-range product plan. Don't be intimidated into relinquishing your input.

I evaluate the success of a new car or truck launch, first of all, by whether the customer likes our product and, secondly, on how well we met our budget—the plan we submitted to the board of directors. If there are variants, I will ask myself, "Can we explain them, or were they simply mistakes?"

Success also will be measured in quality terms. What is our measurable quality in the first 12 months of service? I've always felt manufacturing should be 100% responsible for the first three to six months in service; then it becomes more of a reliability issue and gets more into design engineering specifications and supplier capability from months six through 12. At that point, you move into durability issues. An engine, for example, if it's really durable and well maintained, will last 20 years, but if it's not, you will see problems in the first five.

Looking at specific launches: the K-car in '80, the minivan in '84, the Dakota in '86, and the LH in '92. What do they have in common? First, ask if the customer wants the product. The answer is "yes" for all four. Was the quality in the product what they wanted? For the K-car, no. For the minivan, yes. For the Dakota, yes. For the LH, time will tell. Then, what were their costs? We missed the budget significantly on the K-car, we beat it on the minivan and Dakota, and time should tell if we were close on the LH.

Engineering changes? With a system developing dynamically, cooperatively, and progressively for the last dozen years, there should be a dramatic reduction in engineering changes on new products today, in the '90s, compared to the early to mid-'80s. We had a lot fewer engineering changes on the minivan than we did on the K-car because we had learned from the K-car launch. I've always felt that life is a continuum of learning and if you must learn the same thing twice, you're either lazy or dumb. I can't give you the numbers of changes on the LH, but they continued down on that learning curve.

Picking the Players

A team is no better than its players. Interviewing potential employees is important because your record as a leader will depend on how well you make these critical selections.

Beyond the legal, contractual requirements of an employment agreement (for which we rely on lawyers), I always want to know that the persons I am about to deal with live by their word and will live up to any such contract.

Beyond that, I quickly get down to attitude, capacity, merit, ability, and fit. Those are all subjective but crucial issues in selecting potential employees, from hourly employees to intermediate management to technical engineers to senior executives.

The key things I always look for are *character* and *competence*. If there are character problems, I do not want the person working for me, nor would I want to work for a person not of good character. As for competence, I ask myself, "What are the assignments we are asking these individuals to fill? Are they qualified? Are they competent? Are they experienced? Do they have stamina? Do they have health? Will they stick with us for the long term?" In short, I look for integrity, character, competence, stamina, and innovative skills. I look for chemistry and for good fit.

I also want to know about any athletic experience or interests because that tells me if they like to compete. It's not just if they ever were an athlete, but which sport. Did they play hockey? Did they box? Did they wrestle? Did they play football? These are very demanding sports where you are willing to risk getting hurt. This type of person must like competition. They must like battle. If they have chosen other fields of competition, such as a debate scholar or journalist, I will respect that also, but I still want to know what turns them on.

The point here is that in my 27 years in manufacturing, I never had an athlete quit on me. Not one ever failed to do the job I asked them to do! To my thinking, this confirms that this criterion is important.

Visiting the Troops

It is essential for manufacturing officials to keep their fingers on the pulse of the plants and operations. Depending on the nature of a plant, I reviewed it at least once and as often as 12 times a year.

If the top manufacturing executives don't go to the plants, the plants' staffs eventually feel abandoned. It is essentially the same when you do not visit your own parents, family members, and friends. If neglected, these relationships deteriorate and everyone suffers. Just as these relationships shrivel and die, a neglected plant also will wilt and die.

On plant visits, involve as many colleagues from supporting departments as possible. I always wanted people from finance, design, engineering, purchasing, labor relations, and sales and marketing with me. I knew their support was essential to successful production. I wanted them to see firsthand the impact of their decisions on plant and product success. By involving them in plant reviews, I moved them to a more intense level of support and teamwork. I also felt that the realism of their decisions dramatically improved if they could be based on what they saw and heard at the plant.

The entire attitude of a plant is set by the captain of the ship, the plant manager. The first thing I look at is attitude. It's crucial to find out the realities, to see if a plant has a good, healthy environment—a positive attitude generated by the employees within that facility. Are the people sensitive to the plant manager's objectives and goals or are these seen by them as just whipped cream on the cake?

It doesn't cost one penny to have a positive attitude. If the people in the plant don't have one, I expect the plant manager to take that as an assignment to get people positive, in focus and responsible, and to develop a catalytic-type managerial approach.

I always began these visits with human-relation issues, such as number of unresolved grievances, which people had been moved from one position to another, and who needed to be moved and why. We then covered product quality, discussing customer concerns about the product or processes and measures taken to correct these problems. Inventory turns and supplier relations always formed a major part of my review, as did maintenance in three critical areas: reactive, preventive, and predictive. Of course, we always reviewed budgets and variances to financial forecasts and recovery plans.

I always expected a plant to maximize the efficiency of the hand that they were dealt. If a plant manager had a manually processed body shop,

---

How To Do a Good Plant Review

- Involve colleagues from other disciplines.
- Conduct a plant operating review and emphasize product issues.
- Discuss human relations issues.
- Discuss maintenance.
- Spend at least 60% of the review on the shop floor.
- Walk, don't ride, the tour.
- Wander into corners; get where the sparks are flying.
- Talk to the floor workers.
- Discuss accomplishments.
- Discuss problems.
- Discuss the future of the plant.
- Emphasize world benchmarking.
- Follow up!

I did not compare him to a plant with a fully robotized body shop, but I would compare him to his own track record.

Next, I ask if their capability is improving, remaining the same, or declining. Is local general waste being reduced, things over which the plant manager has influence or control? That can range from paint shop sludge to cardboard and debris from dunnage to scrapped body panels. Obviously, if there is innovation or vision there—if people are creative, ingenious, and working as a team—then there should be constant improvement.

I ask how they get along with their audience. By this, I mean all the people that support that plant, including the union leadership, employees, suppliers, dealers they are servicing, and even the utilities supplying the energy.

Because I believe in *self-help*, I expected the plant staff to present five problems they corrected in the past 30 days, without involving corporate staff. I expected the local people, led by the plant manager's team, to take the initiative and handle these things themselves. I would leave this totally up to the plant manager, asking, "What are the five things you are doing internally? Because, once you tell me, we're going to review them in the future. I want dates, facts, trends, and the final results." The reason you keep score in any game is to know if you are winning or losing.

We then would address future concerns, such as the local business plan, the build-out of the present model, and preparations for the new model launch.

For anything that had to go beyond the plant level for approval, whether people or machinery related, I would ask them to focus on their top five needs. That way, I wasn't chasing a flock of butterflies. I would have five specific things to take back with me and assist that plant manager and the plant staff to get accomplished. I would ask, "What do you need externally from us? Tell us right now, and we'll close the loop. The clock won't start ticking until we actually deliver what you need."

There are several key things a plant manager could not do without my approval. For example, I would ask, "What do you need to train your people?" I would expect them to lay out a training program, some of which could be handled locally, and some of it would require sending people to our corporate training center. I always wanted at least one of these five things to be people-related and one to be technology. Usually, I wanted a third to relate to material handling, either rationalizing the supplier base, going to Just-In-Time from traditional pick-and-pack, or going to sequenced parts delivery, which is an even more intense, more efficient material system. It is a dynamic approach to management.

I tried to balance the plant review so 40% of the meeting was in the offices and the conference room, and 60% on the plant floor. I took greater control of the review on the plant floor and normally adjusted the walking route recommended by the plant manager. Instead, I strolled into the dark corners, into the body shop where the welding sparks were flying, into the operating-room atmosphere of the paint shop, on the roof, into the powerhouse, and in the bowels of basements.

I always declined to ride vehicles during normal plant tours. It is essential to walk, observe, talk, listen and think.

Walking affords the opportunity to greet the workers, look at the plant closely and, in general, get an accurate sense of its personality. A plant is easy to read when you are experienced.

After breaking bread and relaxing, I wrapped up the review by giving specific direction on issues needing improvement. I would place the burden of accountability on the plant manager, following up later to ensure the issues we discussed were satisfactorily resolved within an agreed-to time. I also made my colleagues from other disciplines aware of their responsibilities on issues related to their areas. We expanded on these privately on the return trip, and I made it a point to sit next to the person who could have the most impact on the plant and on its product.

It was my job to leave a plant more energized than I found it, to keep people going in the right direction, at the right pace, and with focus. As I reminded plant managers, "two-thirds of promotion is motion, so get moving!"

Dauch discusses air quality, general maintenance, and winterization plans on the roof with Chrysler Power Train General Manager Frank Clark and Director of Power Train Manufacturing Engineering Rick Zella (left) during a plant review.

What It Takes to Make Plant Manager

During my watch as a corporate manufacturing officer, I conducted 100 to 150 plant reviews annually. They paid big dividends. Doing so let people know I cared about them, their work, and their product, and that I was always available to support them if they needed it.

When I hired or promoted people to plant manager, I looked for several qualities. Character and integrity were first. Second were competence and high energy. I wanted plant managers who enjoyed a good family life as well. In the uphill, long-day battle, people need peace and support at home to be able to give their best on the job. I looked for balance in them intellectually, physically, emotionally, and in their interests, both professional and private. Did they have the energy and enthusiasm to motivate others to positive, focused, results-oriented action? I also asked myself if the candidate would fit into the system. The plant manager is the spokesperson for the corporation in the community. These were the only considerations that mattered. My plant managers were of both sexes, of every creed and color, and from various ethnic groups. They had to be responsible, positive, and catalytic.

The three best jobs I ever held were executive vice president of worldwide manufacturing, plant manager, and foreman. I first made plant manager at Chevrolet Livonia making leaf and coil springs, bumpers, and brake systems, with 3000 employees. It was a highly diversified operation processing over 50,000 tons of steel a month. This factory was exciting and demanding. My second plant manager job was at Chevrolet Detroit Gear and Axle, producing power train and chassis components, employing over 7000 people. It was a wildly busy inner-city plant.

Based on these experiences, I strongly believe a plant manager must be an on-site CEO with 24-hour-a-day, seven-day-a-week, 365-day-a-year accountability. It requires impeccable credentials and exceptional dedication, determination, and business acumen. It is not for the inexperienced, timid, or mental lightweight.

It is the plant manager's responsibility to identify and solve problems. This person must formulate a business plan that includes key tracking mechanisms to monitor employee safety and health trends; product safety performance; product quality, timing, cost, and performance; employee and union relationships with management; facility maintenance and improvement; production planned versus actual volume to market; budget variances (positive or negative); delivery into and out of the plant (normal mode versus premium); supplier and customer relations; management and organizational efficiency and morale; community relations, and future plant product loading and business strategy. The factory's department heads should assist the plant manager. They must relate with sensitivity to the dealers and customers.

The plant manager also must establish annual and long-term goals and track their progress faithfully. Short-term issues should be dealt with as "risks" and "opportunities." Also, all direct reports must submit, preferably on Mondays, a one-page "hot" list of items that could affect plant performance for the current week.

On Being Set Up

I learned these things a long time ago: Never go to class without doing your homework. Never go to the football field without knowing that your

Tips for New Manufacturing Managers

- Don't come on too aggressively. Let the organization absorb you.
- Don't pretend to know more than you do. Actively and patiently listen. Ask questions of substance and study specific things that can contribute to operational improvement.
- Don't be hasty. Ignoring the adage "haste makes waste" will cause you grief.
- Don't get involved in confrontations. Develop your game plan and decide how to discuss and share it appropriately. Where there are differences of opinion, work them out privately and professionally.
- Don't forget that measurable improvements are critical. Make them happen within the framework of the organization.
- Don't forget that one game does not make a season! You will need a minimum of three to five years of measurable improvement to develop a track record.
- Don't forget that continual, consistent improvement is healthier and more productive than short, sensational spurts.
- Don't ever forget people who care for your growth and future, as well as people who see you as a threat, are always watching and measuring what you do.
- Don't forget image is as important as reality. Develop and maintain an image consistent with your fundamental values and goals.

body is in shape and your mind focused. Never go to a factory unless you have done your studies of the people, the plant, the product.

It's only human nature for people to set up a rookie. When I joined Chrysler in '80, obviously, I knew nothing about their factories. I didn't know the people, I didn't know the union, and I didn't know the product. Everything I was learning was being told to me. Some people will tell you straight, but most people put their own spin on the ball.

So I was always prepared for a "setup" when I first got there. I learned the best thing to do is be very thoughtful, be on time, be an active and patient listener, and observe. Then, using your own good head and your own good experience, sift through all these marbles and decide what you really think is right.

That was my approach: have an open mind, be prepared for the worst, and hope for the best. I planned that somebody would set me up big time and bad, but I hoped they wouldn't. The first few years, however, they had a new kid on the block. A lot of people tried me out, but they learned that plants did close, people did lose their careers, and we in senior management were going to hold people accountable.

Walking the Floor

I always insisted on walking the plant floor and talking to people enroute. The only way you really find the pulse of the plant is to be out there and part of it all—to feel it, see it, sense it, and ask questions. If that required an operator to be relieved from duty, I would ask the plant manager to arrange it so the operator could sit down with the plant manager and me and talk in a relaxed manner.

It was very open. I always carried item cards, noting on them the things being brought to my attention. They were my list of "things to do and follow through" on. If a worker asked for something to be done or considered, I wrote it down and promised that the supervisor would personally respond within three days. I always "closed the loop" with the supervisor first, enabling first-line supervisors to maintain their status as the direct voice of management, the voice of decision.

These shop floor people were talking not just to me but to whoever was in the group. We received great ideas. Many times, these were simple suggestions: "I need a fixture tuned up." "I need something maintained more frequently." "My material is coming in with grease on it." "I'm working in an awkward position and getting a back spasm. It's okay the first part of my shift, but on the second half, because I'm 58 years old, my back goes spastic on me."

These were not things requiring a rocket scientist to resolve. They were usually reasonably simple, straightforward, common-sense things that the people there had been so close to, they couldn't see the trees for the forest. Or perhaps, they thought that operator was "BSing" them. Two-way communications, with patient listening skills, are important.

I wanted more sensitivity from my supervisors. "Hey, that operator's telling you this but you're ignoring her," I'd tell them. Obviously, I had to be careful because there was a sensitive line here between intimidation, and compassion and participative management. I wanted to make the quality of the product better, and if I wasn't getting that through the normal system, I had to stimulate it. I did so knowing that poor guy was muttering to himself, ''This guy's the executive vice president and he's as intimidating as hell. He's 6-feet-2, 235 pounds, and you can't miss the SOB, he's looking straight at you!'' There is nowhere to hide.

Well, when you're eye to eye, you see the soul. Later, that guy had to admit to himself, ''He's got a big heart. He shook my hand. He was sincere. He wrote everything down, gave it to a close assistant and, in a short time, I got a report on it.'' This leaves the power with the first-line supervisors to start doing their work as they should with their first-line operators. The power is in the people.

Caught in the Act

When I was a plant manager, I did similar solo excursions on my plant floor, always varying my course, timing, and shift to maintain the frankness and spontaneity of the interaction on these walks. No one, not even my secretary, knew when or by which route I would traverse the plant. It was my way of keeping everyone on their toes.

Despite these precautions, I was often foiled by a variety of technically advanced plant communication systems. One was devised by crane operators, seated in the rafters, tooting coded alarms with their horns to pass the word on which direction I was headed when they saw me crossing the factory.

In one instance, I had fought hard to get some programs approved at that plant to give the people a new lease on life: five new press lines, a brand new office complex, a new loading dock, a leaf-spring modernization program and so forth. I got the money approved, delegated the work to the appropriate people, and authorized the right contractors to work on it. Every day, I would walk the plant for at least five or six hours but never in the same place or the same time.

After a while, I realized that those crane operators were tipping everyone exactly where I was headed. I figured there's a solution for every problem, and since they are setting me up, I'll just drop in unannounced with one of those contractors landing on the plant roof in their helicopter.

I did that one day in a very key area that I wanted to see—steel fabrication and erection—and quickly learned some things that weren't the way the reports said they were.

From this, I developed my TMTTME theory—Tell Me the Truth and Tell Me Early—because I've always felt that if you and I are always honest with each other, always truthful, we'll never have a problem. But that's a one-on-one situation. That swells when you become a supervisor and it's now 25:1, a general supervisor and it's 200:1, a superintendent and it's 700:1, or a plant manager and it's 7000:1.

Now swell that to 70,000, and you've got the responsibility for corporate world manufacturing operations. You can't go one-on-one with very many people. So you must develop a basic credibility that you are trustworthy. Your people must feel that when you say something, you mean it; when they say something, you'll listen; and when you say you will close the loop, you will. They also must know that if they are not being straight with you, heaven help them!

TMTTME—tell me the truth and tell me early. Believe me, when you work with Iacocca, you had better have a similar philosophy. That's why I liked working for Lee. He was straight, credible, no nonsense, and intelligent. I could deal in engineering terms because he was technically trained.

Tips For Plant Managers

Here are a few tips from my experience as plant manager:

- Select a high-character, competent, dependable, confidential secretary with a positive personality. This person is the nerve center of your communication system and an extension of your image. Do not delegate selecting this person.
- Know your product in detail, your global competition, your process capabilities, and your customers. Visit your customers often. Develop good relationships with suppliers.
- Develop good working relationships with your corporate support staffs. You need purchasing's help to motivate suppliers. You need corporate personnel to help you hire, fire, transfer, demote, and promote people. You also need them to administer compensation and benefits as well as to help with medical, environmental, and union matters. You need corporate finance support on budget plans and approvals, on project control, on appropriations, for business and profit planning, on forecasting and variances, and on tax and fiscal matters.
- Always have your resident engineer, chief metallurgist, purchasing agent, controller, and personnel director brief you before visitors and dignitaries in their areas leave the plant. This is important to maintain good communication and support for your production location. Remember, you are totally accountable.

- Develop and exhibit in a prominent location in the plant a quality product and organization display. It will instill pride in workers about the product they make, and help sell it to others.
- Never, ever, let problems grow. Nip them in the bud. Actively listen to relevant views. Require the players to express themselves with data, facts, trends, and results. Try to get a consensus and decision made at lower levels of the organization, then be decisive and support it.
- I also suggest becoming selectively involved in local community affairs. The corporation expects this of you as its ranking representative in the community. When I was a plant manager, I picked three areas I thought would best serve the plant and the corporation: the Chamber of Commerce; the Plant-City Committee, made up of local business leaders and city officials working on community and civic issues; and a youth program such as Junior Achievement, Boys and Girls Clubs, or the Boy Scouts.
- Finally, protect your credibility. People will try to set you up, so be prepared and professional.

Develop the Big Picture

Working for and with the plant manager are the engineers and supervisors who keep the plant moving. Many of these people carry the title of manufacturing engineer. With them rests the charge of making it work, whether the facility is one of many plants in a large corporation or a small business with one site. They may be a highly specialized group or a multi-hat individual who serves as designer, cost estimator, manufacturer, and maintenance supervisor.

Clearly, it is important for such people to be aware of the big picture. Product is the bedrock of the business with quality the key issue and the price of market admission. No one will stay in business long by producing high-priced and/or poor-quality goods. Engineers and supervisors must know that their decisions and work affect the profitability and, indeed, the viability of the business that puts bread on the table for them and their co-workers. They must realize they are not competing only with the shop on the other side of town, but with a business on the other side of the world. They must be kept informed of market trends, and, in turn, must inform plant management of potential problems as well as improvements in process.

It is important for engineers and supervisors to continue their education and/or training. The corporation relies on them to evaluate and implement the latest technology to maintain manufacturing competitiveness. Education and training do not necessarily mean pursuing a PhD. You can learn by scanning manufacturing-related trade journals, reading books, attending seminars and conferences, and taking plant tours. Meetings with manufacturing colleagues can prove useful in exchanging technical and operating information.

The leadership of manufacturing must provide the right incentives if the company is to compete in the global market. Manufacturing must work with corporate systems to establish global requirements so other disciplines will understand the impact of their decisions on the production process and final product. Using the philosophy of concurrent engineering to involve—up front—program management, design, engineering, marketing, manufacturing, sourcing, finance, and customer service will ensure optimum results in product cycle time, customer satisfaction, and cost control. (I discuss how Chrysler did this in Chapter 7.)

Chapter 4

LEADERSHIP AND MOTIVATION

Persons who find themselves in leadership positions will find it necessary to be a force, stimulus, or influence in motivating the team to the level required to accomplish established goals.

There are various means to instill incentive and drive within an organization. A successful leader must be astute enough to know when to use motive, impulse, incentive, inducement, and when to spur or goad. Sanction and reprisal should be used rarely and then only with a profound sense of responsibility. Each situation will dictate a particular approach.

If you aspire to be a successful manufacturing manager, you will need to develop your innate leadership ability. Sit down and write a candid self-analysis. You need to focus and direct your leadership strengths and develop the areas where you may be weak.

Leaders should conduct themselves in a manner that earns the respect of the people.

Authority brings with it the responsibility to lead, protect, nurture, and encourage those whom one leads. Humanitarian management training emphasizes these responsibilities of leadership because it is the aspect of authority most easily forgotten, especially under the pressure of deadlines and production schedules. Both the carrot and the stick are necessary components of manufacturing management.

A senior executive needs a balance of preach and teach. You must be constantly nurturing and changing that culture to see that you are not relying on pride alone to produce performance. You must grow your people. You must expand them and stretch them. Sometimes growing and stretching hurt but that's how birth occurs. To have any kind of growth, you must go through some strain, some pain, to make any gain.

There's an adage that applies to football and it applies equally well to production. "You have to be agile, mobile, versatile, and flexible, and rarely, but occasionally, hostile." Our employees knew that if they were properly prepared, they would never see hostility from me.

Know When to Show

There may seem to be a dichotomy here between the various needs for motivation to get the results required and the rewards derived from close relationships. That explanation is as simple as the British saying, "Different horses for different courses," or our own, "Different strokes for different folks."

Obviously, it depends on the situation. There were times when I had to use the carrot and a very soft-shoe approach. There were others when stronger measures were unavoidable. It always required personal judgment.

For example, in the acquisition of AMC in 1987, on my first visit to the key plants, Kenosha and Toledo, I called together a private meeting with the top two union officials at those locations, and my most senior executive at that location as well as the divisional vice president or general manager.

In Toledo, I met for about one hour with Dan Twist and Ron Conrad, the two union officials heading up the UAW activities there. We had an honest, forthright exchange as to what we, the new parent, brought to the party and our delight to have them as part of the team. We let them know we would respect their past.

We also made it clear there were some images that must be changed immediately: The image of not working together. The image of strikes. The image of shoddy quality. The image involved with a lack of understanding that the customer is the final boss.

I also told them that one game doesn't make a season. Because you have one great year, don't expect us to come here and hand out lollipops. I challenged them to give us five straight good years. If they did, we would see to it that they had a healthy, ongoing operation. There was, you see, considerable concern about whether Toledo would remain viable. We had a similar meeting in Kenosha with Al Scudder (the general manager), myself, and Rudy Kuzel (the union president).

I had excellent cooperation and leadership from these people. Today, Chrysler has powerful assets at Toledo and Kenosha, building good quality Jeeps and stronger, more cooperative, personal relationships every day. One year after that first meeting, we increased volume from 180,000 to 270,000 Jeeps coming out of Toledo! Anytime you can boost volume 50%, it must be because you have the right attitude and cooperation.

What turned them around? I feel part of it is a management style that is refreshing because it is direct, honest, and sincere. I am bold, with little time for BS. Usually, I look right at a person, rarely blinking for five or 10 minutes. That gets people's attention. As I've said, the eye is the window of the soul.

The people at Toledo and Kenosha knew I was dead serious, and they knew they had a communication pipeline to me. If they needed me, I would be there.

In 1981, I had a similar meeting with the Motown folks at Jefferson Avenue Assembly. This was a tough meeting where I invited senior union officials, local plant officials, and my key lieutenants to a real meeting of the minds.

I have always had the philosophy that if you have something bothering your stomach, burp it up—get the gas off your belly! If you want to call me names, call me whatever you want. When we get done and walk out of the room, we don't have to be in love, but I want our forces aligned.

Although most thought then that Jefferson was doomed, we now have a brand-new, $800-million facility with fully retrained people. How did we do it? First, we had to get their attention. Then we needed action with measurable results—improvement year after year. One year won't do it. After five, eight, or 10 years of good results, then the board and Iacocca could say, "I don't know what you are doing at Jefferson or Toledo or Kenosha, but the data looked great! Let's continue betting on those locations."

Territoriality

Most of us have an innate drive to acquire real estate. Those at the higher levels of the dominance hierarchy occupy the best places and have access to the most acreage. In other words, rich people tend to live on hills, while poor people dwell on the flood plain.

The noteworthy failures of Communist economies attest to the fact that man is territorial. One of Communism's tenets is that the means of production, which includes real property, are the possessions of the state and not of any individual. Most former Communist states are rapidly reverting to some form of capitalism and private ownership. The experience of 70 years of common ownership has shown that man becomes much happier and more productive by fulfilling his need for private space.

Since most people resent authority, a manager can prevent needless problems by downplaying it. Your power and authority come with your title. Everyone can identify with resentful employees who go out of their way to deflate a pompous, swaggering boss. It is, therefore, important for you to be sensitive to the many ways in which dominance and territoriality are communicated in organizations. Armed with such sensitivity, you can gain control over the most overt expressions of animal dominance and territoriality. With greater control, you can defuse resentment.

Sending the Message

Although we usually think of communication as something to do with words, language is merely one aspect of communication, and an imperfect one at that.

Body movements communicate messages that often contradict the words accompanying them. The traditional bargaining session places negotiators at opposite sides of a long table. Such positioning sets the stage for confrontation. The parties will reach agreement with much less friction if seating is arranged differently. A round table further reduces volatile postures and frontal assaults.

Negotiations between the Big Three and the United Auto Workers inevitably begin with a photo session showing the negotiating teams on opposite sides of a table. The table is so large that both chief representatives must bend far over it to shake hands. The management negotiator normally wears a suit. The union man usually wears no tie, often no jacket. The message is confrontation. The table size creates distance, coldness, lack of togetherness. Dress symbolizes authority on one side, rebellion on the other. Such negotiations are staged for failure.

Do you remember the Paris peace negotiations to end the Vietnam War? The first months were spent haggling over the table's size and shape. Eventually, both sides agreed on a round shape to minimize confrontational positioning. In negotiations with men, you get the best results by sitting at a man's side; they are not accustomed to aggressive actions from the side. Folded arms, crossed feet or legs, and lack of eye contact sometimes signals rejection, regardless of verbal cues. How titles, first names, nicknames, and pronunciation of surnames are used communicates the intensity of human relationships and the relative status of individuals. Continuing to mispronounce or misspell a surname always conveys a lack of respect.

Status: Use and Misuse

Wealth or how much you earn is the ultimate status measurement in the United States. In older cultures, formal education and knowledge accrue the most status. A special parking place, a large office with a window or an adjoining rest room, and a large plush conference room communicate the status of the person assigned them. Who talks and who listens also is dramatically indicative of status. Higher status managers talk more and listen less. Although this is instinctive, it is a dangerous weakness.

You must use a proper balance with status symbols. I could care less about where I park or where I eat. What I do care about is the condition and safety of that parking lot and the quality of the food available inside—not just for me, but for everybody. When I came to Chrysler, there wasn't one hot-food cafeteria in any plant in the city of Detroit. When I left, every one of my plants had hot-food cafeterias, not just for the plant managers and staff, but for every worker in the plant.

In addition to the facility items mentioned above, I was not satisfied with other aspects of employee treatment which I encountered upon joining Chrysler. I told myself, "If we are going to turn this company around, this must be changed dramatically." In 1980, I started a cultural change in Mexico through education and training and giving the workers the chance to work on a five- to six-year program to take over their own future.

Then in '81, I found that the people in our North American assembly and stamping plants didn't have hot food, and when I went into the parking lot, it was all cinders and broken concrete. There was no pride! You drove your car in and were afraid the car would get stolen, or you would get mugged on the way into the factory. Once inside, there was nowhere to eat hot food or get a hot chocolate, except from a vending machine.

This bothered me, so every time I submitted my investment budgets, I included some social costs. Now, every parking lot is paved, safe,

67

secure, well-maintained, well-lighted, and close to the buildings. When workers get in the building, they see locker rooms with adjoining shower facilities, with hot water. These things are important to the working man and woman.

I did things to improve employee treatment because I'd been a working man and knew how important people are to any effort where teamwork is critical. I showed compassion wherever I could. When someone would challenge me by saying, "You top dogs get all the perks," I'd respond, "Well, we don't need them all. I'm prepared to give up a bunch of them if it will help our organization succeed."

For example, at Chrysler's Belvidere, Illinois, facility we closed the executive dining room and put in first-come, first-served parking. There were other things, however, that must be kept even though they seem unnecessary. The corporate airplane, for example, is not a perk, it's a tool. When the Federal loan guarantee program "shot down our planes" in the early '80s, I put in 20-hour days to have a four-hour meeting in Huntsville, Alabama. Once we were profitable, and our planes were back in the air, I could have a 10-hour meeting in Huntsville in a 15-hour day, which seemed more efficient to me.

We Need Good Communication

One person cannot know everything to make the decisions required by an increasingly complex world. This is especially true in manufacturing where technologists and engineers can provide a wealth of critical technical information. One of the most important requirements I had for my plant managers was communication. I expected each one to complete a Dale Carnegie course to help them with their communication, personal confidence, and human-relations skills.

The kinds of formal communication devices (newspapers, newsletters, bulletin boards, electronic message boards, etc.), and how often the information they contain is updated, show the seriousness of management's commitment to communication within an organization. I say that the more communication, the better.

The manner in which important messages such as cost, quality, and production performance are transmitted discloses whether the organization is attempting to be inclusive or exclusive. Clear, straightforward reports enhance the sense of belonging and employee participation. Complicated indices, convoluted sentences, and specialized jargon alienate people and make workers more difficult to motivate and manage.

Sales, product, process, profits, and personnel information must be disseminated regularly among the work force, preferably in verbal form and ideally by the plant manager. The Town Hall meeting, where the plant manager addresses an entire shift and the attendees can openly discuss company issues, is a popular forum in Chrysler plants.

Communication from management can be fraught with intimidation because the manager exerts so much influence on the well being of subordinates. Anyone who wields power over others is scrutinized by those impacted by that power. Few managers are aware of the influence this scrutiny has on the attitudes and behavior of subordinates. The values and style of managers will be mimicked by all but those who consciously or unconsciously reject them as leaders. The more successful a manager is perceived to be, the more imitation.

The manager actually creates culture by acting as a behavior model and, with the exception of powerful external forces, is also the only one who can change that culture. Since almost everyone resents authority and seeks to improve their relative status, managers can dispel a good measure of resentment by downplaying behaviors and symbols that communicate higher status. On the other hand, a manager can reward employees by conferring on them the rights to these same behaviors and symbols. By doing this, managers will not only enhance their ability to lead, they also decrease the stress of those individuals of lower actual status.

Many studies show that stress increases down the pecking order. The more stress individuals are subjected to, the more susceptible they are to disease—both mental and physical. People with lower status also die younger than higher ranking contemporaries.

Management Paradox

The private loves the general but hates the lieutenant. The plant manager loves the hourly workers but treats the production manager with caution and suspicion. What accounts for this puzzling behavior?

Humans long for a leader whom they can revere, respect, even love. If such a leader doesn't exist, they will create one, projecting the leadership qualities they crave on a real or imagined figure. To maintain the illusion, the mythical leader must remain some distance removed from those being led because, as the proverb goes, familiarity breeds contempt. The general is far enough away from the private to maintain the private's illusions.

Practicing manufacturing managers should take this proverb very seriously. If managers show too many weaknesses, they destroy employees' illusions. When that happens, the vengeance wreaked upon those who destroy the illusions is terrible. When managers destroy an illusion that they never created, and which they may not even realize exists, the adulation they enjoyed from their subordinates will turn to resentment at best, vicious rebelliousness at worst.

To maintain illusions, you must keep your distance.

Maintaining distance from those you lead is not natural, though. An individual aspiring to leadership is imbued with the desire to be different, to stand out, to be recognized. You get flattery and fulfillment when acclaimed by those who range far below in the pecking order. It is, after all, the primary payoff of power. This explains why presidents forsake bodyguards to wade into a cheering crowd. It accounts for the plant manager's tendency to feel more comfortable among hourly workers than in the presence of direct-report staff. It clarifies the powerful attraction between those of very high status and those of relatively low station. It is a tendency you must rigorously control if you are to manage effectively.

The effective manager limits emotional attachments of any kind with subordinates. Emotion clouds the clear judgment necessary to hire, deploy, promote, and terminate employees according to their talents and the organization's requirements. It must be "lonely at the top" if you are to make decisions that transcend irrelevant considerations.

Evaluating Personnel

Management decisions must be devoid of emotion; none more so than the annual performance appraisal. The appraisal is a very powerful tool for management because it affects everyone. It is very volatile because, in most cases, neither managers nor subordinates like it or feel comfortable with it.

You must maintain distance from subordinates on a consistent basis if the appraisal is to be taken seriously by them. Employees cannot accept an evaluation of their total being from someone they cannot respect. Respect consists of a complex mixture of love and fear. It is virtually impossible to fear a buddy, friend, or lover. Even love is difficult to maintain at close range. Closeness is too damaging to illusions.

The most striking difference between man and animal is our ability to rationalize all thoughts, opinions, and deeds. We will vigorously resist anything perceived as a possible threat to our self-image. Tests and examinations threaten self-esteem. The performance appraisal is the most threatening because it can touch every aspect of a person—from appearance to reliability. Employees dislike it because of its implied threat to their self-worth. Managers dislike it because of the anticipated reactions from employees when their evaluations are recorded in the corporate memory.

The performance appraisal criteria must be agreed to by the employee in advance. Employee consent is tantamount to acceptance of accountability for the duties and responsibilities proposed by the criteria. Theoretical acceptance is, however, quite different from an actual situation that requires accountability. When things go wrong, as they inevitably will in manufacturing, the harsh expectation of Western culture will surface—someone must and will be held accountable.

The bosses are ultimately accountable for everything in their areas of responsibility. The only way they can maintain the integrity of their areas of accountability is by nurturing the most meticulous and even-handed accountability among subordinates. This same principle applies to business relationships.

The principle of accountability must, therefore, be accepted before the fact by every employee. A manager must define, and state in writing, the specific framework and details of the accountability of each individual. Without such advance specificity, finger-pointing, scapegoating, and lying will destroy the very fiber of the boss-subordinate relationship when things go wrong.

The plant manager is responsible for the factory environment and the character and competence of the plant's team of managers. The plant manager, and other managers for that matter, are always subjected to the rigorous, subjective requirement of fairness. Webster's defines fairness as impartiality; honesty; freedom from self-interest, prejudice, or favoritism; and conforming with established rules. Employees expect fair treatment. If they feel they are being handled unfairly they will be demoralized and less productive.

Let's say you are a new plant manager who has inherited a staff. You must accept the reality that they have a perception of fairness. Should you attempt to undermine this with actions that adversely affect one or more of them, you may lose the support of the others. They may feel you are not a "fair" boss. Therefore, learn to play the hand you are dealt. Work with your new staff. Develop them. Agree on achievable objectives. In this way, you will gain their support as well as that of uninvolved co-workers who may identify with the fate of the others.

Factories should strive to present a pleasant, eye-appealing atmosphere, both to the workers and the community. Worker morale can be uplifted by maintaining the landscaping at the plant. Chevrolet Livonia used trees, flowers, and shrubbery to improve its appearance. This sketch also served as the cover of the plant brochure.

Consensus-Builders

Two fundamental objectives in developing a management team consensus are worker safety and plant environment. The most dangerous businesses are mining, construction, agriculture, manufacturing, and sports, in that order. I worked in construction, grew up on a farm, spent most of my adult life in manufacturing, and played organized sports for 10 years, so I am very sensitive to safety.

Whenever I was given responsibility for one or more plants, I took care of safety issues first. Nothing is more gut-wrenching than informing a widow and her children of the death of the husband, father, and breadwinner. It is a task I strived to avoid at all costs by maintaining a safe working environment at the top of my priorities.

Second to safety is worker comfort, which has a major impact on quality and productivity. In the past, many manufacturing plants were gloomy, noisy, and dangerous. Whenever I had any influence on a plant, I attempted to eliminate the darkness either by having painting programs, installing more powerful lighting, or by having windows or skylights built. Chrysler's Jefferson North facility, for example, has windows at ceiling level around the entire perimeter and 36 skylights. They are worth the cost, given the cheerfulness they lend to this state-of-the-art assembly plant. When I was at Chevrolet, I made an effort to provide a pleasant atmosphere at the plant's entrance with greenery and maintenance of outside areas.

At Chrysler in the early '80s, I asked plant engineers to develop a plan to reduce noise levels to 85 dbA or lower. I like quiet plants. My philosophy is to manage smoothly, quietly, efficiently. We used new-generation conveyor technology to eliminate the dingy, uncomfortable pits so many of our workers inhabited during their working hours. We used paint to create bright, attractive interior and exterior environments. We provided hot food in fully enclosed and cheerful cafeterias. We provided clean rest rooms, shower facilities, and locker rooms. We upgraded parking areas with permanent, hard surfaced, well-lighted, and secure facilities.

Our efforts paid off big in 1990, when the Sterling Heights assembly plant, where we first tested these work-environment concepts, was named the best Chrysler plant in measurable quality and productivity. It was also rated one of the top 10 assembly plants in North America. These concepts and systems work!

Pay attention to the little things as well.

I remember walking into a plant and seeing signs urging employees to keep things simple, a slogan also found in memos and, at times, even on coffee cups. It is called "KISS," or Keep It Simple, Stupid!

I have no disagreement with keeping directions, communications, or processes simple. But must we call any employee stupid?

Building Your Team

I have always enjoyed interviewing, recruiting, and putting teams together. It is a thrill to find people with the right talent, temperament, standards, and stamina to work in harmony with others. Teamwork is power.

The leadership roles in sports and manufacturing are very similar. Each requires an innate competitiveness, self-discipline, stamina, resilience, and toughness in the face of obstacles. Each also requires a respect for the team and its pecking order and a willingness to sacrifice individual ego fulfillment for the greater good of the team and its mission.

I totally support teamwork. I love teamwork and I'm a team player, but I also know that teams do require leadership. That's part of good management and it's called "focus." I've always felt part of my strength is knowing how to focus people. Get their attention, get them focused, and get everybody to understand we are all going to win or we're all going to lose. A ship in distress at sea doesn't sink just the front half or back half. If one end goes down, sooner or later the other end goes with it. In manufacturing, you're all in that boat together. You simply must have focused, efficient, open teamwork.

Any team can be too big or too small, have too much time or not enough. Each situation requires judgment. You need balance on teams—both in team size and its skills. Timing and balance are important because you don't want to waste effort or time, or get in the team's way.

Anything worth doing requires a sense of urgency. When we went before the board of directors to sell a new-car, new-engine, or new-facility program, we had to agree on when—two, three, or four years hence—we expected to launch the product to the public. A new car launch takes four. A new engine may take only two, as would a piece of a facility, such as a new press or robotic program. This urgency then gets communicated to the teams that will implement that product launch. Each team's deadlines derive from the executive-officer team's deadline when it commits to the board.

Any team can do better. When a college football team wins a national championship with only 17 yards passing, for example, you can bet they will be working on passing drills the following spring. No matter who you are or how good you may be, you can get better. That's called fine-tuning or working on your soft spots.

Any team must be reviewed. We had operational review meetings and it was my job as the chief manufacturing officer to lead this team. I purposely constructed these reviews to get cross-functional involvement. I didn't have to bring in designers or marketing people, or engineering, purchasing or finance people, but I always did because I felt it was important for manufacturing to be understood by key people outside it. Otherwise, they wouldn't know their decisions had major impacts on us.

Melting-Pot Americanism

Manufacturing, like sports, requires the best contributions from people of both sexes and all creeds and ethnic groups—melting-pot Americanism, something we taught the world.

In 1980, for example, the Chrysler Diversified Operations Group numbered approximately 20,000 people. It included many foremen. Less than 1% of them were college graduates. There were no women. There were no African-Americans above the superintendent level. A Hispanic in supervision was rare. The situation in the Manufacturing Group mirrored that of Diversified Operations.

Ten years later, the president of Acustar, formerly Diversified Operations, was an African-American manufacturing veteran, Forest Farmer. General plants manager of the former American Motors (AMC) assembly plants was the highly motivated, people-sensitive, and results-oriented Dick Donaldson, an African-American. Without the outstanding leadership of another African-American, Roy Smith, director of the paint and anti-corrosion group, we would never have been able to totally renovate Chrysler paint and anti-corrosion systems.

Among Chrysler's African-American plant managers were Dennis Edwards of Newark assembly, Americus Crawford of Sterling stamping, Howard Lewis of New Mack assembly, Paul Foster of McGraw glass, and Murv Enders of Indianapolis Foundry. Female plant managers included Martha Wallace at Outer Drive Pilot Operations, Linda Petro of McDonald plastics, and Sandra Bouckley in the Canadian fabrication plant. By 1990, there were 33 women on the bonus roll in the Manufacturing Group (in 1980 there were none). Many more plant managers will come from the group we developed. Moreover, Vice President Richard E. Acosta, a Hispanic-American, headed up the largest, most important division in the group—the Car and Truck Assembly Division.

Leaner Leaders

With the trend toward lean manufacturing, which flattens the organization and pushes responsibility to the lowest levels, there will be fewer formal leadership slots for employees of merit. This must be compensated for by assigning greater authority to smaller business entities. For example, a manager may now have total productive and fiscal responsibility for a body shop or paint department. Pay for performance is another motivating tool. Further education, travel, and rotation to new assignments are other ways to keep employees interested in their jobs.

Americans must come to grips with the fact that the national economy will probably never again experience the growth it did after World War II. The continual upward mobility we have known, which actually began with the Industrial Revolution, is a fast-fading phenomenon. The first challenge is to compete, to qualify for the available and emerging positions. The next is to keep up with the advances in that field to survive in it. The third challenge will be preparing for newly developing fields, so new careers can be entered when old ones become obsolete.

In 1980, Chrysler had a serious shortage of leaders, so I made a conscious effort to identify and develop those people with potential. I appointed plant managers in Canada who were Canadian. In Mexico, we advanced Mexicans to high-level positions as soon as they could assume such responsibilities. Anthony Pujals, Carlos Lobo, and Roberto Gutierrez developed the fastest. Promotional appointments were based on character, competence, and ability to assume a leadership role and greater responsibility as a matter of course in the maturing process.

To provide experiences that would catalyze this, I rotated many potential leaders through several jobs with ever-increasing responsibility. I even transferred them temporarily to other business areas. Engineering is the discipline offering the most to a manufacturing specialist. I strongly believe that engineering and manufacturing are the twin towers supporting modern industry.

Purchasing is another key area because it deals with manufacturing from a supplier perspective. Purchasing can truly be an extension of the manufacturing process. A short stint in finance can broaden your perspective on how a manufacturing concern finds funds and develops budgets. The same is true of sales and marketing. It doesn't hurt to know how products are being sold, especially in this age of customer satisfaction. Seasoned manufacturing veterans can profit from service in the personnel department where they can learn about negotiating strategy, tactics, and administration.

Foreign experience is valuable to any executive. I was proud to have the Worldwide Manufacturing Group provide the leaders for Chrysler operations in Austria, Italy, China, and, in the recent past, for Chrysler de Mexico. We had developed a global business perspective and understanding.

Teamwork and the Individual

With the exception of the military and team sports, no endeavor requires the rigorous bonding of teamwork more than manufacturing in general and automobile assembly in particular. This bonding occurs naturally at times, in a rather loose form. In the vast majority of cases, though, it must be cultivated and nurtured.

In a collective culture, such as in Japan, all social institutions support it. In a culture based on individual accomplishment, such as in the U.S., you can develop teamwork only situationally with great skill and effort because cultural pressures often oppose it. Nowhere in the world does the individual have the personal freedom found in the United States. Nowhere else is the individual protected so thoroughly from the arbitrary exercise of government power. Only in the U.S. are social institutions expected to practice social egalitarianism in addition to performing their primary functions.

Every blessing, however, brings with it a liability of equal magnitude. Our unique personal freedom is no exception. In the U.S., legal and social preoccupation with the individual weakened those primary groups that promote the high degree of cohesiveness found in other cultures. In some countries, for example, children are taught to weigh every decision they make relative to its community impact. This extreme social consciousness makes it possible to muster resources as efficiently as possible to meet external competitive challenges. No resource is squandered. The total energy of the nation is deployed in one concerted effort.

Americans value individual achievement, recognize individual accomplishment, and reward individual effort. Outstanding individuals understand and take advantage of this situation by excelling in their activities. At times this is resented by those who do not choose or are not able to benefit from this American trait. This resentment may result in an adversarial atmosphere which diminishes productivity to the detriment of all. Some cultures reward or punish an entire group, thereby promoting solidarity and teamwork. Skillful drill instructors practice this kind of team building in U.S. Marine Corps basic training.

The team concept has many advantages over management by an individual. In addition to the variety of skill, experience, and perspective contributed by individuals from several different disciplines, team members are motivated to greater achievement when operating in a forum of their peers. They attempt to show the best they have to offer, thereby enriching the entire group. The process forces them to reveal their ideas in a nonthreatening manner, since the group expects each team member to speak with equal openness. Openness, which is not normally practiced when individuals are held strictly accountable, breeds intimacy. Intimacy builds esprit de corps and solidifies team unity.

In addition to the wealth of ideas generated by team interaction, team decisions are more likely to result in action because the members created and authorized the strategies in question. The more numerous and effective teams become, the more efficiently the business should run as more people have taken responsibility for their own destiny.

Teamwork and participative management are inevitable evolutionary steps in management practice. Decision-making in manufacturing is too complex to be entrusted to a single person. Participative management releases considerably more vigor and genius. The company benefits from the increase in ideas to meet the challenge of competition, and individual team members benefit even more. The acceptance and visibility of their ideas by other team members enhances their self-esteem. More important, the individual is delivered from the loneliness characterizing rugged individualism.

A great deal of lip service is paid to teamwork in the United States. To a great extent, however, awards, raises, and promotions are conferred on individuals, often for political reasons. If we continue propagandizing in favor of teams, yet promote individuals, the duplicity will result in a loss of credibility that may prove fatal to team efforts. (In the next chapter, I will discuss how we used teamwork to our advantage during Chrysler's comeback.)

Spotting Trouble

Spotting trouble before it happens is an important aspect of any position in manufacturing management. I used several techniques during my career. First, communication from employees is key. Walking the plant floor is critical. What is the mood of the employee? How does the equipment appear to be functioning? Is all the equipment functioning? What is the general pace? As part of the plant review, a meeting with plant leadership is critical. Second, evaluate all statistics. I found statistical process control provided the process feedback I needed to spot problems in their infancy. Third, evaluate production and/or sales reports. These valuable tools provide additional statistics of progress.

If you are thrust into a situation you didn't anticipate, follow these steps to manage the crisis:

- *Formulate a recovery plan.* You may have plenty of time to accomplish this task. You may have little. Evaluate your deadlines and get moving.
- *Evaluate your people resources.* Do you have the available talent needed to correct the situation? Look for character, competence, and trustworthiness in the crisis.
- *Talk to people.* They must make the solution happen.
- *Project both confidence and sincerity.* Conduct yourself in a manner consistent with the means established to manage the crisis. Convey a winning attitude by emphasizing the positive. Believe in yourself and get the staff believing in itself. As the leader, be decisive. This is one area where image is important.

- *Establish priorities.* Attack the problem (or a part of the problem) that can produce the most significant, quick, and positive results.
- *Don't re-invent the wheel.* There is usually no time.
- *Continue to evaluate.* This allows you to be certain you are not on the wrong course and thereby compounding the crisis.
- *Evaluate resources.* If the machine is down, do you have another resource? Can work be re-routed? Will overtime be needed? Can your vendors help?
- *Rally the troops.* Give them a pep talk if they need it. Project an image of calmness, but be enthused. This is not the time to assign blame. This is the time to take notes and judge who is performing.
- *Don't confuse effort with results.*

These tips worked for me. They will work for you.

Chapter 5

TEAMING WITH UNIONS AND SUPPLIERS

Meeting all my constituents eyeball to eyeball was one of my most important missions as a manufacturing manager. Honoring such a commitment requires a great deal of time. It also entails major risk. You must listen carefully and actively. If you fail to act on a significant number of employee-offered proposals, you risk losing your credibility and their confidence.

Most senior executives are reluctant to meet workers on the workers' turf, an attitude which is at the root of many labor problems. Workers are more likely to develop anger at an unseen power than at someone whom they have seen and, perhaps, spoken to. At the least, workers must know there is some accessibility to an authority figure—even the illusion of accessibility makes them feel they are worthy individuals, that they are part of the action. To ignore them is to deny them dignity—which is unforgivable.

Looking Back At Unions

Unionism in America came about because management was unfair to the hard working blue-collar laborer. Unions were born on a negative note. In the early years, unions were barred from the auto industry. Consequently, long, bitter strikes and deaths occurred at GM, Ford, and Chrysler in the '30s.

When I entered management in the early '60s, a second and third generation of unionized auto worker was in the factory. They were taught by their parents and grandparents not to trust management and to be confrontational and adversarial. It wasn't necessarily the management of the moment that was stirring them up—precedents had been set.

I was reared differently from most managers. Workers saw I knew how to work. When I was a supervisor, if somebody couldn't rivet a side rail properly, I'd take the rivet gun and work with him until the problem was solved. If I had to use a 16-inch drift pin with a three-pound hammer to align the rail, I knew the parts weren't mating properly, and we needed an action plan to correct this problem quickly.

If you are involved with traditional North American business or industry, you will inevitably work with unions. Personnel or industrial relations people typically handle most union contract issues. If the company requires radical change, however, this may mean involving operations management directly.

Union leaders prefer dealing with operations managers because they feel they will get greater concessions from them. They think of company labor relations officials as contract lawyers whose job is to hold the line and who have little shop floor experience. Yet, it is the operating management and supervisors who must live with the daily consequences of any agreement.

Aligned for Power

I will always honor how Doug Fraser, head of the union Chrysler worked with, aligned with Lee Iacocca. They did not exactly fall in love with each other but they aligned for power. Each was a force; together they were a power. It was certainly rare in America for a union president and a company CEO to align forces and go to Congress and the President of the United States. Through good salesmanship and persuasion, led by Iacocca but supported by Fraser, the Chrysler Loan Guarantee Act was jointly secured. One crucial covenant of that was major concessions by the union to the manufacturer, Chrysler, so that the government could ask the taxpayer to support the Loan Guarantee Act.

That set a tone for everybody in the UAW Chrysler Department and everyone on the Chrysler management team. If those two leaders could work together, it was time for everyone else to do the same. This turned the tide and began the change from confrontation toward cooperation, from adversarial relations toward teamwork.

Initial Confrontations

When I arrived at Chrysler, my first action was to take a quick tour of all operations. We did a series of quick field tours, and then I came back and wrote down the good and bad of it—a type of asset ledger, deciding what went on the good side and what went on the bad.

I soon concluded we had dirty, filthy, inefficient, and haphazard operations with people who were dispirited, unfocused, undisciplined, undereducated, ill-trained, and ready to quit. They thought this company would soon be dead.

That was the hand I was dealt. I didn't cry about it. I asked myself: "What in the world can we do about this mess?" I met with senior staff people, counseled with key plant managers and other executives, talked with labor people, and finally took the ball into my own hands (which I sometimes do). I called directly to Solidarity House, the union headquarters, and asked to talk to Marc Stepp, the Chrysler Department vice president.

I must have shocked him somewhat when I asked if I could have the privilege of meeting with him. He was kind enough to agree. We had a confidential discussion, detailing the conditions and observations I just mentioned. I looked him straight in the eye. He didn't flinch.

"Dick," he said, "I've been here 30-plus years and appreciate your wanting to see me. We do have a joint set of circumstances and problems that fate has put us together on. As you develop your plan, maybe you can take certain things into consideration. Maybe we can find some way to walk together and work together."

I found him to be a man of his word, as he did me. Lee Iacocca's installation of Doug Fraser on the board of directors helped my credibility in getting to know Marc. We started to develop a relationship of union/ management respect, and augmented it with an awful lot of field travels together. We had our own "road show."

People immediately took notice. Who was that traveling together? Stepp and Dauch, UAW and management. "My God—salt and pepper—on the same stage, helping each other," they said. They knew we were together when he and I started calling each other "brother." I had played for 10 years on sports teams where blacks and whites worked together for a common purpose with no discrimination, no segregation. I knew firsthand how such teams worked. At Chrysler, for over 60,000 workers, it was time to change work habits, attitudes, and work culture on the factory floor. Manufacturing is a game of competing, and what

Brother Stepp and Brother Dauch were preaching was, "Here is the competition. Compete to beat, or prepare to die. If that sounds brutal, we mean it."

None of us was prepared to do that, to lose our livelihoods. We even told *The Wall Street Journal* to take their predictions and go to hell. We were not about to die with dignity, we were going to survive and grow, and we in management were going to lead our people to that victory.

We traveled to every Chrysler assembly, stamping, and power train plant in the United States, as well as many of the component plants. Well over 150 times, we went privately to these plants with just a few members of Marc's staff supporting him and two or three from mine.

We would go in, stop operations, and talk to the people. Marc has the ability to communicate in his own special way, telling them bluntly, "No quality, no sales. No sales, no jobs." Saying this when he was standing arm in arm with a management guy, especially an executive vice president, got attention. Then, when I'd come on after him to speak, the audience didn't fall asleep. They listened. After that, we conducted an open exchange, and they weren't exactly telling us, "We love you, Marc and Dickie." These discussions were frank and tough. These were rough and tumble, two-a-day drills for a long time but it helped relieve tensions—get the gas off their bellies, so to speak—and they began realizing they could trust us.

I told them then, "Ladies and gentlemen, I'm looking you straight in the eye and telling you, if you continue to improve with measurable data on quality and productivity, I will find, together with senior management and the board's blessing, a new product to put here. When we do, we're going to modernize this plant, train each of you, put in new, modern technology and processing, and new materials management systems."

They looked right back and said, "Dauch, you're full of it! You've been here hardly a year, while we've been here 30. You don't know what the hell you're talking about!"

I replied, "I wouldn't have come here unless I had already worked out some policy and strategy for this plant with top management. I only had leverage with Lee Iacocca once. That was before I went to work for him. However, I did get his support before I came here today and we're going to do what needs to be done to turn this plant around!"

They soon found we meant it. Our message—delivered in these Town Hall meetings—was teamwork, cooperation, quality improvement, and responsiveness to the market. Every time we put in a new product, starting with the minivan at Windsor, we put in a balanced program. In

Tips for Working with Unions

1. Meet workers on their turf. Let them feel they have some accessibility to you.
2. Create a personal, yet professional relationship with the union leaders. They would rather deal with operations managers than labor-relations specialists.
3. Conduct public demonstrations that convey an image of equality and cooperativeness between managers and union officials.
4. Communicate often with the union membership on company goals, performance, and needs.
5. Seek local solutions to local problems. Plant cultures differ. A uniform approach is rarely appropriate for all plants.
6. Share company successes as well as failures with the membership and their leaders. Be credible and fair.
7. Maintain solidarity in the management ranks. Bickering and competitiveness among managers is a ticket to disaster.
8. The integrity of the management representatives dealing with the union must be impeccable.
9. If you feel you are being unreasonably restricted in your ability to manage the company, "draw a line in the sand" and take the necessary risks to maintain management viability.

Windsor, we spent $400 million, with $25 million of that just for training. We started that training two years before we launched the vehicle. We put the remaining $375 million into the facility and tooling including in-line sequencing and Just-In-Time materials management.

As a result, people started saying, "By gosh, what that guy told us two years ago is actually happening!" Then when this modernization fever spread throughout the organization—from '83 through '90—and we converted eight assembly plants the same way, they knew this was for real.

In 1981, I recommended involving a local manufacturing official in every negotiation affecting factory operations. Tom Miner, our highly respected, no-nonsense human resources vice president, and my boss, Steve Sharf, then executive vice president of manufacturing, backed me on this. Chrysler used the tactic until 1991. It helped customize agreements to the needs of the local organization, as well as rendering them more effective since local management shared total ownership of them for the first time. This pleased the union because it no longer compelled its leaders to work totally through a third party. The system was now more personal, flexible, and realistic. A personal touch is important in team building. The positive effects on quality, productivity, profit, and morale were dramatic.

Unions, Pro and Con

Most Japanese-owned U.S. plants operate with employees who are not unionized, and this provides flexibility that is to their definite advantage. The concepts and principles of managing manufacturing operations are the same, however. A union is just one factor among many to a manager, though a costly one. The negotiation and administration of contracts and related matters takes time and money. Large organizations in particular require staff specialists to ensure contract-related activities are handled professionally and in a way that does not impair management's ability to run the company.

Some pundits argue that unionization forces management to manage better. It does indeed require that actions relating to employees be sound and justifiable. Union presence forces management into greater awareness of employee interests. Unions typically react to management actions rather than initiating action in a vacuum. In a climate of good relations and well-informed, coordinated management, unionization need not be an obstacle.

In the early '80s, as I have said, the militant Windsor Assembly union was represented by Ken Gerard. It had a history of striking each time an agreement expired, which typically was every three years. The relationship between management and union was confrontational. It was against this bitter background that I stuck my neck out in recommending we build our new minivan there. When I first told Gerard that I thought we should replace the rear-wheel drive New Yorker, Y-body Imperial, and J-body Cordoba and Mirada with a vehicle with no history of high volume, the minivan, I can't tell you what he thought of my mentality and my mother!

With the help of the Canadian personnel staff (then headed by Bill Fisher) and the factory's top management (headed by Plant Manager George Hohendorf and Production Manager Ron Gagnon), we set out on a campaign to win plant employee support and establish a better relationship with the union officials at Windsor. The team's accomplishments were remarkable.

I decided to get to know Gerard better, this 300-pound bear of a man, and try to overcome his bitterness. It took time but we eventually developed a good relationship that carried over to other key union represen-

tatives. These efforts were crucial in the success of the plant modernization and minivan launch—massive expenditures critical to the union's job
security and Chrysler's survival.

When the vehicle made automotive history, it was important that the
union and its leadership share in the credit. Producing the one-millionth
minivan was a proud moment for management and stockholders, and a
gallant one for the workers. It delighted me to share that podium with
Gerard, who beamed like a proud Papa Bear at the celebration. He spoke
glowingly of my mother after that.

Bargaining Breakthrough—the MOA

There were other situations at Chrysler where union relations were
particularly critical. In 1983, for example, the St. Louis Assembly Plant
II had been idle for three years. Chrysler needed a plant to assemble the
rear-wheel-drive Fifth Avenue and related vehicles which were being
taken out of production at Windsor Assembly to allow renovating the
plant for the minivan.

Since there were no employees at the St. Louis II plant, negotiations

*Dauch shares the speakers platform with Canadian Auto Workers official Ken
Gerard (speaking) at a celebration commemorating the production of the one-
millionth minivan.*

on a collective bargaining agreement needed to be hammered out with the International Union. If Chrysler was to resurrect the plant, it was important to have a good local contract. The union, in turn, wanted to put members back to work in the St. Louis area. St. Louis II was our first opportunity to construct an MOA (Modern Operating Agreement) from scratch because there was no labor force—the plant was vacant and in mothballs. It enabled us to redesign job classifications more rationally with our plans for flexible manufacturing.

Most people don't realize, however, that I first started reducing job classifications at our Saltillo, Mexico, engine plant shortly after joining the company. We were in the process then of taking a one-fourth scale model of our Trenton (Michigan) Engine plant down there.

Trenton had about 70 job classifications and those same 70 were in the process of being transferred to Saltillo. I said, "Hold it right there! I may have just arrived here this month but there's no damned way I will tolerate all those classifications! I want this rationalized to the skill level of the people there. I want to get rid of these exorbitant costs of everybody in our labor force having only a tiny slice of the job they can do with no adaptability or flexibility to do the kinds of jobs these men and women are capable of doing."

With that admonition, we were able to cut the number of classifications at Saltillo to less than 20—a huge drop! That was a precursor to the St. Louis II MOA, and the first time we were able to make a big reduction in job classifications by simply refusing to transfer the status quo when we had the opportunity to do something better.

Back to St. Louis II. In 1983, after working four years on PQI, we were developing a positive relationship with union leaders. Instead of always fighting, now Marc Stepp, Steve Sharf, and I were traveling together, literally and figuratively. By '83, we said to the union: "We are prepared to put some money back into the St. Louis II plant that has been mothballed for the past three years. We will do this if—and only if—we have a different labor agreement." With that leverage and our improving relations at that time, we made it happen.

Our St. Louis I plant, only 200 yards away, had over 100 job classifications, yet we were able to start up St. Louis II with only 27. That was before we came up with the MOA acronym. It was simply a case of manufacturing people—labor and management—recognizing, "Hey, we've got to compete with the world!"

With the new St. Louis II MOA, former narrow classifications were no longer barriers preventing the efficient assignment of work and limiting the development work force skills. We could apply higher pay rates to the smaller number of broader classifications, and supervisors could now effectively assign work. Such progress could not have been made without General Plants Manager Al Scudder, St. Louis I Plant Manager John Burkart, Personnel Manager Lou Morris, and staff members who established a solid working relationship with the union leadership. They created a team in the face of confrontation.

By 1986, we were working with the union to improve the concepts developed at St. Louis II, and implementing them at the Sterling Heights (Michigan) assembly plant (down to 16 classifications), Newark (Delaware) assembly plant, and Detroit's totally new Jefferson North assembly plant with only 10 classifications. Locations operating with MOAs allow flexibility in managing the work force while enhancing employee opportunity, incentive, earnings, and teamwork.

Skilled Negotiations

The traditional agreement between Chrysler and the UAW covering skilled trades was one of many classifications and restrictions. Apprentices were chosen primarily by seniority. Target apprentice percentages were specified by classification; however, during Chrysler's financial struggle, specified percentages were not maintained on the rolls. The union insisted that Chrysler employ apprentices. Management felt the classifications were no longer appropriate and the limitations on the apprentice pool too severe.

I saw this as a situation where both parties could win. The corporation would need skilled trades employees. I got corporate approval to employ hundreds of additional apprentices. We reached agreement to reduce the number of skilled-trades classifications and ease the restrictions on selecting apprentices. At the same time, we reached an understanding on a commitment to employ specified numbers of apprentices. Al Bucci of the UAW and B.G. ("Bob") Mathis of Chrysler's Manufacturing Group human resources department were instrumental in our success here.

Even a good union relationship at one organizational level cannot always overcome problems at another level, however. Automotive stamping operations, like the Twinsburg, Ohio, facility typically supply sheet-metal components to assembly plants. If a stamping plant has a production interruption, the assembly plants must shut down in short order.

Twinsburg had a history of labor problems since 1959. The union local

89

was militant and management was rigid. Historical local agreements were not canceled or superseded by later agreements, making it almost impossible to determine what provision of which agreement covered a particular matter. The parties bickered constantly. I often wondered what Coach Mollenkopf ("Jack The Ripper") would have done with that bunch.

I felt granting the union's demands during the 1983 Twinsburg negotiations would create unbearable costs, while management would lose the ability to assign work effectively and manage the plant. The demands for additional workers and work-practice restrictions were extreme. I decided we must take a stand. We drew a line in the sand. A short strike ensued. Iacocca backed my position and, fortunately for us, a quick settlement canceled all previous local agreements and contained none of the excess manpower and work practice restrictions the union had sought. The union leadership was replaced in the next local election, the plant now has a much improved labor relations climate, and Twinsburg has lost no time due to a strike since 1983. (More on this in Chapter 12.) Leadership does count.

It is important to achieve the company's objectives in ways that are politically attractive to union representatives and, at the same time, beneficial to the employees. Look for, create, and seize opportunities for progress or to correct existing problems, but when your ability to operate effectively is threatened, take a firm stand.

Self-Directed Success

An important innovation during my watch at Chrysler was the birth of self-directed teams. Although there are many organizational variants of this, in general, a team controls everything from schedules, purchasing materials, and quality to hiring and, sometimes, firing.

As early as 1981, we began using self-directed teams at the Newark, Delaware, assembly plant. We chose the paint shop phosphate and prime area to pilot the concept, expanding to other plant areas and operations later. The skilled trades proved ideal for the approach. These employees are capable, proud, quality-conscious, action-oriented people. We found they could accomplish incredible things. Such teams must have access to needed information and open lines of communication with management, however. They also must have management support and direction in their objectives and requirements.

Team-Building Tips

1. Establish a sense of equality by abolishing privileges symbol-izing status differences (i.e., job titles, time clocks, reserved parking places, executive cafeterias, etc.).
2. Push decision-making to the lowest possible level.
3. Provide incentives for all employees to continue their training.
4. Communicate critical information often and in various forms to all employees.
5. Reward groups rather than individuals for outstanding accomplishments.

I have seen skilled trades teams accept major challenges and perform with great success. Here are a few examples:

- Teams accomplished the unstacking, transfer, restacking, and put-ting into operation of stamping presses safely, ahead of schedule, and under budget. Production then took over a turnkey operation.
- Teams have removed, transferred, and reinstalled multi-million-dollar machining lines with excellent results.
- Teams reroofed entire sections of a manufacturing plant.
- Teams dismantled, rebuilt, and reinstalled engine and transmission testing equipment, and taught operators how to use it effectively.
- Self-directed teams also are successfully running various parts and service production operations.

In 1985, Chrysler was seriously considering closing the New Castle, Indiana, machining plant which was our oldest factory. Together with the UAW, we decided to take a shot at saving it. Our primary effort centered on the self-directed team. Workers were renamed "technicians," fore-men became "team advisors," time clocks disappeared, and manage-ment parking spaces were eliminated.

The plant now has 77 teams, each with authority to organize work flow, assign tasks, reprimand poor performers, communicate directly with customers, and even change shift start and finish times after con-sultation with the plant labor-management steering committee. Extra pay motivates workers to enroll in training courses. Absenteeism fell from over 7% in 1988 to an all-time low of 2.9% in 1991. New Castle's 1988 high of 1000 annual grievances plummeted to 33 in 1991. Defects per million parts produced declined from 1000 in 1988 to just 20 in 1991.

Two members of the Belvidere Assembly red-coat "concurrent engineering" launch team provide input during their training sessions.

Cost containment is keeping pace with quality improvement. The self-directed teams learned how to operate the plant with business acumen and positive results.

I thoroughly enjoyed meeting and working with the fine men and women of New Castle. The U.S. work force, properly managed (or self-managed), can perform far beyond what you might anticipate. In many instances, self-directed teams can provide the necessary motivation.

Team Launch

In 1986, Chrysler Area Manager Ray Lash faced one of the biggest challenges of his career in launching the Dodge Dakota 4×4 midsize pickup. He sought volunteers from the hourly work force and developed a list of training needs. The Dakota Launch Team was selected based on past performance and ability to train others. Training included reviewing the operation description sheets and assembly and disassembly of the truck. The process created a group of experts who could pass their knowledge along to other workers. Before the team went to the factory floor, every member was given a red jacket and hat which allowed them to be

The Dakota launch ceremony included representation from corporate leadership, union officials, and the government. Pictured here are (l to r) President of Chrysler Corporation H.K. ("Hal") Sperlich, Lee Iacocca, Michigan Governor James Blanchard, UAW President Owen Bieber, Vice Chairman of Chrysler Corporation Gerald Greenwald, and Dauch. (Chrysler photo)

identified easily by any worker with a question about a Dakota process. They also were required to work closely with production control and industrial engineering to assemble the right parts on the right job at the right location. Staging parts in the correct bay is very important to a successful launch.

The team worked so well that the new Dodge RAM full-size pickup (T-300) has a similar team associated with its development. Some of the top team members, including Guy Holstine and Dave Simmons, moved from the Dakota to the RAM team. Phil Roberson, also a member of the Dakota team, was reassigned to help launch the Dodge Viper which required his team building skills. Once training in team building is successful, you can fan it out through the company.

Suppliers as Members

The outside supplier is another key member of the manufacturing team. Supplier performance is more crucial for Chrysler than for Ford or General Motors. GM buys only 30% of its automotive parts from outside suppliers; Ford outsources 50%, but Chrysler depends on noncorporate vendors for 70% of its parts. Stated another way, Chrysler quality is 70% dependent on the quality supplied by vendors. In 1985, that totaled $7.6 billion in purchases, climbing (as our sales increased) in 1991 to $20 billion!

The Japanese Keiretsu system embraces suppliers in the manufacturer's family and gives automakers vast influence on supplier quality and finances, a tremendous advantage. Europeans still have a quasi-adversarial relationship with vendors, although this is changing, and both North American and European suppliers are typically located much further than the Japanese from the assembly plants they supply. Distance makes it more difficult to respond to quality or engineering problems rapidly.

Vendor quality is critical. The importance to the manufacturer/customer lies in product cost. The importance to the supplier lies in economic survival. The following chain of events illustrates the impact of vendor quality.

- In a good year, Chrysler assembles 8100 vehicles per day from 33 million parts. Annually, that is almost two million vehicles and more than eight billion parts. If only 1% are defective, more than 330,000 rejected parts per day or more than 80 million per year must be managed by Chrysler assembly plants. The plant must remove each one from the material flow and replace it with a good part. Cost increases. The entire JIT material flow system then must be updated, and the defective parts stored in space that could be used for more productive purposes.
- If the part supply threatens to interrupt production, a supervisor, clerk, and one or more workers in the quality department must unpack the parts, sort the good from the bad, send the good ones to the line and, perhaps, rework others. The crew also must repack those that cannot be assembled. Sorting or reworking often requires overtime. The quality department must contact the vendor for a disposition of the defective parts. Will the vendor come to the assembly plant, verify the defect, and make immediate corrections? Does the vendor want the parts shipped back or should they be scrapped on the spot? If they are scrapped, production control must arrange for their

Supplier Success Summary

1. Choose a supplier in close geographical proximity; it will expedite solutions to problems and reduce transportation costs.
2. Keep the total number of vendors as low as possible.
3. Choose only vendors whose records demonstrate they are routinely capable of delivering defect-free products.
4. Apply the same cost and quality standards to outside and in-house suppliers.
5. Use "target pricing" rather than competitive bidding when choosing a supplier.
6. Involve both the engineering and the manufacturing departments in the selection of a new vendor or termination of a present vendor.
7. Commit business to suppliers for periods of up to five years. This will motivate them to a greater degree of cooperation.
8. Integrate your quality and delivery systems with those of the supplier. This is especially important in product testing and validation.
9. Involve the supplier as early as possible in the design process.
10. Require suppliers to certify their own parts. This eliminates the need for an expensive receiving inspection apparatus.
11. Audit suppliers regularly for conformance to your requirements in the areas of leadership, technology, quality, delivery, and cost. Reward those who perform best.
12. Aid suppliers by consulting in the areas of new technology, statistical methods, maintenance, CAD, and CAM.
13. Communicate often, and in depth, with your suppliers on company goals, performance, and global competition.
14. Create situations that enable your employees to communicate with their supplier counterparts.
15. Aid and encourage supplier R&D efforts.

disposition and adjust the material releases for the vendor location. The quality department then sends the paperwork to the plant controller who writes off the material as a loss and charges it against plant productivity.

Changing Suppliers

During my tenure at Chrysler, we began a new way of managing supplier relations to assure vendor quality progress that matched or exceeded our own. It is an area you must constantly review.

First, we established a program to significantly reduce the number of suppliers to our assembly plants. At the same time, we set a goal of zero defective parts coming from outside and from captive corporate suppliers. We vowed to reduce the supplier base 10% by 1984, 20% by 1986, and 40% by 1988. Costs would drop; quality would rise as vendors who stayed with us went for a larger piece of the pie or even the whole pie.

We met areas of strong resistance as we began changing cultures and standards. Culling the vendor base impacted companies, careers, and job security. Persistence, reasoning, and fairness were most important in the effort. We also had internal resistance because we began to apply the same zero-defect criteria and cost goals to internal corporate suppliers. It is important to do what is right, even if it is not popular.

We won most arguments by using uncontestable data and trends. For example, 41% of our average expense per unit tested at the Chrysler Proving Grounds in Chelsea, Michigan, resulted from failed components. Three-quarters of these components were from outside suppliers. During the 1984 model year launch, the assembly plants had to manage a whopping 140% increase in defective material over the 1983 model year. Through June 1, 1984, the assembly division detected 41.9 million defective parts for the 1984 model year which began the previous July. More than 28 million of these parts came from outside and 13.7 million from internal suppliers.

Defective material in an assembly plant undermines the entire manufacturing system. It prevents building a vehicle in station. Defective material disrupts and retards commitment to JIT materials management and in-line sequencing, which demands zero-defect material. Just one bad part can shut down an entire operation.

Defective material also undercuts the ability to meet customer quality demands. It adds to the cost of inspection, repair, sorting, rework, inventory updating, shipping, and warranty claims. Worst of all, defective material squanders resources and time that assembly plant personnel should be using for operations directly relating to the process they are expected to control.

Assembly plants are not equipped to detect casting defects, metal stress cracks, plating irregularities, improper heat treating, and other imperfections. When parts with such defects arrive, they are installed. By the time the problem is discovered, all of the defective parts must be replaced. I have seen as many as 2000 cars waiting to be retrofitted because of quality problems that we, the builders, were not equipped to detect. In one extreme case, we had to strip the usable parts out of 1300 vehicles in

1983. We then destroyed the cars, baling them into scrap. The thought of scrap is still repugnant to me.

For these reasons, we established a department of vendor quality engineering. Our engineers spent more time in vendor plants than they did in their home office. They helped vendors isolate faulty processes, correct obsolete methods, and solve other complex problems with the aid of Chrysler's technical resources.

Reliable Relationships

When deciding to shrink our supplier base, we knew we had to create a new kind of relationship with the remaining vendors. In our struggle-for-survival mode, these vendors remained loyal when payments were either reduced, late, or both. The company now began moving away from a confrontational, lowest-bid-gets-the-job philosophy to a Value Managed Relationship (VMR), which operates by these principles:

- Commit to supply sources for extended periods.
- Purchase from the few suppliers most capable of improving the manufacturer's position.
- Decide sourcing on actual costs plus profit (or target pricing of a component or commodity) rather than competitive bidding.
- Integrate supplier and manufacturer quality systems to prevent defects as well as discover them early in the value chain.
- Manage the delivery system to reduce inventory levels.
- Involve the supplier's engineering department in the design process as early as feasible, including both design and manufacturing engineers.

We began our VMR efforts with a pilot program concentrating on wiring harnesses, an area where vendor proliferation had created a nightmare. Tom Stallkamp, then director of production purchasing, headed the task force piloting VMR. The Vendor Quality Engineering group under Dennis Langlois was largely responsible for its day-to-day operations, with primary responsibility for rapid intervention and resolution of outside supplier quality problems.

We did not rely exclusively on VMR to improve supplier performance. We also increased functional testing of vendor parts. Part suppliers who failed were brought in to determine whether they were adhering to our engineering standards. We held 20 to 30 such meetings weekly, many of them follow-up sessions to verify that recommended corrective action actually took place.

We also organized the Corporate Manufacturing Reliability Center to do supplemental durability and reliability testing on critical components. This complemented normal engineering reliability testing—in effect, double-teaming the problem. Starting in 1982–83, the Sterling Heights Vehicle Test Center (SHVTC) removed defective parts from company-owned product evaluation and lease cars and forwarded them to the responsible suppliers and Chrysler engineering for analysis and a recommendation for corrective action from the Vendor Reliability Improvement Group. Gino Giocondi, vice president of Parts and Customer Service, assisted me in getting support from local Chrysler dealers so we could use this valuable information to attack warranty problems. Mike Monicatti, a local Detroit area dealer, led the support from the dealer group. Jake Bass, manager of SHVTC, and his work force made a powerful contribution to Chrysler vehicle quality improvement.

In our 2000-piece certification program, we instructed suppliers to identify and ship the first 2000 pieces required for a new launch. This material was 100% certified against blueprint dimensions and specifications, as well as manufacturing performance standards. Manufacturing further requested that the Supplier Quality Assurance (SQA) group investigate and approve all new suppliers and reinvestigate and reapprove existing suppliers with a poor or even fair quality record before awarding new business to them. The customer and competition were requiring everyone to chin a higher bar.

We pushed for a change in corporate purchasing practices from unilateral sourcing by the Procurement and Supply Department to a process including input from the engineering office and manufacturing's Quality and Product Engineering Department. This effort was eventually accepted. We needed strong arguments to prove our point. In the 1984 model year, we documented supplier shortcomings such as lack of facilities and equipment, lack of engineering support, inadequate racks, inadequate paint and carpet application processes, inadequate packaging, lack of coordination with subsuppliers, lack of engineering design and process capability, inadequate staffing and personnel training, facility timing and readiness failures, inadequate component development, late or substandard quality approvals, and late or substandard equipment installation and calibration.

Helping Hand

We pushed, even helped, vendors install state-of-the-art testing equipment to verify their products against their own engineering standards as well as Chrysler's. We asked, even showed, suppliers how to implement statistical process control for key production processes. We encouraged and helped them establish sound, regular maintenance programs for their production equipment. We also found that working together effectively was a tremendous boost to morale and organizational strength between the supplier and Chrysler.

We began introducing suppliers to computer-aided design (CAD) and computer-assisted manufacturing (CAM) so they could communicate directly with Chrysler electronically in a totally paperless environment. This contributed to our concurrent engineering efforts. We showed vendors how to set up a *prevent* rather than a *detect* quality control system and demonstrated corrective action strategies and techniques.

We worked on major cost and design objectives up-front, in a partner level that was very proprietary and confidential where both parties could share the improvements later. It was not selfish. We also wanted this effort to be very proactive, so we welcomed their thoughts on how we might improve our designs or our processes, change our packaging or scheduling, or eliminate specifications that possibly were redundant and not required. We wanted to move beyond the confrontation of the past to new levels of cooperation and still have a business arrangement that was fair to the charter of both companies—Chrysler and each supplier.

We conducted roundtables and formed supplier meetings as early as 1983. We brought in vendors en masse, in a very respectable environment, so members of Chrysler management (starting with the most important, our vice president of procurement and supply, Dave Platt) could review what our new products were; what components, materials, or supplies they could provide, and what the required engineering specifications would be, including the quality standards that were definitely going to be at a much higher level. It was a total team effort.

We always had our products on display outside of the auditorium so vendors could see the finished cars and trucks. Inside, we had the power trains, engines, transmissions, componentry, castings, and many of their products. Displays of supplier parts included wire harnesses, bulbs, connectors, or crucial elements with which we were having problems, such as reliability, or warranty, or quality defects.

Another important communication avenue we created cooperatively was to allow our production workers to visit and communicate directly with the vendor's operations people. When they get the chance to interact, the first-line troops of each organization solve problems quickly and efficiently. This opened eyes quickly.

We encouraged vendors such as Detrex, PPG, and BASF to create their own technical centers where they could perform research and development. They could design formulas or components and materials on their own or in cooperation with Chrysler designers and manufacturing engineers. We shared a great deal of responsibility with them and received cooperation and leadership critical to our cost containment and quality improvement efforts. These efforts peaked in 1988 with the founding of the New Mack Process Development Center. There, with vendors, we jointly financed and proved new processes and machinery before installing them. New Mack also provided a comprehensive technical training center equipped with robots, coordinate measuring machines, and laser welders. Dodge Viper design and development owes much to the New Mack efforts. Also, New Mack provided the facility and space to assemble the vehicle. Especially critical was the excellent work of our composite materials development group under Dr. Subi Dinda.

This was not all milk and honey. There was strong resistance to these actions. We instituted a system of chargebacks for vendor failures to reinforce our recommendations, proposals, requests, and requirements. We did meticulous cost studies to calculate the total expense to Chrysler when a vendor failed to perform. Included in the debit were such things as: line stoppages, handling, system updates, storage, inventory holding costs, record keeping, sorting, reworking, unpacking, repacking, and supervisory costs. We grabbed the supplier's attention by subtracting these costs from submitted invoices. Once we had their attention, we got action!

In addition to working with vendors, we reworked our own related internal systems, especially the Corporate Audit System (CAS). By 1984, CAS was 35 years old. It indicated product quality daily but did not meet corporate goals for durability, quality, and reliability. For example, Best-in-Class objectives for one vehicle were being met by the corporate audit standards of the time. In field performance ratings, however, this vehicle came out Worst-in-Class! After the vehicle was in service eight months, warranty claims were 64% over target, with a lifetime assessment of 6.3 warranty claims per vehicle—300% to 400% higher than the Japanese competition. It is important to deal with facts.

Manufacturing supported creating a corporate audit verification team to audit a plant monthly rather than daily. The emphasis shifted from 80% on in-process quality control to the 40-20-40 audit of the three major influences on automobile assembly: 40% for incoming material quality, 20% for in-process quality control, and 40% for the outgoing product. The corporate audit was eventually revamped to reflect these priorities. Tradition is hard to change.

The Make/Buy Battle

The final thrust was to transform the make-or-buy decision. Purchasing departments tend to support a large number of vendors and a high percentage of outsourcing because that provides purchasing jobs, influence, and career paths. Manufacturing departments, for similar self-interest reasons, tend to produce as many components as possible in-house. The referee in this territorial fight is the finance department. It is finance, in concert with the company president and chairman, that eventually determines whether an item is produced in-house or purchased.

Since purchasing exerts greater control over outside vendors than manufacturing does, the emphasis in make-buy decisions traditionally has been on cost rather than quality. The attitude ''they talk quality but buy price'' is changing but is still there.

With greater control over in-house corporate vendors, manufacturing can put emphasis on quality and productivity rather than only cost. Our thrust in manufacturing, therefore, was to produce the components that influenced quality and productivity to the greatest extent—final vehicle assembly; engine and motor block production; transmission, transaxle, and transfer case production, and related castings; exterior body stampings; interior body structural members; and electronic controls.

The toughest battles to bring production in house were over the V-6 front-wheel-drive engines, external stampings, and vehicle electronic components. When the Power Train Division came under my guidance in 1985, I worked with the UAW's Marc Stepp and Human Resources Vice President A.P. St. John to put together an MOA (Modern Operating Agreement) for the Chrysler Trenton (Michigan) engine plant and the Chrysler Indianapolis foundry. (The same Trenton plant, you will recall, where the classification-reduction battle began in '80.) We agreed with Vice Chairman Gerald Greenwald that if we could get this agreement ratified by the union rank and file, we could source 50% of the V-6 FWD engines in house. The remaining 50% would still come from Mitsubishi . . . for now. The union did ratify the agreement, another breakthrough. Today, 50% of the production of this most important component is built by Chrysler's Trenton engine plant, and the Indianapolis foundry supplies the engine blocks. Times are changing.

We kept much stamping work in-house by requiring our stamping division to *bid* on all work while being held to the same quality and cost requirements as outside suppliers. Division management had chosen the parts it wanted to make and outsourced the others. The new practice required a more astute business sense. Greenwald's "holding our feet to the fire" with that policy change was an excellent strategy. Thanks to the creative efforts of Jim Lyijynen, Jim Clancy, Jim Unis, and Mel Young of stamping and production engineering, we adjusted to the new system and became truly competitive.

I watched the U.S. electronic industry slip into Japanese hands and was determined not only to save, but to enhance, our Huntsville, Alabama, electronics complex. In 1980–83 pressure to sell or close it was strong. Fortunately, we saved and enhanced the operation, building the entirely new Huntsville Electronics City and expanding the business. Today, Huntsville fulfills most of Chrysler's electronic needs. (More on Huntsville in Chapters 6 and 9.) You have to be bold and brave to provide meaningful leadership.

Chapter 6

OUR QUEST FOR QUALITY

In 1987, manufacturing consultant Jim Harbour wrote in *Automotive Industries*:

> In the past when Lee Iacocca would go on TV and say "If you can find a better quality car, buy it," that generally meant you had to drive to the next dealer. But recently, Chrysler's product quality has actually achieved what Lee has been bragging about for years.
>
> The new Sundance and Shadow and the new "J" bodies from St. Louis represent a level of quality never reached before by Chrysler.
>
> How has Chrysler achieved this high level of quality when just a few years ago it produced the lowest quality in the industry?[1]

In the same issue, *Automotive Industries* editor, John McElroy, in the 1986 Industry Report Card, wrote:

> For the second year in a row, Chrysler has come out at the top of the class. The Pentastar people are running one very well-oiled machine, and they made the big improvements across the board. In the Quality Category, which is based on J.D. Power's Customer Satisfaction Index, it took a big step forward and earned an "A."
>
> Coincidentally, Chrysler's improvements in the Productivity and Inventory Turns Categories are factors that would also have a positive impact on quality, which reinforces the fact that their improvement here is no fluke.[2]

No fluke, indeed. The quality levels were the result of detailed planning, years of hard work, wise investment, teamwork, and precise focus.

Journey to Excellence

We started where I always begin with any improvement—the people, specifically the group in the styling area because in manufacturing, quality begins with the product's design. The favorable impact on the quality of your end product is a 100:1 return in product design, 10:1 in process engineering, and only 1:1 in production.

Tom Gale and his designers drafted, and Jack Withrow and his engineers developed, entirely new products for future production. A related approach had to be implemented for vehicles and components already in production. These products represented 70% of our output for the next five years. Manufacturing had its hands full with present production but, nevertheless, expended substantial effort on the future. We knew such action would determine the long-term health of the corporation.

As in any cultural change, quality will improve in direct proportion to the emphasis and direction given by the top executive and other high-level company executives. The top executive must visibly support your efforts to achieve major improvement. Without it, you're dead in the water!

Recognition of accomplishment is an essential element in any quality improvement program, and the organization must be changed to reflect the new emphasis on quality. A top executive must lead the quality improvement effort. This cannot be done effectively, I believe, unless that executive reports directly to the CEO.

Here are other elements of a successful quality improvement program:

- You must post quality indicators for all to see and confer recognition and awards on the basis of performance against these indicators.
- You must reinforce the vision at regular intervals in the form of Town Hall meetings, recognition ceremonies, articles in the company paper, etc.
- Most importantly, top management must support the culture change by breaking bureaucratic logjams and providing the resources necessary to support change.

Chrysler manufacturing was fortunate to have Lee Iacocca's support in all critical areas. He introduced culture change in a top management meeting and circulated a videotape of his remarks throughout the corporation. His framed quality policy became the model for quality policies written at every location. It states:

> The quality policy of Chrysler Corporation is "To be the Best."
> This policy requires that every individual and operating unit fully

understand the requirements of their customer, and deliver products and services that satisfy these requirements at a defect-free level.

Iacocca also created the position of vice president of quality and productivity reporting directly to President Hal Sperlich. The Chairman's Award was created to recognize stellar quality achievement. We instituted our own recognition system in the manufacturing group and submitted our candidates for the award.

Productivity Incentive Plan

America has gone through many decades of jaw-boning—just talking about how manufacturing needs fixing. It wasn't until 1984 that this country actually did something about rewarding productivity accomplishments with national recognition. At that time, Congress established the American Productivity Award.

One plant I fought furiously to save was Huntsville Electronics, in Alabama. This complex makes Chrysler radios, proprietary electronics, and computer devices. We earned the first-ever American Productivity Award in 1984 at Huntsville. Meanwhile, we had a sister plant—Chrysler's oldest factory worldwide—in New Castle, Indiana. A lot of people told me that New Castle also could not be saved and it reminded me of an old saying, "The one who says it cannot be done should never interrupt the one who is doing it."

After Huntsville's transformation, I went to New Castle, met and worked with them and, in 1992, they won a second American Productivity Award. My point here: The power is in the people if we challenge them to compete! You must let them know exactly where they stand, that management is not mad at them, but how they compare with other plants within the company are the hard facts. Then tell them it isn't good enough to compete with the Big Three anymore because GM and Ford aren't necessarily the best. Maybe it's Toyota, VW, or Honda.

There's only one standard today—the world standard. When we used that approach, it didn't matter if I was talking in Huntsville, New Castle, Kokomo, or Motown. They wanted to compete because Americans like to compete. We need more efforts to recognize the winners in competitions critical to America's ability to compete worldwide.

We need to continue revitalizing America's competitive spirit.

Changing Chrysler's Culture

In 1985, George Butts, our quality and productivity VP, with the support of top management, introduced the Quality Improvement Process

(QIP) to Chrysler. The brainchild of quality guru Philip B. Crosby, QIP involves the entire corporation and suppliers in a mass approach to total quality management. All of top management and much of middle management were trained in QIP at Crosby's Quality College in Winter Park, Florida. Corporate trainers then educated the remainder of the salaried employees and thousands of hourly employees in their own plants.

Crosby's approach synthesizes a plethora of quality ideas and strategies. He defines "quality" simply as conformance to requirements. A requirement is specific, measurable, achievable, and negotiated between supplier and customer. All of us are customers as well as suppliers, and we agree on the requirements we live by. This quality system also stresses prevention. Quality is designed into the product and process upstream, not built in later with inspection, rework, and retrofit in final assembly. Crosby's performance standard is zero defects—the only standard that makes sense.

When I announced our new supplier quality assurance program on June 17, 1982, I told our suppliers, "We build an average of 5000 vehicles per day, each one containing 4000 parts. That equals 20 million parts assembled every day. You supplied over 16 million of these. Our supplier defect rate is 10%, and that means we are managing nearly two million defective parts every day! The effect on quality and productivity is disastrous." We demanded zero defects, the suppliers responded, and we were nearly there in May 1991.

Crosby's method for measuring conformance to requirements is by a term he calls the "Price of Non-Conformance." In other words, the more you pay for reworking, retrofitting, replanning, redesigning, rewriting, and other kinds of waste, the lower your product quality. As he writes in his widely read book: "Quality is free. It's not a gift, but it is free. What costs money are the unquality things—the actions that involve not doing jobs right the first time."[3]

The Quality Improvement Process required significant investment in training. We bit the bullet and made the investment. We also made training a top priority for each of Chrysler's launches. Our hourly and salaried work forces received one million employee-hours of training. Much of the training was provided by the advanced technical training group from the human resources department where Tony Rainero and Keith Green prevented many costly defects at launch time.

These efforts were bold and innovative but were not accepted immediately by all of our Chrysler colleagues. We overcame some resistance simply because the relatively new manufacturing team was not associated with events that brought Chrysler to the brink. This was a major advantage.

Listening to Dealers

The way you continue to grow market share is to have something new in your showroom that's different from and better than what your competitor has. That's the first rule of marketing. The way to improve your market share in the "car-war" years of the '80s was to improve your relationships between your front-line troops in this battle—your dealers—and your manufacturing team.

Chrysler has a long-serving Chrysler-Plymouth dealer council and a Dodge dealer council. We listened to their chairmen and their committees because they were representing the 4000 dealers servicing and selling Chrysler products in 1980. They were independent principals, all with their own network, and they were going bankrupt as fast or faster than Chrysler. We were in the same boat and that boat was gushing and taking us onto the shoals.

We took a look at their priorities, and Number 1 priority was driveability. We had to solve that by design. Most quality items are solved with design. We had to perfect, as best we could, the fuel system of mechanical carburetion, but we also planned a 10-year hill climb to solve the real driveability problem with a new electrical fuel system then called "fuel injection." We started with in-body (carburetor) injection. We then went to multi-point injection, and finally to sequential multi-point injection (and that took us from 1980 to 1990).

The next dealer concern was our rust-bucket image because of our dramatic failures with products where fenders rusted out and other body elements had no substance or reliability of body structure. We fixed that again by major design changes, like changing from cold-rolled steel to four varieties of pre-coated steel. Coated steels are a challenge to work with. We had to decide how to work with it in manufacturing, and the only body panel that we kept out of precoats was the cold-rolled steel roof (it's very hard for road salt to get up to the roof). Statistically, we recognized there were certain areas of our country or markets that were dramatically worse than others. For example, some states do not allow road salt or calcium. Others lay down up to 40 pounds per running foot per year! It took about 10 years to fully solve the driveability problems,

A Message to Manufacturing from Sales

As an automobile dealer, I consider myself a key player on Team Chrysler. Sales and service is an important element of any business, whether you are in automobiles, appliances, sports equipment, or household goods.

In 1984, I toured the Sterling Heights assembly plant with other dealers—an idea developed by Dick Dauch. The boom of the welding equipment and the frantic assembly line pace are two experiences I will never forget. I was impressed with the application of automation. The tour gave all of us a better understanding of the product we were selling and assured us that quality was a commitment at the factory.

A sales staff—however large or small—presents the product to the customer. We are the final representative for every manufactured good and the major link to customer feedback. Dick insisted that reports from customers coming through dealer service departments get channeled to manufacturing. If there ever was a recurring problem with a vehicle, this direct line helped correct it quickly. Manufacturing people even arrived in my service department to explore ways of resolving customer complaints through better manufacturing execution. This undoubtedly saved Chrysler manufacturing dollars and enhanced the resulting quality of our product. Some of these people were right off the shop floor. It was a unique experience for me to see builders meeting service technicians.

If you are a manufacturer, do not discount the role of the people whose livelihood depends on selling and servicing what you make. If you are in sales, make an effort to see how the product is made. After all, you are part of the team too.

—*Seymour Kliger*
General Manager
Garrity Dodge
Hamtramck, Michigan

and four to seven years to really solve the problems of rust and corrosion protection.

So that we could each better understand customer needs, we asked our dealers to come to our factories and give us some constructive criticism and to open their doors to our hourly and salaried people. The message that came from this was, when the car gets to the dealership, it must drive smoothly, quietly, efficiently, and reliably, with no coughing, surging, and dying problems. The body must have beauty and integrity and the paint must have luster and depth of image—a finish that is impeccably applied, because *people still buy with their eye*. If they do not like the looks of it, they will not come to the dealership and drive it, or even consider buying it. This cemented our resolve to upgrade our painting systems.

The First Step: Design

Our first step in manufacturing was to win the support of senior management and colleagues in product design, product engineering, product planning, and program management. We knew true quality improvement depended on product design, so in 1981 we placed an eight-man team in the design department called the Manufacturing Feasibility Group (MFG). We chose a career man as MFG team leader—Jim Clancy, an experienced, low-keyed, cooperative, professional manufacturing engineer, expert in planning, tooling, die development, prototyping, and pilot and production build. I knew he was a person who could promote the kind of balance between process and design that would lead to the types of products customers expected. He also had to be tough as nails; his job was to change a bureaucratic system that existed for decades. It had to change because, as the saying goes: "If you do what you always did, you'll get what you always got."

MFG formed our front-line assault in this battle for process-driven design. It concentrated its initial effort on body systems, led by Roland Mueller, who reported directly to Clancy. It recommended eliminating lead solder, beginning with our 1984 product launches and confirmed our need for upgrading body panels from cold-rolled to pre-coated steel to give us the best corrosion protection in the industry. It developed new sweeps on side body panels reducing the visual vulnerability characteristic of flat surfaces. It began to reduce the manufacturing processes required per panel, a development requiring many years to fully implement. It led the way in replacing welds with adhesives, beginning with the rear liftgate and the side sliding door of the minivan in 1984, and expanding the application through other product lines. Excellent teamwork and leadership were provided by Marion Cumo, Tom Gale, Bob Marcell, Joe Nigro, Robert Sinclair, and Leo Walsh.

The group simultaneously began developing a CAD/CAM program. Although Chrysler had been a leader in CAD, there was no computer-assisted manufacturing whatsoever. I had become familiar with CAM in my Defense Division days when we launched the XM-1 (Abrams) Main

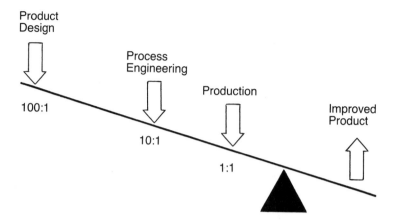

Quality in design is important. You can attain major savings by correcting problems early in manufacturing. The ratio of gain in quality improvement follows a rule of 10. In this example it is 100 times less expensive to fix a problem at the Product Design stage than at the Production stage.

Battle Tank at the Lima, Ohio, plant—an experience that helped me deploy CAD/CAM effectively in automotive manufacturing.

Sperlich and Executive Vice President Jack Withrow provided technical help when we were struggling to establish a CAM capability, and Iacocca approved funds for the purchase of the hardware and software we needed to get going. Dr. Frank Plonka and Jack Thompson helped me lead this critical new manufacturing charge.

The Second Step: Finer Finishing

Our second step to improve the quality of Chrysler vehicles involved paint systems. From my days as a foreman at GM, I knew painting cried out for automation. When I went into a spray booth and found how quickly that solvent-laden environment bothered my eyes and lungs, I knew something had to be done to correct it. We could not gloss over this. We had to find a solution and at the same time fix our poor vehicle-finish reputation.

Paint shops today have become a critical issue. This is one thing I brought to the attention of senior management early. Paint shops played a role in which plants were closed because of the importance of finish quality and the difficulties in meeting the stringent requirements of the Clean Air Act, VOCs (volatile organic compounds), and RACT (reasonable available control technology).

This was tough explaining to a chairman who is a marketing guy; a vice chairman, Greenwald, who is a finance guy; and a president, Sperlich, a product guy. So the burden was on me to really know painting technology and to communicate its seriousness to people who get quickly bored with manufacturing details and don't want to find out that painting is an expensive poker game. To put in a new paint shop, I was talking about spending between $100 and $240 million, so it was a high-stakes game.

In doing my reviews, I confirmed that the factories' paint systems and the resulting final product were deficient in finish quality. We were not even coming close to meeting customer expectations. We set out to radically change Chrysler's reputation for peeling, blistering, and substandard finishes before the minivan launch. Sperlich supported me in the founding of the Paint and Anti-Corrosion Group in 1981.

I always think of Roy Smith, a marvelous young executive who was terribly frustrated when I first found him at Chrysler. He was thinking of leaving the company. He was embarrassed because he felt he was working for a loser that had no future. In meeting with Roy, I found that he, along with another young man, Leroy DeLisle, had the right technical chemistry, the right fit to do something big here. By putting those two together, along with another young man named Bob Piccirilli, they came up with a game plan to turn our painting problems around.

Under Roy's leadership, this group performed miracles in Chrysler paint facilities, reducing paint warranty claims 85%! They showed me how the right technical, sociological, supplier, and financial investment could, over time, totally transform the worst performance in paint and warranty conditions into the world's best, 10 years later. We got three marvelous performances from these men who showed they could work as a team and unify for a purpose. In 1990, Iacocca presented the Paint and Anti-Corrosion Group with the Chairman's Award before a gathering of top management. This recognition was well deserved.

Waiting for Paint to Dry

Paint shops are not only expensive—the most expensive system in assembly plants—they require the most time to build. Any commitment to their overhaul is a monumental risk. In planning the paint renewal effort at Chrysler, we vowed our paint shops would be bright, hospital-clean, cheerful, and efficient. Air exchanges would provide fresh air for line operators. We would have a nine-to-eleven-stage, full-immersion phosphate bath. The anodic process would be upgraded to a more powerful cathodic version into which the entire vehicle body would be immersed. Our conveyor systems would be of the inverted, power-and-free variety wherever possible so debris could not drop onto the vehicle being processed. By 1992, every Chrysler paint shop was following the model we envisioned in 1980. (Chapter 10 more fully details what Chrysler accomplished with this technology.)

We also worked with paint vendors to ensure a high-quality finish. We reduced the number of paint suppliers per assembly plant. For example, paint suppliers dropped from as many as five down to one, and that supplier had to commit to JIT delivery by developing satellite facilities within a few miles of the plant. They had to develop their own R&D capability rather than doing their experimenting in our paint shops. This was an important structural and policy change. We received excellent support from Fred Rhue of PPG and Larry Jameson and Dan Logan of BASF.

To reduce complexity and cost, we outsourced painting small parts. To achieve a high performance level in both body and paint systems, we changed the way the processing equipment was designed. We had to bring our planners, tool designers, and manufacturing engineers together in one facility with the sophisticated technological support essential to modern engineering. In 1982, we refurbished an idled stamping plant with the latest computerized technology. It contained a pilot assembly plant with a portion of a state-of-the-art paint system. This facility, called the Outer Drive Manufacturing Technical Center (ODMTC), let tradespeople, designers, and manufacturing engineers exchange ideas and support each other in stamping, body, and vehicle processing. This is now being done at the new Chrysler Technology Center.

Doors Off

A major part of quality consideration is how your product is processed, or how it's transported within the factory. This affects both assembly and paint finish.

Consider one example. As your product comes down the line, how easy is it for your assembly people to work with? How can your workers affect product quality? My experience is, of course, with automobiles, so this example involves vehicles on the assembly line.

I always felt that the doors should be removed when a vehicle exits the paint department. A typical auto moves down the line with the doors

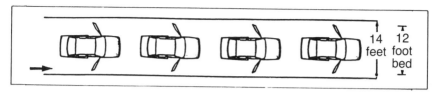

With the doors on, vehicles to be assembled require more space and the interiors are much less accessible for the workers. This is typical of many assembly facilities. In this case, the vehicle rests on a 12-foot bed and requires 14 feet of space. Damage occurs more frequently.[4]

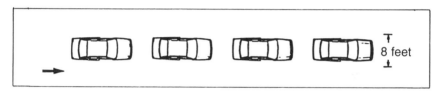

With the doors off, vehicles being assembled require less space and are more accessible for the workers. Vehicles assembled in this manner require only eight feet of space and are more easily accessible to the workers. Damage is minimized.[4]

open. This means the clearance is 14 feet. The lighting to workers inside the vehicle is diminished. As the automobile moves along the line there is potential damage to doors, paint and, in later operations, the door trim. Finally with the door opening at 60° there is a restriction of access for the workers who need to get to the interior of the vehicle.

Now consider the benefits of taking the doors off.

The clearance reduces from 14 feet to as little as eight. There is much improved lighting inside the product for the worker who can now better see the work. There should be no damage to the doors or the paint of the product. Workers have better access to the inside of the vehicle. Automation becomes very practical, which usually improves quality. You can also reduce the size of your plant. This helps reduce cost.

Consider how your product is assembled, the steps, the process, the design. Should your doors come off? Do you have a similar challenge? Re-evaluate your assembly process seriously and often.

Statistical Process Control

SPC measures the repeatability of a manufacturing process within certain control limits that are both tighter and differently configured than traditional engineering blueprint tolerances. SPC measurement shows what a process is capable of producing and whether or not the process is performing to capability. By enhancing standardization, it helps ensure the repeatability and thus predictability of manufacturing processes. This, in turn, makes it easier to manage quality precisely. In assembly, I first introduced SPC in 1983 with the launch of the minivan at Windsor. We introduced SPC into all other plants and divisions in 1985. Allen Rae helped me train tens of thousands of workers in statistical methods. They now routinely employ process capability indices to measure processes and equipment performance greatly empowering the employee while improving product quality.

To teach SPC at Chrysler, we offered eight-hour courses for top management and 16-hour courses for middle managers. Supervisors and hourly employees, the people who would actually implement SPC on the factory floor, attended courses for as long as a week. After we gained experience with SPC, we began teaching and practicing Design of Experiments, a more sophisticated technique.

For our 1986 model launch, we issued the following seven inviolable rules.

- Chrysler will launch to a quality target, not to a quality curve.
- Chrysler will not vary or deviate from the agreed corporate program if product quality is at risk.
- Chrysler will not vary the mix during the launch period.
- Chrysler will not retrofit any part that compromises product quality.
- All Chrysler plants will resist, or keep minimal, rework of material to bring it up to specifications or quality standards.
- Chrysler will not build out of station or out of sequence if product quality is at risk.
- Chrysler will not build vehicles without approved parts. If quality parts are not available in station, we will shut down the assembly plant.

It was shortly thereafter that Jim Harbour and John McElroy of *Automotive Industries* reported their findings of Chrysler's major improvement in accomplishing high levels of product quality. The game plan worked.

I've mentioned the joint union-management Product Quality Improvement (PQI) partnership. PQI steering committees, jointly chaired by each plant manager and local union president, still meet regularly to identify quality issues, deploy teams of union and management personnel to address them, measure progress, and muster support for quality non-conformances that require cross-functional or multi-plant cooperation in their elimination. This partnership was an industry first, empowering the people at a time when such initiatives were unheard of at other American manufacturers. Our quest for quality was leading the American automobile industry.

References

1. Harbour, Jim. "Building Quality the Chrysler Way," *Chilton Automotive Industries*. Radnor, PA: Chilton Co., April 1987, p. 10.
2. McElroy, John. "1986 Industry Report Card," *Chilton Automotive Industries*. Radnor, PA: Chilton Co., April 1987, pp. 40–43.
3. Philip B. Crosby, *Quality Is Free*. New York: McGraw-Hill Book Co., 1979, p. 1.
4. Drawings adapted from : Otis, Irvin. "Learning from the Japanese: A lesson for American Managers." Southfield MI: Irvin Otis, 1991, p. 5.

Chapter 7

REVENGE OF THE PLANT RATS

Many engineers and designers tend to be prima donnas and very thin-skinned. Now that they have to compete globally, they are going to have to develop an elephant skin on their butts. In manufacturing, you have to get that thick skin your first year out, or you don't survive the next two or three.

It's like being a Big Ten fullback. You know you're going to get the donkey crap knocked out of you every time you go off tackle or throw a block. But that's the position you play, you're like an eighth lineman and rarely the star. The quarterback is the designated star.

In the automobile business, marketing is the star, and finance is the superstar because everybody respects money. America fell in love with marketing and finance after World War II and fell out of love with manufacturing and engineering. Now we are all finding out that if we really want to make this country solid again, the twin towers of strength are manufacturing and engineering.

I said manufacturing first, because manufacturing must drive engineering. Engineering doesn't like that arrangement because they've always been the ones driving manufacturing. Now, as these roles reverse, the design engineers are starting to develop the thicker skins they will need to match ours. Eventually—within our lifetimes—these roles will merge.

Manufacturing engineering and design engineering will become one profession.

First Signs of a Merger

The Dodge Viper—rolled out in 1992—is a good example of cross-functional teamwork in action in a concurrent engineering environment. The core development group for this limited-production sports car included all facets of design, manufacturing, and related support groups. Team Viper members, all volunteers, were selected for their expertise, racing enthusiasm, and desire to broaden their engineering talent. Not only did they like to race cars in their off hours, they got a professional kick out of beating the clock.

In 1989, Chrysler put most of this multifarious crew of 80 in one large room, literally tearing down walls to create the open space necessary for cross-pollination of professions and good communication. Only mechanics working on the test car with noisy power tools were kept separate.

There was no need to organize the group into specific teams; it did this itself by consensus. A technical policy committee that allocated the budget for capital expenditure and R&D oversaw the project. As long as it stayed within budget, however, the group could decide how to spend its money, reporting quarterly to the committee. Maintaining the bottom line—rather than department allocation—was what was important.

This approach cut through complicated approval routes and authorizations. Vendors were brought in very early and the team made good use of their expertise. They received team rosters and Chrysler expected them to contact anyone they needed without asking permission. Team Viper held weekly meetings with vendors.

To cut lead time, Viper parts were released directly from layout or models with only functional dimensions. Certain suspension, engine, and body-panel designs were on CAD systems to save time and streamline the process. The team, however, also worked with clay models that were not on CAD. Component work envelopes were primarily made from layout drawings.

The team evolved into three engineering subgroups: chassis, body, and synthesis. The synthesis group ensured that components came together to produce a vehicle with balance and integrity. Responsibility for synthesis rested with team management, where it became a daily concern.

Team Viper reached beyond design and manufacturing engineering to include the shop floor workers who would build the car. Over 600 hours

Viper production team celebrates rollout of the first production vehicle. That's Howard Lewis, plant manager, in the passenger seat. Directly behind him (in the tie) is Manufacturing Engineering Manager Bill Smith. Viper design and production is a major example of concurrent engineering at work.

of training and the ability to build a complete car from scratch made these people another breed, a far cry from the traditional assembly line worker restricted to a single repetitive task. Each Viper assembler had wide responsibilities and routinely pointed out potential production problems to engineers.

Central to the Viper project's success was the fact that the group got the credit and shared the blame for mistakes. If something did not work, it was not manufacturing's fault; it was the team's responsibility. The company is now spreading the lessons learned during Viper's development throughout the organization.

Us Against Them

The Viper experience reminded me how, not so long ago, engineering and manufacturing were still dug in on opposite sides of the wall. When

I began working for Chevrolet in 1964, there were two groups of people preparing new models for launch. One worked in offices, labs, and test tracks that were spacious, bright, sometimes pastoral, sometimes sumptuous. Their dress was casual, their work pace leisurely, never interrupted by the need to produce tangible results immediately. These were the stylists, designers, and product engineers.

Somewhere else—often in trailers and test garages stuck onto an assembly plant—you could find a motley crew of ex-mechanics, ex-diemakers, and ex-millwrights with mismatched ties hanging askew. Their loud voices, clipped sentences, and bad language marked them as plant rats, weaned on the factory's din, smoke, and grime. All day long, they heard the shrill protests of workers who spent their days in often dangerous, usually uncomfortable jobs. They were hardened to the relentless pressure of production quotas made more unbearable by specifications that bore little relationship to the realities of manufacturing processes. They had learned to improvise, lie, and cheat to survive. Manufacturing and production engineering plant rats were just one step away from the hell hole of the production line.

Ivory Tower Thinking

In the auto industry of the '60s the product engineers worked in "chimneys." The brake engineer worked on the brakes of the A-body, B-body, C-body, or whatever body was currently in design. The suspension engineer did the same, as did the bumper engineer, instrument panel engineer, piston engineer, crankshaft engineer, and every other engineer in this land of bizarre toys. When they finished designing the 1964-model brakes, suspension, bumper, instrument panel, crankshaft, or whatever, they began working on the 1965 version.

About four years after work began on a new model, the engineering documents supervisor would fill a van with layouts and detail drawings— some on mylar and others printed in faded brown and blue—drive a dozen miles to the dismal lair of manufacturing planning, dump the whole mess unceremoniously at the feet of the receptionist, mumble "prints for the '65," and flee back to his ivory tower.

Summoned by a telephone call, a perspiring ex-mechanic would be muttering to himself even before he stooped to retrieve the wads of paper that would sour his life. These manufacturing people felt about product engineers the way an infantryman feels about a commander who orders him onto the battlefield while cowering in a bunker out of artillery range. Those who have not experienced it cannot appreciate the fury induced by this system. When a vehicle turned out well, you can be sure success came out of the hides of those plant rats.

Breaking Down the Wall

Chrysler's turnaround depended on changing this system. Back when I was with GM, their 1971 GMC CK pickup was a very key truck. Thanks to Fred Caffrey, our plant manager, we in manufacturing were allowed—for the first time—to go upstream two or three years earlier than the launch of the product to work with the chief engineer and his key lieutenants. This was a precursor of what everybody is so in love with today—concurrent engineering—getting engineering, design, suppliers, and manufacturing working up front together, and not just a year, but two or three years ahead of time.

I remembered that experience. When I came to Chrysler a decade later, that's exactly what I tried to do. I brought that thinking to Chrysler. That's why I met with Don DeLaRossa in design on my first day there, after my first meeting with Iacocca. I asked if I could actually put some manufacturing people into the design studio, not for just one car or one truck, but for *every* car and truck. The renaissance had begun!

That was when the real product-development revolution started, when we started working together every day. Today, every vehicle is done with process-driven design, concurrent engineering or whatever you want to call it.

The Manufacturing Feasibility Group (MFG—an acronym loaded with meaning) planted in the bowels of design engineering in 1981 was the first step toward concurrent engineering. As I mentioned, significant cost savings resulted from shrinking the time between conceiving a design and introducing it into production. Higher quality levels were now possible because parts production did not strain the manufacturing system, as it used to. Our studies showed that quality starts with design and that one-third to one-half of product quality problems are traceable to poor design.

Concurrent engineering's benefits began cascading throughout Chrysler Manufacturing. A fender that required nine or 10 stamping operations, for example, now required as few as two! Fewer press operations meant fewer presses and related equipment on a line, significantly

Year and Body Style															
78	80	83	84	84	85	86	86	87	88	88	89	90 N	91	92	94
L	K	E	G	S	H	P	N	J	C	A	Y	EXT	S	LH	PL
Percent Process-driven Design 25	30	35	45	45	45	45	50	45	50	50	50	55	50	80	90 +
Percent CAD-designed Significant Panels 5	12	50	78	0	80	82	0	46	87	92	90	100	100	100	100
Percent Dies Machined by CAM (panels) 0	0	0	0	2	0	0	0	2	12	26	30	30	80	100	100

Chrysler's improvement in concurrent engineering (process-driven design) and CAD/CAM. Each new model at Chrysler was the end product of the increased interaction between design and manufacturing.

reducing the investment in capital equipment, and cutting the time needed to get product to market. Reducing the number of production stamping operations meant more uptime and, therefore, more output. Uptime and maintenance are related: the more machines and tooling producing a part, the more breakdowns. Stamping plants with the lowest possible number of press operations can run at 75–80% uptime. With a high number of operations, uptime can drop to below 50%.

Optimizing product design for manufacturing brought other savings. We could now see ways to reduce size, structural strength, and complexity for die shoes, walls, ribs, and wear-plates. In many cases, we cut the number of inserts and used less costly welded edges.

The MFG pioneers tenaciously prodded, pushed, cajoled, and plied product and design engineers with favors to prompt them to take manufacturing realities into consideration. Each new model bore more of their fingerprints, culminating in the outstanding quality and cost improvements achieved in the '80s and early '90s.

The products of the LH design series (Chrysler Concorde, Dodge Intrepid, Eagle Vision) realized the dream. Although we are still a few steps away from putting product engineers and manufacturing engineers on the equal footing that true process-driven design demands, they have traveled leagues together since the days of the country clubs and trailers.

CE and the Rule of 10

Whether you call it process-driven design, concurrent engineering, simultaneous engineering, design for manufacturability, design for assembly, quality function deployment, dynamic manufacturing, quality engineering, synchronous manufacturing, or producibility engineering, it means the manufacturing engineer sits next to the product and design engineer. Before product engineers draw a line, they answer such questions as, "Can we cast this configuration in the foundry?" "Can we machine this contour on our mills?" "Can we stamp this flange consistently with our transfer presses?" "Can we weld this flange within the tight tolerances required by robots?"

Physical proximity is essential. Face-to-face interaction elicits greater responsibility, urgency, and even tolerance. A team member can get up from the design terminal and walk a drawing or part over to an associate from another discipline to get a three-dimensional demonstration, avoiding the misunderstandings typical of exchanges over the telephone.

With CE, you can get a physical prototype of your concept within days (sometimes hours) of proposing it. A three-dimensional, solid prototype can be made from CAD data using a laser and a material such as resin polymer in the stereolithography process (which Chrysler used extensively on projects such as the Viper exhaust manifold). Rapid prototyping bypasses the problems of human interpretation, machining, and inadequately cut sections. For example, interpretation of blind holes, complex interior passageways, or complex curved surfaces may lead to difficulties between the designer and the manufacturing engineer. The process solves such problems through improved part visualization. Some part testing may then proceed within the material's physical limits.

The Rule of 10 drives the CE effort. This fundamental law of concurrent engineering says it is 10 times as expensive to implement a change (or correct a design mistake) when a product has reached the next stage of development. For example, the cost to fix design problems at the plan step is 10 times that at the design stage. The cost to fix the problem at the manufacturing stage is 10 times that at the plan stage and 100 times that at the design stage. When the product is in the consumer's hands, the sky's the limit.

Player Profiles

A CE team needs a forceful and experienced, yet democratic, project manager. Up, down, and lateral communication is of utmost importance

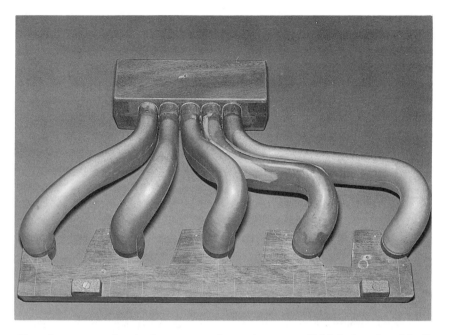

Complete pattern for the inner core of an exhaust manifold designed and built with stereolithography. Stereolithography was used by the Viper program to reduce costs and save considerable time for the exhaust manifold development and increase accuracy in the development of prototype parts. Stereolithography is one tool that can be used to bring design and manufacturing functions closer together.

if the product designs are to be as good as they can. All disciplines must not only be heard, but their ideas absorbed in the final design.

I look for these personality traits in a CE leader: good people skills, assertiveness, openness to change, analytical ability, good understanding of product costing, determination and persistence, good understanding of manufacturing processes and their relative costs, knowledge of the overall organization and the roles of various functional groups, and, if possible, expertise on the specific product.

Many people in manufacturing and engineering will insist they are not creative. When you consider their problem-solving abilities and ability to deal with budget and cost, you will find this is simply not true. Too many people believe creative individuals are only those who can draw well, write music, or write for publication. Most people are creative. They have a wealth of knowledge and ideas that is typically kept hidden. At times, those ideas are suffocated by negative comments or "killer statements."

Statements That Kill Initiative[1]

"We don't do it that way here."

"I'm sure that's been considered."

"We've been through all this before."

"Let's think about it for awhile."

"That was ruled out a long time ago."

"Last time we tried it, it didn't work."

"There's no personnel to put on it."

"It must be interchangeable."

"UL would never approve it."

"Our customers won't buy it."

"This isn't the right time for it."

"That's not to our standard XYZ."

"That's manufacturing's problem."

"We have the best system already."

"Designing our products is different."

"They are not on our qualified suppliers list."

"We are already using design for assembly."

"It's a good idea, but I don't like it."

"Sure it costs more, but we'll have a better product."

"We can't change that, Industrial Design won't allow it."

"The cost doesn't matter, it's time to market that's important."

"You can't fight success."

"No!"

"We're different."

"We're too busy."

"I don't like it."

"It's impractical."

"That's old technology."

"I didn't budget for that."

"That's been tried before."

"Be practical."

"We can't risk that."

"That's not my job."

"It's been tried already."

"We'll get to that later."

"We tried that years ago."

"Our business is different."

"It's not a proven design."

"The schedule won't allow it."

"We can't afford it."

"But our customers want it this way."

"Process mastery has not been proven."

The CE team enhances the motivation of its players. I mentioned the engineering "chimneys" of the past, where engineers identified only with their specialty. Now they take ownership of an entire vehicle. The fruit of their labor is visible, tangible, measurable, driveable, washable, and polishable. They can discuss what they've made with friends and neighbors who are not automotive professionals.

In the automotive industry, a CE team can number over 1000 people. Under the old system, the project group was small in the beginning and grew larger as the project neared production launch. Now CE teams shrink as they solve problems before production begins. Although these teams disperse after completing a given project, in the auto industry, a stable cadre remains together on each platform team specializing in a certain type of vehicle.

In planning your journey to concurrent engineering, be sure you have answers to these questions:

- How will team leaders identify potential team members? How will they get their resources?
- How will job assignments be made in cross-functional teams, and what will happen to the member when the assignment ends?
- Will groups that must work together be located in the same place?
- To attract the best talent, teams should be viewed as mainstream assignments. Does your organization see them as an exception to the rules? How do they alter existing career paths and patterns?
- Will a team member's contribution be judged individually or collectively?
- Will the judge be the team leader or the member's functional organization?
- How can a cross-functional team's success filter through a hierarchical organization?
- Team members must tolerate having work inspected by people outside their function at every stage of an assignment. They, in turn, must examine and critique the work of other members on the same basis. They must negotiate tradeoffs (price versus performance) with other team members. How will you get people to change their ways of working?
- Design engineers are judged on the elegance and performance of their designs, manufacturing engineers on how inexpensively the product can be made, service engineers on mean time to repair, and so on. How will you overcome functional stereotypes and status differences?
- How are you preparing design engineers, accustomed to working alone until an assignment is complete, to work in tandem with manufacturing engineers? What new skills have the team's manufacturing engineers learned to replace throwing it back over the wall?
- When a design feature boosts performance but increases manufacturing costs, or a manufacturing process boosts savings but decreases serviceability, how will the team decide?

- When a team decides it must select or build a new set of tools for its project instead of using existing ones, how do you overcome the not-invented-here syndrome?
- How can management monitor strategic direction while allowing teams to take initiatives and solve daily problems without interference?

Contributing to the CE team is the member from finance who calculates the design cost and determines whether the project budget can cover it. Sales and marketing team members represent the customer's needs and desires. Top management steps aside so the team can hear the customer's voice. Service and parts-department members watch out for the interchangeability of components and systems. The team member from purchasing identifies suppliers who can produce the parts in question economically, with precision, and needed volume. Concurrent engineering demands involving major suppliers in a new product project at the inception, eliminating many of the past adversarial relationships.

Expecting more of individual suppliers reduces their number and potential shipping points, and this can mean major savings. Stephen E. Plumb noted this point in *Ward's Auto World*:

> Turning over complete systems to suppliers enabled Chrysler to reduce dramatically the number of vendors with whom it does business. The company used only 230 parts and material suppliers, including wholly owned Acustar Inc., and 285 shipping points on the LH. This compares with 456 suppliers and 626 shipping points for the current New Yorkers in production in Belvidere, Illinois, and 490 suppliers and 680 shipping points for the Windsor, Ontario, minivan plant.[2]

CE also enhances union-management relationships. Traditionally, workers didn't see the new vehicle until the first pilots were built on the line. Now, they are involved from the concept stage and provide direct input into the work processes and assembly techniques they will have to live with when the vehicle is in production.

Involving manufacturing engineers and production employees from the concept stage saves a great deal of money and time. Their familiarity with manufacturing equipment and processes prompts the salvage and re-use of automation that would have been torn out and replaced under the old system—a tremendous boon in this era of tight budgets and niche marketing. Including process and manufacturing engineering staffs at the outset of a development program also provides advance warning that technological innovations will be required. Obviously, the earlier the warning, the better the chance that the style intent will be implemented optimally, at the lowest cost, and with the highest quality.

What's more, adding manufacturing personnel to Chrysler's Design Engineering did not inhibit the design process. Our conclusion was corroborated by other automakers surveyed in a University of Michigan product development study: "Effective automakers do not sacrifice imaginative styles by integrating styling, design, and production functions, or by having styling share authority with other functions."[3]

The Tools of CE

I've found the following technologies and methods important in helping a CE team achieve its goals:

- Feature-enriched solids modeling systems.
- CIM systems with integrated database and good cost-estimating subsystem.
- Local and wide-area network communications.
- Critical path method systems to schedule complex multifunction tasks and provide master timing charts for the network coordinators.
- Pareto analysis.
- Matrix diagrams to identify correlated or excluded items.
- Value analysis engineering to analyze value added by each design component.
- Cost-sensitivity feature analysis to evaluate the cost to downstream functions of each design feature.
- Tolerance splitting programs to calculate stock allowances and their tolerances.
- All the "Design for's": Manufacturing, Assembly, Testability, Reliability, Maintainability.
- Robust design evaluations via Taguchi's Design of Experiments.
- Engineering/strength/deflection/thermal analyses to design for forces encountered.
- Failure mode and effect analyses to evaluate seriousness, probability, and likelihood of detecting failures.
- Process design and simplification analyses for plant machinery layout and staffing.
- Rapid prototyping.
- Manufacturing process simulation and animation.

- Quality function deployment.
- Benchmarking to validate goals, technology, and processes in comparable production environments.
- Continuous improvement to identify machining and assembly problems today and to hit marks established for the future.

As you can see, the computer plays an important role here. Networking personal computers or workstations helps eliminate confusion, misunderstanding, and wasted time. Computer-integrated manufacturing can transfer critical process information to the product design, business, and production areas, providing current and accurate data, where and when needed. The plant rats have been heard and are now well respected.

References

1. Bakerjian, Ramon, Editor, *Tool and Manufacturing Engineers Handbook,* Volume 6. Dearborn, MI: Society of Manufacturing Engineers, 1992, p. 8-5.
2. Plumb, Stephen E., "Suppliers Offer Bench Strength," *Ward's Auto World.* Detroit, MI: Ward's Communications, Inc., March 1992, p. 55.
3. Industrial Development Division Product Development Study. *A Key to World Class Manufacture of Automotive Bodies*, Volume 1. Ann Arbor, MI: The University of Michigan, 1991, p. 22.

Chapter 8

COMPUTER-AIDED EVERYTHING

Chrysler Product Engineering started developing its computer system over 20 years ago. Robert "Bob" Sinclair provided key leadership and direction. Currently, more than two-thirds of its design and drawing output is done entirely by computer-aided engineering. Most applications are mathematical surface definitions, design and engineering, drafting, solids modeling, vehicle package studies, NC milling (die models and hard tools), material nesting layouts, and test controls and analysis.

Chrysler has one of the largest integrated technical computer systems in the world, with over 27 interlinked large-scale computers processing more than 64 billion instructions a second! This network supports more than 1000 terminals, 500 of them with interactive graphics capability, running mostly on Chrysler-generated software.

Chrysler's manufacturing engineers now can access all data generated at Product Engineering. Their own computer systems complete tool and fixture designs, plant layouts, model building for simulation studies, and CNC machine programming.

All die models are made with CNC milling machines. Using surface information from the CAD database, a computer develops the machining commands. The surfaces are accurate and can be easily mirrored to make left and right matching parts.

The Sterling Heights assembly plant uses its computer to communicate with the central corporate manufacturing engineering computer, putting the plant in a real-time relationship with product and die changes and *ending* waits for paper engineering changes or part prints.

Computers also develop material nesting layouts and pass them on to the interior trim manufacturing plants. The system generates instructions that drive the fabric cutters to assure correct pattern alignments and minimum waste.

Computers check all sheet-metal subassembly tolerances to ensure dimensional specifications achieve world-class fit-up. The data also help in the design of checking fixtures with realistic tolerances for stamping and assembly plants. Standardizing the design of assembly fixtures for two- and four-post weld presses allows the computer to merge a body design into an automatic framing fixture, saving weeks of design effort.

Chrysler creates and edits over 25,000 operation description sheets yearly that tell downstream support operations how to assemble a vehicle. A computer automates the process sheet updates. The next-generation system will be capable of including video disks to show each plant operator motion pictures of the assembly process. A CAD database for all plants allows fast, accurate evaluation of new designs to be produced in existing facilities.

In 1982, our manufacturing engineers used CAD/CAM to develop the robotic paint process for the interior of the T-Wagon minivans, Plymouth Voyager, and Dodge Caravan. After determining the conveyor and paint-process requirements, a computer helped design the robot specifications.

Manufacturing engineers could preview and simulate every robot move before it happened, using the computer to find the most efficient path and prevent interference. Before starting construction, they even did computer simulations of the assembly plant processes to ensure that JIT material delivery, tooling, material handling, scheduling, and facility design would work as an integrated system.

Running an accelerated computer model of the plant provided years of production experience in days! We found that we could reduce in-process inventory at Windsor Assembly by 50% over earlier K-car plants while maintaining production at or above program requirements. Simulating the plant's JIT material delivery system established optimum shipping/ receiving dock space and stock loading/unloading requirements.

The engineers also put their best ideas into a proposal incorporating the newest process and tooling developments for the layout at our Sterling Heights assembly facility. We developed a computer simulation to evaluate and test how the plant would function, again gaining years of production experience in days. Because we knew the output of various process configurations, we could tell plant managers how various production strategies would impact operations.

Computers also are helping Chrysler in areas such as defective material tracking, trouble reports, audit items by detail, computer-aided body layout, performance feedback from all areas, on-line random sampling, and in-yard quality audits.

Closing the Loop

Computer-controlled processes and equipment require computer-supported information systems to measure and monitor factory performance, so we installed a Performance Feedback System (PFS) at the Sterling Heights plant.

PFS is a menu-driven program that provides minute-by-minute information on who is working and what they achieve. It records who called in sick for the day, who entered the plant at what time, what total plant staffing is, and who is on each job. It describes the job assignment of each workstation and the modifications required if the production schedule or mix changes.

Workers report any problems via a data terminal so management can dispatch immediate assistance. Most important, PFS creates a complete record for each vehicle as it passes through each process/assembly station in the plant and does not allow a vehicle to leave until the assembly and testing process is certified complete.

PFS is a key tool for managing the plant because it continuously updates production counts and quality information and presents the data in bar charts. A computer-driven tracking system—which includes the plant's component suppliers—keeps tabs on quality, quantity, mix, and location of every part. This system allowed us to respond rapidly to changes in the production schedule and significantly trimmed inventory from three- and four-day stockpiles to just a few hours of material or, in some cases, a few minutes.

Installing sophisticated equipment and adopting in-line sequencing and minimum inventory between stations makes preventive maintenance and monitoring systems mandatory. We designed and installed state-of-the-art Factory Information Systems (FIS) at Windsor and Sterling Heights enabling the plants to work predictably. Built around an IBM Series I computer and more than 120 programmable controllers, the FIS ties into major production areas throughout the plant, as well as into conveyor systems, robots, transfers, spray booths, and ovens. Nine status monitors provide instant crisis recognition on screen as the graphic of the affected machine changes color. Every production machine in the plant is part of a data highway system providing these real-time alerts to workers. Forty video terminals tell maintenance staff which part in the "down" machine failed and where to begin repair.

Formulating the Future Factory

After the minivan launch at Windsor proved many of our manufacturing theories and provided us with capital to continue our efforts, we began dreaming about our "Factory of the Future." I put our best planners together and asked them to brainstorm—to come up with ideas that would enable us to leapfrog the competition and create plants that would serve as benchmarks for global manufacturing excellence.

The ideas that passed muster had to meet two stringent criteria: the net present value of the discounted cash flow over the life of the project had to be greater than zero, and any proposal had to fit into a plant-wide strategy that provided for the growth of the automation network without islands. Only a systems approach could provide the control, diagnostics, and adaptive feedback required to maintain high-quality production and take full advantage of the hardware and the software in the system.

I had 10 general principles in mind for our Factory of the Future. We would:

- Establish a policy of zero defects.
- Reduce the direct labor content of designs.
- Reduce product and process complexity.
- Minimize work-in-process inventory.
- Streamline clay-to-die and tool systems.
- Adhere to the master timing schedule or accelerate it.
- Minimize product changes.
- Match plant personnel skills to tasks.
- Maximize flexible automation to minimize new-model changeover time.
- Perfect in-line sequencing, JIT material delivery, and our FIS.

The plan that our think tank came up with uses automated guided vehicle systems (AGVS) and inverted power-and-free or linear motor conveyors to carry assemblies and bodies through the plant as products are processed. Parts travel in magazine-type, reusable containers to the line from automated storage/retrieval system (AS/RS) areas to keep pace with the body. Robots load parts from this system to the body. Parts flow from the automatic accumulator, selected by job number, using in-line sequencing. There is to be *no storage on the line*.

In the future factory, composite tooling pallets, used for locating the parts in the body shop, will carry parts and assemblies through robot-operated fixtures while robots weld the assemblies. Fixtures will be the quick-change type, picked up by gantry robots and held over the tooling pallet in a close relative location. They will then capture the roughly located details and place them into a finite, relative position. High-capacity gantry robots will change fixtures on-line while the AGVS is indexing. Robots performing assembly processes (such as welding) will change programs and sometimes even tools while the AGVS indexes. A machine-vision system will help AGVS repeatability, will correct the robot programs, and will help robots load parts to the body.

An AS/RS will collect and store all produced parts for subsequent release to the assembly line on a first-in, first-out basis. It will receive all incoming JIT shipments, distributing them by part number to the AGVS which will transport the material to the line.

The system will eliminate stock storage and associated cardboard, wooden packing, and steel banding materials in the plant. Because assembly workers will no longer have to select the appropriate parts, they will assemble a greater product variety and may even be able to customize products in mass production operations.

Our think tank specified a new fixturing concept in assembly that called for welding a complete hinge to the door and body while the door is held in the body opening in the precise assembly position. Machine vision guidance would be needed, and the product would be redesigned for welding accessibility.

Expensive power-and-free conveyor systems will be replaced in the future factory by linear-induction-motor-driven pallets with optical recognition and microprocessor controls. They will index, accelerate and decelerate, and position precisely fore and aft.

A vision-guided robot will seam-track the roof-to-aperture joint and will MIG-braze the joint in one pass while compensating for metal fit-up variations. Another robot with a grinder or sanding disk will finish the joint after brazing.

The future automotive factory will use light but strong composite materials in tooling pallets, body trucks, paint trucks, conveyor belts and carriers, and trim trucks, reducing the load on conveyor systems and electricity consumption. More composites in the final vehicle will require modified paint systems. Think tank engineers expect adhesives and heat staking to replace traditional rivets and screws as preferred fastening methods.

One technology I particularly liked in our future factory was a universal discrete-point, three-dimensional, laser gaging fixture mounted on a six-axis programmable robot. It would eliminate manual gages in both stamping and assembly, and check principal locating points and associated critical surfaces. A network of these systems in a plant could audit tooling performance at least 10 times per shift. Using the speed of the laser and an associated computer system, a stamping will pass through an on-line "laser car wash." The laser will record surface dimensions and compare them to official CAD surface data stored in the system. Variations greater than the prescribed limits will signal the need for die adjustments.

Our planners also wanted to replace the conventional leak test. Pumping a vehicle body full of helium, then letting a robotic "sniffer" detect escaped gas, would reveal body leaks and accumulate statistical data to drive corrective action.

Though the factory will have no fork trucks, its truck receiving docks for JIT delivery will triple. (Right now, the new Jefferson North 1.7-million-square-foot assembly plant has 56 perimeter docks.)

All of the things I talked about and/or researched can be done today. We did them at Jefferson North in the body shop, paint shop, and materials system, but chose not to go whole hog in general assembly. We also moved into modularity, that is, bringing in a whole instrument panel as one module and a whole suspension, something we never did before. We decided it was best to creep before we crawl, before we sprint, so to speak. The era of the computer is here.

Chapter 9

GETTING OUR MONEY'S WORTH

What's it cost to make a good small car these days? According to a June 1992 report, Ford Motor Company produced its small cars for $5415, with Chrysler close behind at $5841, and the cost at Toyota was $6216. The other three Japanese car makers were higher. Ultimately, the low-cost quality producer will win this competition.

To stay in the game, however, manufacturers need a consistent infusion of capital for equipment purchases. Here are six rules I, as a manager, used to prepare my pregame plans.

First, I looked for a connection between my project or new equipment purchase and the company's strategic goals. Would it expand the business, cut costs, or improve product quality?

Second, I put a realistic numerical value on project benefits and costs, keeping in mind the fact that numbers don't always have to be "financial." Maintenance records provide good data, for example.

Third, I drew up an implementation plan and timetable, with clearly defined milestones. The plan would discuss implementation, team members, and the training required. Remember, the devil is in the detail.

Fourth, I discussed the human factors involved in my new process or equipment: What workers would be involved? What training would they need? What would it cost? What worker benefits do I anticipate?

Fifth, I did not give up easily. I expected roadblocks, expected to rewrite my proposal, expected tough questions. I knew I would not win every battle. Neither will you, but if your financial assumptions are correct and your presentation is solid, you may be on your way to improved quality, productivity, and flexibility.

Last, I maintained a file of rejected proposals on the principle that their time might come. This year's reject may be next year's shoo-in as technology advances or the financial picture changes. In my time at Chrysler, we added modern stamping and metalworking equipment, automated body shops, world-class paint systems, a modern impact mold foundry process, state-of-the art conveyor systems, and new material management systems—all precisely planned and executed within an integrated corporate system. It took 10 long, tough years to get these investments approved. My philosophy is anything *neglected* eventually will demand to be *corrected*.

Start with Strategy

A manufacturing-investment strategy should start with a long-range product plan formulated to fit your company and industry. Chrysler uses its long-range product plan and the answers to the following questions to determine its manufacturing-investment strategy.

- *Sales Average Annual Rate.* What will be the total industry volume for a given year and market?
- *Individual Company Market Share Plan.* What percentage of the total market do we expect to command? How many product units does this percentage translate to? How do they break down into specific product lines?
- *Capacity.* How many units of a product, and of what type, can we produce? How can we maintain reasonable stability despite expected cyclical demand based on historical performance?
- *Facility Utilization.* Which facilities are most productive? Which are best suited for which product because of quality, location, flexibility, cost, age, work force, or other variables? Which should be consolidated, idled, or even demolished?
- *Automation.* Where should new automation be deployed to expand capacity, enhance productivity, improve quality, or improve systems? What kind of automation should be used?
- *Methods Changes.* What can be done to make the thousands of little

improvements that can be realized daily to continuously enhance efficiency and productivity?

- *Adding or Insourcing Work.* What jobs should be brought back into the corporation to re-employ laid-off workers, jobs bank people, and use facilities operating at partial capacity?

Once we had accurate assessments concerning these issues, we set our investment plan and budget in place.

Manufacturing investments do not lend themselves to planning based on 10-day sales periods, 90-day financial reporting periods, or even annual shareholders' meetings. The vision must extend at least five years, and 10 years or longer is preferable.

A major weakness of Chrysler's financial planning had been myopia, so I pushed to plan capital investments with approvals that were firm five years out and directional for another five years.

The outstanding quality gains of the '80s and early '90s at Chrysler were accelerated by technology investments in:

- body shops ($30–90 million each),
- paint shops ($100–240 million each),
- assembly plants ($250–500 million each, except for Jefferson North plant, which cost $800 million),
- stamping plants ($80–200 million each),
- foundries ($25–100 million each),
- engine plants ($25–300 million each),
- transmission plants ($200–500 million each), and
- the Outer Drive Manufacturing Technical Center, which cost $60 million.

Rebuilding Chrysler's manufacturing capability cost a total of $3.5 billion and was one of the best auto industry investments ever made! It was also less than Saturn's cost alone to General Motors. Chrysler's was for worldwide manufacturing capability.

Autonomy to Spend

Autonomy must be earned. As plants developed maturity, added good skilled people, and gained my personal confidence in their manufacturing-engineering, master-mechanic, tool-and-die, and plant-engineering type jobs, we gave them more autonomy.

We obviously couldn't give autonomy to Windsor assembly in 1980–1981 in robots, for example. They hardly knew what a robot was. They didn't understand computers. They didn't know about lasers. They didn't understand the new paint processes or turbo-bells. So I couldn't give these factories much latitude from 1980 through 1984, but as we built skill levels over that period, we started transferring more decision making to the local level. From '87 through '91, most of the plants controlled their own equipment purchases. During that period, they deserved it because they were more qualified than we in central office were to make those decisions. We had successfully driven the decision making process closer to the real action. Decentralization was evolutionary.

From '79 through '85, individual plants at Chrysler couldn't control much of their own destiny because they had been decimated, had not been replacing obsolete equipment, and most of their top people were only high school graduates. There were few degreed engineers, let alone someone with a specialty in computer technology, for example. By the late '80s, nearly all my plant managers and MEs were either college graduates, engineers, or had specialty degrees. We had infused much more education, confidence, and credibility into the system. I would say plants had minimal authority in '80, moderate authority by '84, and maximum authority by '87.

Each plant still was required to get corporate okay to do something major, but *how* they did it was up to their discretion. They still had to work through purchasing to define their specifications because we did not do direct buying. In a major corporation, the manufacturing people establish their specifications, and purchasing negotiates with vendors to determine who will build the new factory and who will supply the conveyors, machine tools, welding equipment, paint system, power plant, etc. I didn't let anyone make those decisions without final review from me. After all, my butt was on the line. Our factories were always able to run. Balance is important.

The Huntsville Saga

In 1980, our Huntsville electronic-component facility in the Diversified Group was on the bubble. The majority of our analysts thought Huntsville should be sold or mothballed. America was losing the war in home-built consumer electronics to the Japanese and, Europeans, and they wanted me to throw in the towel for Chrysler, too.

My approach here was somewhat emotional. Huntsville was electronics, not electrical, and that's as big a difference as there is between my heart and brain, and the rest of my body. I remember telling the policy committee: "I cannot win this case just by pleading numbers. Sometimes numbers lie or can be misconstrued. I cannot give you a case to save Huntsville solely on the basis of the numbers."

As I will explain in Chapter 11, our plant-closing decisions were based 70% on hard numbers and 30% on subjective judgments. So here, over two-thirds of the argument was against me, and I had to base my case on resorting to salesmanship to gain their attention.

"Gentlemen," I said, "in 1979, Chrysler cars had no computers in them—absolutely zero! Yet, we brought out the Imperial in '81 with three computers in it. What do you think the trend will be by 1990? We're going to have at least half a dozen computers on the equivalent K-car then, and guess where you will want to build them? Right here in Huntsville! Computers and electronics are a vehicle's heart and brain. Now do you really want to outsource your heart and brain?"

Somebody must have listened. Instead of selling the plant to RCA, or Siemens, or Bosch in Germany (which had expressed interest in buying it) or their Japanese equivalents, we kept Huntsville. At the time, that plant had 2000 people and was two different factories separated by 100 yards. It made everything from radios to power antennas. It must have been doing something right because it was a key contributor to our company going from a $7 million a day loss to a $7 million a day gain. In 1988, we built and dedicated a brand new plant, called Huntsville Electronics City. I believe in doing the necessary right, not the popular wrong.

Automation's Proliferation

The massive automation deployment in refurbished Chrysler plants represents a major investment in process control and consistency. These advances were harvested from the seeds of cutting-edge technology and worker training. As an American, however, I am troubled by what I recently learned from a National Center for Manufacturing Sciences (Ann Arbor, Michigan) study. NCMS reports it takes 55 years for 90% of U.S. manufacturers to adopt a new technology. In Japan, it takes 18 years. The old "slow-walk" financial system and people still control American manufacturing.

The reluctance of U.S. manufacturers to innovate was most obvious in the past decade in robotics. Joseph F. Engelberger, the chairman of Transitions Research Corporation (Danbury, Connecticut), who is considered the father of industrial robotics, noted his frustration with U.S.

foot dragging in leading-edge manufacturing technology in a letter to the editor of *Manufacturing Engineering* magazine:

> For me, the biggest manufacturing technology disappointment is the failure of robotics to permeate production. Even the irresponsible forecasts of media sensationalists and financial pundits should have come to pass by now.
>
> What happened? In the heat of the chase, the giant latecomers bought in and treated robotics like a commodity. After losing prodigious amounts fighting for market share, GE, Westinghouse, United Technology, IBM, and such quit, leaving the little guys in disarray. Japan, with incremental advances, took—and now dominates—the industrial robot market. Meanwhile, no one was fundamentally advancing the state of the art.
>
> If we had made our robots autonomously mobile, sensate, articulate, and imbued with artificial intelligence, the stand-alone robot worker could have become reality.
>
> But, not to worry. To perform in service activities, robots must be more humanlike. That is where the action is today, and the smarts are right here in the U.S. Ten years from now, we in service robotics will magnanimously share robotic intelligence with manufacturing folks who have relegated robots to being just another automation subset.[1]

Although Engelberger makes a good point, as a manager I was faced with a practical problem: introducing new automation technology into a manufacturing operation that had been paralyzed for 20 years. The technical and social obstacles were formidable. For example, a 30-year-old worker has some fear of robotics, a 40-year-old has more, and a 50-year-old a heckuva lot more than that. A 60-year-old is usually totally paranoid about this new technology!

Awakenings

We began by using computer simulation to design and lay out a completely new manufacturing system. Power-and-free conveyors eliminated assembly line pits and ramps. More than 1500 once-manual welds, per vehicle, were now performed by precision-programmed robots. Weld integrity was monitored by computer through our new Factory Information System with terminals located at almost every workstation.

The FIS helped head off problems before they affected the product and production process. It pinpointed critical machine nonconformances as they occurred and provided early warning of potential problems, monitored quality, and gathered machine performance data for planning preventive and predictive maintenance.

Windsor was the first North American auto assembly facility to coat body interiors with spray painting robots. As early as 1981, we had decided to never use any human to apply paint to the interior cavity of the vehicle. There were three reasons: It was one of the most horrible jobs I had ever experienced in my foreman and superintendent days. No human beings really want to get into a vehicle and spray paint that is going to blow right back into their faces and their lungs. Robots, on the other hand, never become fatigued and their lungs never get fouled with overspray. The programmed spray quantity and force improves paint application quality. Second, we felt we could use conveyors, paint-booth, and robotic programmability technology to do this and get the person out of that unfriendly environment. Third, it would improve product quality. G. Paul Russo, director of manufacturing engineering, did an excellent job in leading this successful project. We produced three million vans at Chrysler without ever asking a person to spray any of them on the inside. We had no warranty claims for interior paint on those three million units. That proves the minivan's paint quality is outstanding, as is the productivity.

Workers freed from spray painting can work on safer, more comfortable operations, but displacing people has social implications. We studied worker attrition at the plants being considered for retooling with robots. It ranged from a low of 3% to a high of 14%, with about 6.4% of our manufacturing group people lost annually.

During the period when we were deploying large numbers of robots, our work force was growing within our 40 remaining factories. Between 1980 and 1986, for example, annual output increased from 1.0 million units to 2.3 million units! We were on a roll. Simultaneously, automation and other factors were prodding us to an ever-more complicated product mix. We gradually replaced small, fuel-miserly engines with six-, eight-, and even 10-cylinder engines. In response to consumer desire for power and performance, intermediate, large, and luxury cars replaced large volume, subcompact vehicles, creating work assignments for people who otherwise would have been displaced by robots and other automation. Using robots in manufacturing required upgrading employee skills, but we tried to avoid layoffs.

To gain greater control of quality, we began increasing in-house fabrication of sheet-metal parts and subassemblies, creating more jobs. We also began building more of our own engines, gradually eliminating purchases from Volkswagen and Peugeot. We then decreased purchases

Robot arms reach inside the vehicles to spray interiors. (Chrysler photo)

of the Mitsubishi V6 from 100% of the total required to 50%, and prepared to sell engines and transmissions to Mitsubishi and Diamond Star Motors.

Robot Lessons

Our first robots were hydraulic-mechanical. We had about three dozen of them at Belvidere Assembly (Belvidere, Illinois) for the launch of the Omni and Horizon in 1978. We doubled that number for the K-car launch at the Detroit Jefferson and Newark, Delaware, assembly plants in 1980. At that time, they were used only in the body shop for resistance welding. We eventually deployed robots in stud welding, brazing, and arc welding, and then moved into applications in the paint shop, in body sealing, material handling, gaging, fusion welding, and small and large subassembly.

From 1980 to 1983, we increased the number of robots in our plants from just over 100 to 1000, making sure every stamping and assembly plant had at least one for safety training and maintenance preparation. Robots can be dangerous if not treated with respect.

In our planning and experimentation with robots, we looked for ways they could reduce danger to workers, reduce monotony inherent in certain manufacturing jobs, and enhance worker comfort by reducing fatigue through ergonomic improvements. They could also improve quality dramatically, as we found when we applied them to framing, which determines a vehicle's basic geometry. The respot line—dubbed "the turkey farm" because of the hundreds of herky-jerky movements of several dozen of these mechanical creatures—added strength and integrity to the vehicle body with a flurry of precisely timed movements that explode into a fiery multi-colored shower of sparks.

Together with the Robotics Industries Association (RIA)—an Ann Arbor, Michigan-based trade organization of robot manufacturers—we established our 50-Hour Rule, whereby a new robot must perform flawlessly, under simulated production conditions, for 50 consecutive hours before we accepted it for delivery to one of our plants. If the robot malfunctioned for even a second, the entire sequence had to be repeated. Because the vendor invoice came due only upon actual shipment, we had the leverage to enforce the rule. Life is leverage.

My manufacturing engineering managers scoured the world for the most reliable, precise, flexible, durable equipment (a key issue in robot applications), traveling to Sweden, France, Germany, Italy, Japan, and all over North America. These trips expanded our knowledge of robot applications into areas we had not previously considered.

We used hydraulic robots for applications requiring high strength, power, force, and reach, such as loading and unloading, or where pressure is great, such as in press welding. In most other applications (about 80% of robot usage), however, we evolved to electric robots, although we couldn't use them in paint shop applications until they had been rendered absolutely safe for environments where a spark could cause a problem. Once the safety issue was resolved, we expanded our deployment.

Electric robots can operate with greater precision because their electric power is at full capacity milliseconds after the switch is thrown. A hydraulic unit hesitates while the oil pressure builds to full power. The same is true when power is cut: the electric device releases almost immediately, whereas the oil of the hydraulic unit returns to its inert state more slowly. Electric robots also are simpler and easier to maintain, which increases uptime. Because they are smaller, electric robots can be deployed in spaces too limited for hydraulic robots and they can be suspended from a ceiling, hung from a wall, or mounted on a light pedestal. You must floor-mount hydraulic robots.

Tips for First-Time Robot Users

1. Respect safety.
2. Require all technology suppliers to meet your performance parameters.
3. Buy the best available technology regardless of the country of origin.
4. Start the robot in a department whose manager and staff are positive toward robots.
5. Involve your technical staff and other employees in the selection and purchase.
6. Buy the robot to meet current needs.
7. Train robot operators thoroughly.
8. Consider maintenance and software issues as critical.
9. Dedicate one robot for training and maintenance purposes.
10. When available, upgrade to new technology to stay current.

It's not that we never had any failures with robots. We had a couple of instances where we were taking more risk or "stretch" than we or the robot manufacturer could handle. I would say we were 98% effective with robotics. On about 2%, we had to do work-overs or do-overs, but nothing that put the "patient" at risk.

The primary reason we needed robots was simply that they improve quality and flexibility. They help replace people in jobs that are unattractive. If you have ever welded, you know it is no fun to do nine hours a day, six days a week for the rest of your life. Before I left, we had converted nearly 100% of our welding to robots and other automation.

If I'm going to put in a robot and displace a person on each shift, plus half a person for maintenance, that's 2.5 people. What will I do with them? I was compassionate enough to use these people, Molly and Joe, to replace Johnny and Suzy who were retiring. But that meant Molly and Joe would need training. You can plan these things and do this in a business fashion, even when there are thousands of Mollys and Joes.

Technology Training

In their desire to be "modern" and their fascination with gadgetry, many companies rushed into automation in the '80s without proper training. As a consequence, many expensive efforts to automate failed. *That didn't happen at Chrysler.* Before introducing high-level automation, we

146

knew the work force who managed it had to be receptive and trained to use it.

It is no secret that U.S. workers are ill-prepared to deal with the complex machinery of contemporary manufacturing. U.S. managers cannot assume people possess the ability to read and follow directions for assembling, calibrating, and operating complex machinery. Nor can they assume that workers have the simple mathematical skill necessary to calculate speeds, feeds, and appropriate tolerances.

You must assess the general educational skill levels of the work force before introducing automation. Based on your findings, you can modify your plan to exclude more complex components, simplify others, and/or embark on a training program to enhance reading, mathematics, and communication skills.

Long before introducing new automation on the factory floor, a sample (a single robot, for example) should be available for familiarization and training. As I said before, many workers are terrified of new machinery and technology. If you introduce these workers to the new technology early and allow them to become accustomed to it over long periods, they will be more likely to operate it properly. Be sure to include some introduction to software programming in that familiarization.

Remedial math and reading probably will not be necessary for skilled tradespeople. Rigorously train them in the assembly, disassembly, maintenance, troubleshooting, and repair of the new machinery for as long as you can. If you have decided to automate but haven't decided what you will purchase, your workers can still get up to speed in the principles by attending generic courses such as those at community colleges.

A contract to purchase automated machinery should include extensive training by the equipment vendor, to begin as soon as your company issues the purchase order. Require qualification tests of all personnel working with the new equipment.

Many automation programs have been ruined by cut-rate, poorly executed, or nonexistent training and substandard education. The massive investments required by automation warrant the insurance provided by education and training. It is as important a component of automation as electricity, hydraulic power, and sophisticated mechanics. (I have more to say on training in Chapter 14.) We enjoyed getting our money's worth.

References

1. "Challenges Facing Manufacturing," *Manufacturing Engineering*. January 1992, p. 85.

Chapter 10

FOCUS ON FLEXIBILITY

On each launch of a new or changed product or process at Chrysler, manufacturing and assembly flexibility was part of the picture, reflecting the worldwide shift from mass to specialized production. Flexible systems allow faster changeovers, run several products on the same line, bring new products to market more quickly, and change production schedules and product mix as circumstances require. We built S-body vans and station wagons on the same line at Windsor Assembly, for example. At Sterling Heights Assembly, it was a mix of Chrysler and Dodge H-bodies and P-body Plymouth Sundances and Dodge Shadows. Warren Truck Assembly built full-size Dodge Ram pickups and mid-size Dodge Dakota pickups using flexible assembly technology. We even produced convertibles on the same line as coupes and sedans.

Flexible assembly allows expanding capacity by adding cells as production requirements increase. Routing assemblies through the system is software-controlled and can be modified as changes occur in the process. Each machine can operate at its maximum output potential. Line-balancing problems are minimal and you can use equipment from different vendors in the various process operations.

Stamping Out the Good Old Dies

General Motors, Ford, and Chrysler once dominated the U.S. automobile market to such an extent that they could produce and sell under several product names vehicles constructed with the same sheet-metal stampings. Pontiac X differed from Chevrolet Y only in the grill, head lights and taillights, chrome moldings, wheel covers, and internal trim. The same was true for Ford X and Mercury Y, or Plymouth X and Dodge Y.

Then the world changed. The Big Three were suddenly competing for the American consumer with over 30 other automobile manufacturers. Buyers were no longer satisfied with these minor makeovers. Manufacturers had to satisfy consumer demand for greater *product differentiation* or face extinction. They also had to keep down costs, which, of course, affected their suppliers.

The standardization that made mammoth regional stamping plants, long press runs, and leisurely die changes economical ceased abruptly. Press runs had to be shorter to produce variety. Capital, once tied up in vast inventories, was now needed to design new vehicles and options. The stamping portion of the business had to change. Time was our enemy—time to change dies, stamp parts, and ship them to the assembly plant. In the past, we could take a shift or two to change dies in a six-press tandem line. Now, we had to do it in minutes. We designed, built, and purchased new equipment and processes. Contests were organized to motivate improvement. Our die change team at the Twinsburg, Ohio, stamping plant replaced the dies in a huge five-press Schuler tandem line in two minutes, 35 seconds, beating the closest industry competitor by eight seconds. Video cameras can help manufacturing engineers analyze and enhance the die-changing process.

Here's a sampling of the innovations this activity produced.

- We standardized press line sizes. When we could, we used only long-stroke presses to reduce expensive variability in fixturing and die-change equipment and processes.
- We deployed synchro-mesh drive presses to reduce cycle time and general wear and tear.
- We used more progressive dies to do several operations with one hit, maximizing die and press efficiency.
- We automated material loading and stacking because press automation is quicker and less expensive if stackers are uniformly controlled and properly calibrated.
- We routed master scrap conveyor systems to appropriate plant areas.
- We constructed die repair areas at the end of the press lines to speed repair and increase plant efficiency by eliminating the movement of large dies through the plant.

Synchronized press lines meant productivity and quality improvement in Chrysler's material forming efforts. In this photo, workmen were developing a line of presses at Warren (Michigan) Stamping. Five Schuler presses are in the background. They formed the synchronized line. The line of presses allowed us to stamp parts in a progressive manner. (Chrysler photo)

- We decentralized tool and die cribs for greater accessibility.
- We eliminated shear collars, used for hydraulic overload protection, wherever possible.
- We added pendulum controls on cranes so they could be operated from a position on the floor close to the spot where material needed to be picked up and placed. This reduced the time needed to move dies and equipment, improved safety, and minimized tool damage.
- We automated part handling at the end of the line.
- We fitted presses with drip pan systems to contain oil leaks so production could keep moving until repairs could be made.

151

A transfer press at Chrysler's Sterling Stamping plant. These large presses increased the automaker's quality and productivity by performing more than one material forming function in a single piece of equipment. (Chrysler photo)

- We increased the number of die-tryout press lines.
- We constructed automatic steam-cleaning booths to accelerate and improve die cleaning.
- We added body-panel illumination stations in each bay, with green-light fluorescent bulbs that highlight previously invisible defects, with significant quality gains.
- We designed and built storage areas for progressive die strips, form-die spotting racks, master blank templates, and last-hit evaluation panels, so they could be protected from damage by custom nesting and workers could locate them faster.
- We based maintenance programs on the number of dies and quality desired, rather than on production numbers. Preventive and predictive maintenance, based on computer-assisted statistical methods, buttressed our stamping modernization program by increasing equipment uptime and reducing bad hits due to excessive press ram motion. Poorly maintained or over-stressed dies must be very durable to withstand abuse—which means added expense. Good maintenance

lets us use lighter, well engineered dies. Maintenance also improved part quality enough to let us reduce or eliminate quality control equipment and certain inspection processes in our stamping plants.

- We enhanced stamping process control by establishing an SPC training, charting, and monitoring system.
- We installed rolling bolsters to improve die-setting efficiency, used hydraulic die clamping, installed die pushers and rails between presses, and deployed trolley cars for moving dies between plant bays.
- We installed tonnage monitors on our press lines for better control.

Pressing Together

To achieve optimal cost, quality, and inventory advantages, stamping plants must be linked to assembly operations organizationally, geographically, and operationally. North American automobile manufacturers traditionally used regional stamping plants to supply a large, geographically dispersed market, originally by rail. When product life cycles were long and volumes large, extended stamping production runs made economic sense.

Now product life cycles are short, volumes more fragmented, and high customer expectations render in-transit damage unacceptable. The cost of repairing transportation damage, coupled with greatly inflated transportation costs, made the regional stamping plant obsolete. Concurrent engineering also demands that stamping and assembly be unified geographically and organizationally.

The ideal arrangement is to locate press operations within the product assembly plant. This, however, requires an extremely large capital investment and a complete restructuring of the stamping organization infrastructure. Most manufacturers are unwilling or unable to effect such massive, radical change, so they compromise.

In 1983–84 Chrysler's compromise was a dedicated stamping plant next to the assembly plant. Two ready-made solutions, at least geographically, already existed. The Warren (Michigan) stamping plant was next to the Dodge City truck assembly plant, and the Sterling Heights (Michigan) stamping plant was near the Sterling Heights Assembly Plant.

Flexible Scheduling

Despite manufacturing automation's proliferation, assembly means people. People do much of the assembly by hand or guide the automation, making judgment calls that affect production rates and quality. As a recent headline in *Automotive News* put it, "As Assembly Goes, So Goes Reputation."[1]

In 1982, in the interest of quality and flexibility, we replaced tag relief—relieving regular workers on the line temporarily with semi-skilled utility workers until the regulars returned—with mass relief in all assembly plants. The utility workers were clearly not as proficient in the details of a given job, and tag relief inevitably led to quality lapses. Mass relief reduces these lapses because all workers take breaks at the same time. Mass relief maintains work continuity and consistency. We needed time to enhance the skill level and quality commitment of our utility work force.

I also introduced a "swing plant" concept, which idled one assembly plant as it was retooled for the next new-product launch. This practice would "swing" from plant to plant to accommodate the product cycle and market requirements.

A traditional U.S. assembly plant runs for two eight-hour shifts, five days per week. There is some flexibility to daily and weekend overtime. The first shift usually begins around 6 a.m. and ends around 2:30 p.m. Normally, there is an hour or more between shifts so the parking lot can empty, making room for second-shift employees, who begin at 4:00 p.m. and work until 12:30 a.m.

Salaried support workers usually work from 7:30 or 8:00 a.m. to 4:30 or 5:00 p.m., with a lunch break. For routine equipment repairs, the maintenance department uses the pauses between shifts, break times (20 to 25 minutes in the first and second halves of the shift), and lunch (30 minutes). More extensive maintenance and special material adjustments are done during the four-to-six-hour span between the end of the second shift and arrival of the first shift.

Because the cost of building or refurbishing assembly plants skyrocketed with the advent of automation, robotics, and environmental requirements, we sought ways to keep plants loaded, fully utilized, and running. Another innovation—called the alternate work schedule (AWS)—had an amazingly positive effect. When the work force at the Chrysler St. Louis II assembly plant approved the AWS, it signaled a trend. This method greatly enhanced assembly plant utilization. Simply stated, AWS uses the plant more hours each day. In Chrysler's case, more vehicles could be built in the same plant, increasing profit without investing in constructing a new plant, expanding an existing facility, or gutting and refurbishing older facilities.

Chrysler's AWS program began in early 1992 after lengthy planning. Teamwork was important. I picked a four-member study team led by the vice president of assembly, Richard E. Acosta, and the vice president of employee relations, A.P. St. John. They were assisted by Abid Ghuman, general manager of manufacturing planning, and George Chomakos, director of manufacturing administration. Acosta, Ghuman, and Chomakos reported to me. The team was successful. Mr. Acosta was successful in implementing the AWS plan. The first in America.

We began by benchmarking General Motors Europe operations in Zaragosa, Spain, and Antwerp, Belgium. We chose our St. Louis II plant to launch AWS because it assembled the popular, profitable long-wheel-base minivan: the Dodge Caravan, Plymouth Voyager, and Chrysler Town & Country. The one-shift production increase under this schedule added roughly one-third to the work force. The addition let us bring back laid-off employees.

AWS brought real advantages for the workers: paid hours, including contracted overtime, rose approximately 12%. In addition, we hoped to improve quality by training and deploying the best work force available. Increasing employee free time would make continuous training possible and enhance home and family life. Overtime and fatigue would be reduced.

The advantage to the company was the increase in production: from an annual range of 205,000–218,000 units, we went to 250,000–265,000 units. That's 50,000 more units per year! The labor cost per vehicle rose approximately 4%; however, annual revenue and variable profit rose much more than that.

They chose a schedule calling for three crews working six days per week; two of the three weeks. On the third week, they work only five days, thereby enjoying a two-day weekend. Sundays are always free. Saturday shifts are eight or nine hours long. The schedule provides a 10-minute break in the first and second halves of the shift and a 25-minute lunch. Maintenance takes place during relief and lunch breaks and between shifts, as usual. Quality at St. Louis II has improved since introducing AWS. Employee performance improved because overtime fell and the work environment stabilized.

Successfully launching an AWS requires planning the smallest details. The program management team must be forward-thinking, flexible, and compatible. The union must be brought in at the earliest stages to negotiate a new or significantly modified contract. Vendors must change their traditional supply practices as well. Capital investments must be made in every part of the facility, beginning with the parking lot and ending at the shipping dock.

Both the UAW (for St. Louis II) and the Canadian Auto Workers (CAW) (for Windsor) negotiated agreements to use alternate work schedules when market conditions will support them. They are vital for market share, profitability, employment, cost competitiveness, and optimal capacity utilization of a facility and work force.

Making It Modular?

Modular assembly simply requires vendors to design and process components into subassemblies and integrated systems to be shipped as modules to the assembly plant. Examples include chassis systems, drive train systems, seats, and interior trim. The Dodge Viper was designed to be built using modular assembly principles.

Modular means you avoid the large investment in an assembly plant; the expensive body and paint shops are no longer on site. High-priced organizational design and labor costs are reduced dramatically. Early involvement of vendors cuts the time from concept to production. But it has its disadvantages. For example, the final vehicle manufacturer virtually gives control of a percentage of product design and product processing to vendors, which causes a mammoth coordinating challenge.

The manufacturer must guarantee that powerful companies outside the organization will adhere to the standards of their vendor partners. Due to the vastly divergent philosophies and cultures of modern industrial organizations, this can lead to disaster. Vendor failures, vendor labor problems, and even vendor price extortion can wipe out cost advantages overnight. Then too, automobile business history has shown that manufacturers that become nothing more than "kit" assemblers, like Studebaker, Packard, and American Motors, will perish. Although modular assembly has its advantages, it will probably never be practiced on a wide scale in auto-making. I feel it is best suited for low-production niche products such as the Viper.

Painting a New Future

If the stamping improvements and body and assembly innovations at Chrysler in the '80s could be called a revolution, what happened in the area of paint systems technology was the creation of a new universe. From 1981 through 1991 and the launch of the Grand Cherokee and

Wagoneer, Chrysler invested $1.5 billion to bring its paint systems up to state-of-the-art technology. The results were astounding. Warranty claims declined for cars by 45% and for trucks by 38% between 1985 and 1989.

The Paint and Anti-Corrosion Group, formed in 1981, developed cost savings on paint operations of $264.8 million between 1985 and 1989 and designed recurring annual savings of $115.5 million into the system! Good legal leadership and environmental compliance was provided pro-actively by the design of the organization. Fred Neumann and Peter Gilezan provided solid, intelligent guidance for our legal and environmental issues.

The public responded to the effort. Rogers Research rated 1986 Chrysler cars better than both Ford and General Motors on paint appearance. Several Chrysler vehicles were rated best in class for the least foreign material in the finish. The LeBaron Coupe was judged best in class for its resistance to stone chip damage. The 1990 Consumer Attitude Research survey of early 1990 model new car buyers rated the Chrysler Imperial paint appearance the best among domestic nameplates. Chrysler corrosion protection has been recognized since 1985 as the industry's best.

Back at the plants, by model year 1989, paint shop emissions were reduced by 450 tons from 1985 levels. Cumulative emission reductions in paint shops now amount to more than 2200 tons per year. Dedicated paint shop environmental engineers monitor processes meticulously to ensure compliance. Paint sludge is recycled into body sealer.

Here's a sampling of the paint system achievements and innovations realized during the '80s:

- We converted every U.S., Canadian, and Mexican assembly plant (except Pillette and Lago Alberto) from straight shade paint processing to base coat/clear coat.
- We launched the first automotive application of powder anti-chip to body sides. Powder anti-chip is more durable than any available liquid and has a smooth appearance that does not detract from the finished product. It is very low in volatile organic compounds (VOCs) and has extremely high transfer efficiency.
- The first computer-controlled infrared flash-off for water-borne basecoat is operating at Belvidere Assembly. Water must be removed from the basecoat before the solvent-borne clear coat can be applied. The computer allows a uniform heat distribution about the body, which smooths the basecoat and improves image depth.

- Chrysler is the only U.S. automotive manufacturer to rely on high-build E-coat rather than a primer surfacer. The low-film-build E-coat reduces cost, while the low temperature allows processing different plastics on the body through the entire paint system.
- Introduction of recycling technology for purge solvent was complete in five U.S. assembly plants by the end of the 1991 model year, resulting in an average saving of 40 cents per vehicle.
- A low-cost color offset for interior surfaces resulted in an annual saving of $500,000.
- A changeover from zinc phosphate to manganese modified phosphate was accomplished during the 1991 model year. The new phosphate provides improved electrocoat adhesion and increases the product's ability to resist corrosion by lessening the rate of undercutting.
- During my time at Chrysler, we found the powder coating process effective in several areas. In addition to producing a high-quality finish, this process offers better process economics. The elimination of solvent emissions assists in reducing overall finishing costs. Recycling powder can prove efficient and cost effective. Note, however, that custom coaters may make several color changes daily and special powders may not be well suited for reclamation.
- Chrysler has the only U.S. automotive assembly plants with staff dedicated to documenting and assuring compliance to EPA regulations. These personnel provide daily emission compliance demonstration via a unique computerized program and also do in-plant transfer efficiency testing. We enjoyed being innovative and providing leadership.
- Chrysler was the first automobile manufacturer to eliminate paint sludge from going to landfills.

Environmental Efforts

I am not what some might refer to as a "tree-hugger," but I do believe manufacturers cannot—and should not—continue fouling the air or landfills with their waste. We need to be socially responsible. Even in a throw-away society, industry must find ways to re-use materials and keep hazardous wastes to a minimum. It is simply good business. And it is everyone's business in the plant, including management, design people, and manufacturing engineers.

Nonhazardous recyclable powder from sludge. More than 5.2 million pounds of paint sludge have been processed since Chrysler began its recycling operation.

One of the largest, most effective environmental projects that Chrysler tackled during my watch was the sludge drying process at the Dodge City assembly plant in Warren, Michigan. During the '80s and into the '90s, an environmental and economic problem surfaced: what to do with the huge amount of paint sludge generated by overspray from painting operations. U.S. automotive manufacturing plants generate 30 million gallons of wet sludge per year. Fast-diminishing landfill sites, skyrocketing disposal costs, and government mandated womb-to-tomb responsibility and liability for waste compound the problem.

Chrysler adopted a three-fold waste management strategy: eliminate or reduce waste at the source; recycle or reuse what cannot be eliminated at the source; and provide appropriate "end-of-pipe" controls for waste and/or emissions that cannot be eliminated or recycled. Our initial approach was to reduce paint usage by using a high-build electrodeposition primer, eliminating intermediary spray surface primer, and using high-solids paints and high-transfer-efficiency equipment.

Because of the fast-depleting landfills and the 1986 Resource Conservation and Recovery Act, we initiated a search for technologies that would reduce sludge disposal volumes and generate a recyclable waste. The most suitable was sludge drying. At this point, Chrysler contracted with Haden Environmental Corporation, led by Arthur Geiger, to pursue joint developmental work for two years. The Chrysler/Haden venture pioneered improved sludge removal from the water recirculation system and ultimate drying of the sludge to 100% solids.

In 1988, Haden contracted to install a full-scale sludge drying system at Dodge City Assembly. The plant was selected because paint use on the large truck bodies built there was high compared to other plants, so it generated larger volumes of sludge. The unit began operating in November 1988, the first in the automotive industry. We constructed the Dodge City 500,000-square-foot paint shop in 1986. The trucks are processed through automatic phosphate and electrocoat machines and sprayed with topcoat paint in four spray booths, including reprocess operations. Overspray from painting is collected by recirculating water over trays located at the bottom of the booths.

A detackifying chemical enables the water to remove the sludge, and it is collected in two 300,000-gallon sludge pits. The sludge floats and is removed by a movable weir. The 1%-solids sludge is concentrated in a flotation cell to 30% solids, and a rotostrainer removes the remaining free water. The sludge is pumped to the drying system using a positive displacement pump.

Hot organic oil, circulating in pipes, heats the sludge by convection, and the volatilized water and solvents are removed into an afterburner. The sludge is removed to a bagging station for collection and storage. Patented modifications to the screw dryer and supporting equipment make the system self-cleaning, so it can be run for an indefinite period with no fouling and no need for manual cleaning.

The Dodge City drying system processes 1800 pounds of 20% solids sludge per hour, yielding 2000 pounds per day of powder. Dryer operation began in September 1988, and the system processed 5,791,986 pounds of sludge generating 707,687 pounds of powder through May 1991. As a result, we didn't send five million pounds of sludge to landfills! Instead, it is recycled into roof mastics, concrete blocks, polymer concrete, and underbody coatings and sealers. The powder substitutes for calcium carbonate or other inert fillers and pigments. Dodge City Assembly now recycles all its powder. It takes guts and vision to lead.

Even if disposal were selected over recycle, the benefits would be reduced quantities (87.7% at Dodge City) and reduced costs for shipping and disposal due to the nonhazardous nature of the powder. This work proves *the feasibility of eliminating all paint sludge from landfills*.

Environmental regulations—whether they concern air, water, or solid waste—are complex, but if you have hazardous-waste management responsibility for your company, you must take time to meet with legal counsel, understand, and correctly apply the regulations to your operation. Manufacturing managers making this effort will make informed, cost-effective decisions (and stay out of jail).

Things That Flopped

Success has its down side. Not everything we tried to do worked the first time around, the second, or even the third. Here are some memorable miscues:

- **Oh Horsefeathers!** We wanted to remove air-borne contaminants (dust, lint, fibers, etc.) from primed auto bodies between zones before final painting. One of the concepts we picked up from our benchmarking trips abroad was brushing off the bodies using ostrich feathers fed from a large roll the width of a car or truck. We piloted the approach at Dodge City, never could get it working to satisfy our process-control people, and we had to give up on the idea. We went back to pressurized air rings and manual wipe-off. (Probably all for the better anyway; sooner or later we would have run out of ostriches!)
- **Holy Locomotive!** In renovating a paint-processing building at Dodge City, we had to modify final construction to include an air-makeup house. We chose to use some adjacent land that we purchased from a steel company. During site preparation, much to our surprise, core samples revealed we would be sitting on top of buried locomotives, heavy slag, steel-melting ladles, and structural-steel remnants. This sent us back to the drawing boards, and we ultimately had to relocate the air-makeup house on safer soil.
- **Robot Butterfingers.** Automatic parts loaders are critical in transferring between presses and feeding the assembly line. Although we perfected this new technology in our power train line, we had great difficulty getting reliable robotic unloading in some stamping presses. The result was downtime and major wait time for downstream operations. The only practical solution was to add extra workers to monitor these processes to maintain continuous flow, stepping in where necessary when the robot drops one.
- **Bending's New Twist.** Making our commitment to fight our rust-bucket image with precoated body materials was much easier said than done. Once we dove into it, we had problems with just about everything: forming, welding, and final finishes. Galvanized buildup, either on the die or the part, couldn't be detected by the human eye until too late—after the panel was painted. Die design—getting the right spring back—and die maintenance—improving reliability—had to be completely re-learned. Our welding equipment, from transformers to gun tips, had to be replaced with the latest technology. It was a long, hard learning curve to follow—we had to throw out just about every-

thing we knew about metal bending and body building. It was well worth it, however, when Chrysler was able to offer seven-year warranties, the best in the industry.

- **Mucked-Up Robots.** Robotic application of heavy sealers, undercoating, and flowable gasketing materials proved difficult. Robotic sealing of pickup-truck boxes had to be discontinued because the automation was not reliable. Nozzles applying deadener and undercoats were clogging at some point at our assembly plants. Skips in the laying down of power train gaskets could not be tolerated. Quick solutions for the simpler applications were expandable sealing materials and newer undercoat formulations, but further development will be required for the tougher ones.
- **Lost Seed Corn** We were getting too many early drop-outs in our college-graduate-in-training (CGIT) program. The new blood we needed to vitalize manufacturing was being lost to other departments. Some of these young people even left the company. We took a hard look at this and modified our CGIT program, redefining training assignments to get better bonding with mentors and moving these people into manufacturing earlier. Keep a sharp eye on process flexibility.

Reference

1. Keebler, Jack. "World Class depends on the plant," *Automotive News*, August 24, 1992, p. 26LH.

Chapter 11

CLOSE DOWN OR COME BACK?

After joining Chrysler in 1980, I had to evaluate the future viability of various manufacturing operations. Chrysler was in no position to continue operating plants that would hinder its ability to recover from near bankruptcy. In those areas where operations were to continue, I knew developing a good relationship with the union was critical.

As a result of apartheid and other considerations, Chrysler elected not to continue participating in South African operations and subsequently disposed of its holdings there. In contrast, operations in Mexico and Canada were highly important to our future. Some top Chrysler officials favored discontinuing operations in Mexico. I felt otherwise and vigorously lobbied to retain and expand those operations. My plan included being the first automobile manufacturer to produce cars in Mexico for sale in the demanding American market. The plan was approved.

Close-Down Criteria

Why is one plant or operation chosen for enhancement while another is sold, idled, shut down, or demolished? It takes an extensive, well defined, and disciplined method of evaluation to answer this question.

In analyzing the viability of a plant situation, you start at the top by figuring what your industry SAAR will be; that is the Sales Average

Annual Rate. Let's say you are projecting annual domestic sales of 15 million units as your working number. Then, say, for example, you wanted a 10% market share. (When I joined Chrysler, it was an 8% market share company. A 10% share then would have required 25% growth.) Taking 10% of 15 million leaves 1.5 million units a year. Then, you decide how to make up that 1.5 million. It could be 500,000 were K-cars in those days, 250,000 were trucks, and 300,000 were minivans, 100,000 rear-wheel drive vehicles, and so on.

In 1981, a year after I joined Chrysler, my job was expanded and I suddenly had 11 assembly plants assigned to me. The average assembly plant can produce 250,000 units. So I had 2,750,000 in capacity, but since only 1.5 million of this was needed, I had to make some serious cuts in assembly capacity. Somebody's ox was going to get gored!

So then I had to say, "Give me the measurable characteristics that are important." First, I wanted to know who had the best people relations. I was looking at attitudes and relationships. Who is not fighting, on strike, or experiencing any sabotage or slowdowns? I also had to examine their skill levels. Can this work force be trained fast enough with the skills our new technology demands?

Next, I looked at measured quality from actual customer warranty claims. Who is building the best product for the customer? I looked at actual costs. I looked at relative volume, and found huge differences, in some cases, between a plant like Pillette, able to run 100,000 a year, and Dodge Main at 500,000.

I then looked at facility and technology. Vertical height to the lower truss-chord is a critical measurement. Some plants were 16 feet and others were 28 feet. So there were huge differences. One plant may have 20 feet by 40 feet column spacing and another 12 feet by 20 feet column spacing. It's very important to be able to install new technology. You just can't get it into some plants. Many of Chrysler's plants were built between 1900 and 1950 with huge architectural differences in construction.

So, I focused first on people—how well they work together. Second, the results of their work—the customer either likes or doesn't like their quality. Third, cost—who is building a car at least cost. Fourth, volume—capability. Fifth, future technology—whether we could put it in at a reasonable cost or would it be cost-prohibitive.

Much of this was factual and objective. I would say about 70% is number crunching and the other 30% subjective, based on my own experience.

Ask These Questions When Evaluating a Plant's Future

1. What product is manufactured? Are sales expanding or declining?
2. How much time would plant conversion take?
3. How high is productivity?
4. How much does transporting raw material into the plant cost? How much does shipping the final product to market cost?
5. How good is product quality? Can it be improved?
6. What machinery must be moved, stored, reinstalled, or scrapped if the plant closes? What is the cost?
7. What skills and education does the work force have? What is the history of employee relations?
8. How old is the facility?
9. How flexible are the work rules? Is the management/ employee relationship flexible or adversarial and antagonistic?
10. Will local government provide training, tax breaks, or other financial incentives to keep the plant open?

Another key point is flexibility. One plant may be adaptable to run cars, trucks, or minivans without requiring many changes. Another may be absolutely inflexible. You must look at process flexibility, which is strictly an equipment issue and has nothing to do with people.

Another consideration is transportation costs. If you are on the East Coast at Newark, Delaware, and have to ship your components there and then ship final vehicles back, you have extra shipping costs both ways.

These are some of the critical things to evaluate when reducing a 2.75 million capacity down to the long-term plan of two million. I knew we had to close three assembly plants. We closed Dodge Main (or as it was called then, Hamtramck) and Lynch Road, and mothballed St. Louis II from '80 to '83. We selected plants with the worst quality; highest costs; least capability to adapt to future technology; lowest work force skills, and the most ancient, least adaptable facilities—factories that time had clearly passed by.

How tough is it to make a plant-closing decision, and then announce it to the people involved? Very tough, but there is something I consider personally even more difficult: breaking the news to the spouse of someone who has just been killed at one of my plants. When we had a fatality in a plant or a serious accident and I had to break the word directly or through my people to that spouse or family, that was the worst thing I ever had to do.

The second worst thing was when I had to go to a plant and break the word that they were on a kamikaze mission.

No Time for Ultimatums

There are times when you can give a plant an ultimatum: "Shape up by such and such a date, or we close the place down." If you can, you do it this way.

But there are other situations when you don't have time to do that, and the early '80s at Chrysler were exactly that. Our manufacturing system was hugely responsible for the company bleeding at a rate of $7 million a day of red ink! How can there be much patience when you, the patient, are hemorrhaging that much blood. That's a yearly rate of $1.5 billion, and our loan guarantee then was for exactly that, $1.5 billion, so you have just one year of potential blood transfusions. I could hardly give a plant two or three years to show me how they were going to get well— there was only a year's worth of plasma!

Shutting down a plant costs big money. Many times environmental cleanup must be done. Machinery must be moved, stored, reinstalled elsewhere, sold, or scrapped. Employees must be bought out, transferred, laid off, or retired. Pension coverage for those eligible also must be provided with financial obligations extending well into the future. It may cost almost as much to close a plant as to build a new one! The social costs alone are staggering.

A plant closing powerfully impacts a community, its tax base, social services, infrastructure such as schools, hospitals, banks, churches, police and fire protection, and roads. The social costs can be incalculable: the welfare burden on the community and the state when unemployment compensation is exhausted; the suicides, alcoholism, and family disintegration, including unwanted pregnancy, prostitution, and crime, that accompany unemployment; the careers and lives that are destroyed. Some will never again be gainfully employed. For many, their financial future becomes uncertain and, in some cases, desperate. You must be sensitive and sensible.

There are also repercussions for the customers of the failed plant or company. If a suitable substitute supplier cannot be found in an acceptable time frame, they, too, are in jeopardy of failure. Obviously, this was not true of an assembly plant, but it is true of a component-producing plant.

When the decision was made to close a plant, I would go there, assemble the people, and say "Here are two plants, yours and theirs. I can only keep one open. I've got this cost here and that cost there. I've got this quality here and that quality there. This is not just my opinion, but hard facts. I need to put this technology in, and it won't work here. By the way, their plant has 50 job classifications, and this one has 100.

"So you've got me roped in with a lot less operating flexibility at this location than that one, and my boss just told me he can't sell more than 80,000 units per year. I'm telling you right now, I'm not killing your plant. However, we are going to have an orderly shut down in X number of months. The people will go on contractual layoff. I cannot promise you we will ever reopen. All I can say is my heart wants to reopen this plant, but only under a different set of conditions."

How to Save Your Job

What can the people on the shop floor do to save their jobs? What actions on their part will affect the plant's long-term viability?

First, they can actively listen and become more aware of what the real problems are. Second, they can speak out with their opinions on how things can be done better at the plant level. Third, they can look around in their own environment at how to do things more productively and eliminate waste. There are a million things, large and small, that can be improved at the factory level by the operators and their immediate supervisory team. How do you remove product for repair? How do you remove scrap? How do you minimize downtime? How do you maintain a safe, efficient work environment? How do you break production bottlenecks? These are things that can get done every day on the factory floor if people react to them, and then act.

The best response a plant can make to reverse a pending closing is to have an open mind, a positive approach, a preparation for change, and a set of specific requirements to consider. Then, they must be trustworthy and execute their fair share of the bargain. That's very important.

Governments may make ingenious concessions to keep plants open. Land is provided, for example, or roads are built, taxes are forgiven, construction materials are provided tax-free, or workers are trained and even paid by the government while in training. The general educational level of the work force becomes more important as automation increases and as statistical methods gain greater implementation.

Again, employee relations is a major consideration in plant closings. Is there a high absentee rate, a history of social problems (such as drug and alcohol abuse), violence, wildcat strikes, or inflexible work rules, all of which decrease productivity? This is why Chrysler rebuilt the 1928-vintage Windsor assembly plant while closing, and then selling the newer 1951 Lynch Road assembly facility. It's also why we refurbished the 1948-vintage Indianapolis Foundry while idling Huber Foundry built in the '60s. Three other plants, Newark Assembly, New Castle Machining, and Kokomo Casting, turned themselves around when faced with the possibility of extinction.

Chaos at Newark

Let's look more closely at the Newark situation. In 1984, the plant was assembling the ''K'' platform, launched there in the summer of 1980. The daily rate was 968 units, using two shifts. Schedule achievement was erratic, quality marginal, and average direct-labor hours were in the high 30s per vehicle.

The model mix was complicated with too many options: pin striping combinations in multi-colors, wood grain or leather here and not there, and a wide variety of sound-system entertainment options. On the same line, we were building Plymouth and Dodge four-door sedans and station wagons, offered in two price classes each, and a Chrysler LeBaron four-door sedan and station wagon in a premium class.

The ''first-time-through'' yield off the final assembly line was dismal, requiring repair of over 62% of the vehicles. The repair department worked more hours than assembly, running two nine-hour shifts, six days per week while the assembly departments ran two eight-hour shifts, five days per week. From an operating standpoint, this plant was in big trouble.

As I said before, the plant also had physical liabilities, having been built decades earlier, and incurring abnormal transportation costs due to its location. We also had some abnormal environmental problems because the East Coast is more populated than other sections of the country, so we would have to redo our paint shops anyway. The plant is very close to a major community, whereas some of our plants are in more outlying areas and are less sensitive environmentally.

What Saved Newark

What saved Newark was its people. Anytime you save a plant, the Number 1 reason is people. The people stepped up and said: ''Mr.

Dauch, you are the representative from Chrysler who comes to talk to us. Please let the right people know that we want to fix this plant. We really want to save it!''

"I hear you," I said. "Now, I'm going to go back, and, next time, I will come back with Brother Stepp." When I returned with Marc Stepp, I asked them, "Now tell me what you told me before, but tell us as a team with my colleague, Mr. Stepp."

We had an open, honest, mature exchange, and they reiterated their pledge. Marc and I then involved Tony St. John, the corporate officer of human resources, and we agreed this was a prime candidate for an MOA, modern operating agreement. We then went to work and secured approvals up to and including Jerry Greenwald. He, I am sure, had coordinated with Iacocca that if we could ensure operating changes in the plant, management would reward that plant with a new product because of the employees' attitude and commitment to making significant progress.

The Newark people were telling us, in effect, "We've learned our lesson. You've shown us data that verify we cannot compete presently internally within the company." They knew they couldn't beat SHAP (Sterling Heights Assembly Plant), Windsor, and Belvidere. If they weren't competitive within Chrysler, they could hardly be competitive worldwide, so they accepted our judgment.

The new product that ultimately we assigned there was the A-car, which is the Dodge Spirit, Plymouth Acclaim, and the four-door Chrysler LeBaron. So Newark got a new car, and we got a new agreement—an MOA focused on quality, cost, operating classifications, skill level development, technology improvement, education, training, and operating flexibility.

The Reformation

We began improvement efforts by analyzing key plant problems. A big one was work-content differences throughout the assembly process in that both the base car and option loading were causing line stoppages and quality problems. To combat this, we formed cross-functional teams in the body-in-white, body-paint, and trim departments to identify bottlenecks and root causes, and find both short- and long-term solutions. We analyzed the order condition over time, so we could develop a build schedule (called a "gateline") to control body styles and options with a major impact on work content.

Simultaneously, we took major steps to improve preventive maintenance and evolve to a predictive maintenance program. Teams were

169

formed including hourly workers from the skilled trades and from production, salaried engineers, and production and maintenance supervisors. They met weekly to discuss new approaches to improving manufacturing throughput.

As machine uptime improved, and our scheduling ability became more sophisticated, further improvement opportunities came to light. For example, traditionally the main feeder systems (i.e., floor pan, engine compartment, body side subassembly, and main framing) had to run at 80 units per hour to supply the body shop net requirement of 68 units per hour, which was 17.6% overspeed.

As throughput improved from 1984 to 1988, overspeed and associated labor and production supplies fell from 80 units per hour to 72 units and we met our goal. Moreover, we completely eliminated the body banking system (about 200 units) and the floor-pan banking system (about 120 sets). That let us close an entire warehouse. Also, because of dramatically improved process control in the metal shop, we eliminated four door fitters in trim and two in final assembly, saving $300,000 annually.

We created area managers to replace the general foreman and superintendent, reducing the management hierarchy from six levels to five and putting the decision makers (area managers) much closer to the implementors (supervisors). The organizational change also forced area managers out of their offices onto the shop floor and significantly reduced the number of meetings. Senior managers were compelled to meet regularly with cross-functional quality and productivity improvement teams and support them with resources. An area manager departmental goal system detailed each quality, volume, cost, training, housekeeping, and safety objective critical to operating efficiency and product quality.

Another key strategy was quality and productivity "walks and talks." Twice a week the plant manager, the manufacturing engineering manager, and the quality manager walked an area of the assembly plant, asking the operators and teams to show what they had accomplished, what they were working on, and what help and support they needed. This demonstrated our continued support for their efforts, allowed worker access to "the brass," and steered their thinking and efforts toward resolving problems and issues they judged important. Union leadership also was involved in this teamwork concept.

The production manager, manufacturing engineering manager, industrial engineering manager, maintenance manager, and production area managers also met monthly with teams from each production department to review what the teams called their "hit list" of quality, warranty, and productivity items. They examined, in detail, the staffing and/or investment required to advance their projects. The group set priorities and allocated local resources as part of Chrysler's self-help program. Very little capital funding was requested or spent. Most improvements were funded from manpower and monies generated from the plant expense budget.

The teams in the paint and trim departments also were active. One concentrated on sealer application to eliminate water leaks and minimize color-coat defects from sealer under the paint. Production, together with engineering and quality, installed a man-assignment strategy in which sealer application and clean-up became a team responsibility. Newark soon began reaping benefits from those efforts. Water leaks at the in-line test diminished by 50% in two years. Deck-lid water leaks all but vanished.

We restructured the plant's system of selecting bodies for paint preparation from the accumulation area. This led to the first real success in the approach we called "block painting" (see Chapter 2). The major saving was in materials, but an added benefit was the elimination of overspray on vehicles during the color-purge cycle. This all happened in just two years. We were running like a frozen rope—flatout.

During this period, the plant installed a new electrode-positioning (uni-prime full-immersion) system and constructed two new spray booths *without* interrupting production. This required immense cooperation. Corrections to sealer and paint applications and reduction of in-system damage let us cut the low-bake paint-repair work force from a two-shift operation to one shift and from 16 vehicle repairs per hour to seven by 1985. Those were hard results which provided hope. Consistently high process quality was quickly becoming a reality!

A paint team and a trim team together decided that certain optional wiring, switch installation, and trunk dressing could be performed in the paint shop on the sedan vinyl-roof line and the station wagon side-wood grain installation line. This leveled the work load between vehicles on the pre-trim line and let us lengthen the line so we could begin using the "hot car" process where vehicle electrical systems were completely checked before the wiring is covered with carpet, door panels, quarter trim panels, garnish moldings, etc. This procedure contributed to the ultimate improvement of first-time-through capability at the end of final assembly from 38% in 1984 to near 87% in 1985. We were beginning to be in tall cotton.

Corrective actions were also in progress outside the production areas. Engineering was working steadily with corporate material handling to develop durable containers to replace cardboard, wood, and steel banding in the plant. Working together and planning packaging upstream led eventually to eliminating the plant's cardboard-baling operations, saving six salaries and ending a maintenance nightmare. It also helped clear away some of the waste cluttering the plant. Every little bit helps when you are trying to save an operation.

In 1984, the average demerits assessed by Chrysler's corporate quality-audit team totaled about 50 per car. As many as three to four of these were major, 10 demerits each. Such a defect, under the corporate audit system, is significant enough to cause a customer to return the vehicle to the dealer for repair and thus create a warranty claim.

Under the Newark plant product quality improvement umbrella, we organized 10-demerit elimination teams of technical people, hourly operators, and skilled tradesmen. By 1987, their efforts dropped the average audit scores under 20 total demerits per car and to less than one 10-demerit car per day!

Newark's accomplishments were *typical* of the thousands of improvements made in Chrysler assembly plants during the '80s. These management strategies and a consistent demonstration of commitment to improvement let people achieve levels they would not have believed possible.

No More Mr. Skunk

It's always tough to accept the hard fact that we must change, and it is tough for a plant to be continually reminded their performance was inferior to that at our other plants. It was also tough for me to be the skunk always bringing them the bad news. It was, "Hey fellows, look who's back! It's Bad News Dauch telling us we're not competitive."

That goes with the turf. In a manufacturing company, the CEO or president turns to the chief manufacturing officer and says, "There's good news, go deliver it." Or he says, "There's bad news, go deliver that." Starting in 1980, and for the next 36 months, I often had to deliver the news that of our 60 plants, we were going to kill 20 of them. That was not pleasant duty, but it had to be done to save the company. Ten years later, we were not only saving the company, we were preparing it to become world class, with plants around the world able to compete with any in the auto industry! We were also adding plants and not closing them. We successfully changed the entire factory management system.

It was plants like Newark—stepping up and changing significantly and sincerely—that helped make this transformation possible. We gave them their second chance, and they proved to us, and to the world, that they are capable of becoming world class.

I used a unique approach to let the Newark team know they had finally won the war, they were not going to have to die, that their plant would have a future. I asked Marc Stepp and his closest associates to meet with me and a few of mine, not at the plant, but at the union hall in Newark. He was curious why, and asked, "Brother Dauch, what the hell do you want to do?"

"I'd like to have a special meeting," I said, "and I don't want to go to the plant first. I want to go to the union hall."

He asked, "Why in God's name do you want to do that?"

I answered, "I want to go to the union hall because there are some crucial things I want to say to those people who met with you and me in the past asking for a new lease on life. You, as a leader, have worked hard with your team and the local to get them to come to some understanding of the potential agreements on an MOA. In the meantime, I have been running my side of the track, working with senior management, the board of directors, and trying to secure, through my human resources group, a new agreement that would give us even a chance to propose a new lease on life and a new product for that plant. I am not authorized at this time to tell you anything other than that."

He looked at me and said, "I think you've told me enough." With that, we flew to Newark, took the plant manager and personnel manager with us, and met at the union hall with the local union president, past president, and their officers.

We had a nice breakfast and I was introduced. I gave the announcement then that Newark had a whole new lease on life; that the A-car program was going to be produced for Chrysler's U.S. and Canadian needs at Newark. You have never seen such a love-in in your life! I was so excited because it had taken me eight long years of persistence—from 1980 to 1987— to save that plant, and it finally paid off. Newark's past union president Bobby Clemente echoed everyone's feelings by saying, "Our partnership of people, productivity, and new product will lead to world-class workmanship right here at Newark!" They did not let us down. The launch of the A car was at Newark.

It was a "near perfect" performance.

Paralysis at Kokomo

Like Newark, Chrysler's Kokomo, Indiana, aluminum casting plant was on the ropes. The 550,000-square-foot facility, the largest of its kind under one roof, contained five furnaces that could hold over 600,000 pounds of molten aluminum at a time. The plant's 114 die casting machines cast more than 700,000 pounds of aluminum per day. An average of 10 die casting machines were shut down and in a changeover mode at all times, leaving 104 to run production. Of those, the plant was running on average only 46 machines per day—only 44% of capacity—usually because of equipment failure, die failure, or management-directed shutdown for out-of-specification and quality-related reasons.

It was 1985, and the plant was running three shifts per day, seven days per week to produce and ship 50 million pieces annually. The 920 hourly and 115 salaried employees were tired, and quality and productivity were declining because there was no time for die or machine maintenance, and new leadership, discipline, direction, and education were sorely needed.

Quality was totally unacceptable. As high as 8% of the products were being returned from in-company customers as defective. Scrap rates in the plant were running 12% on large products and 6.8% on smaller, easier parts. The equivalent of two to three days' production was usually in a sort, rework, or repair bank in the plant. We had Kokomo Casting people out in many customer plants working full-time just sorting and reworking defective products.

To most people in top management, Kokomo's aluminum casting plant was expendable. The feeling was sell it and buy our castings, or outsource them and mothball the factory.

Kokomo is actually two plants; the other half is the Kokomo transmission plant, Chrysler's only automatic-transmission plant. If we stopped that one, we were dead—you can't re-source transmissions overnight. That plant was vital, and the work force there knew it. It was a case where those Kokomo people felt they were far enough from Detroit to think they didn't have to change as rapidly as our other plants.

Once again, I had the responsibility to personally communicate to them that maybe we had to change a little bit. Being a Purdue man, I feel I understand the Hoosier mentality quite well. We talked about where we were: hard data, trends, facts, and results of comparisons with competitors like Ford, GM, VW, Toyota, and other transmission producers. I told them, "You're not bad. You're just average to good, but that's no longer good enough. We must work together and come up with a new program.''

Recasting Kokomo

To do this, we got a lot of people involved. I went to the Indiana governor, Robert D. Orr, and got the state political environment involved at the highest level. I met with the leaders of universities at Purdue, Indiana, and Ball State. Then, we got together with plant management and the leaders of Purdue University, leaders at Indiana University, and Ball State, and the unions. We constructed a plan so that I could go back as a spokesperson to management and secure a $500-million investment. Instead of starting the process of closing this plant and de-emphasizing it, we started to expand it, fix it, and grow it.

That is what I am best at. I do not like to kill plants or people. My mom and dad taught me that it takes a man to make a man, but anybody can break a person. I don't like to break people. I like to be the catalyst of change, to help people improve themselves.

It was obvious from my initial meetings with Kokomo's senior staff that they typically believed low quality and poor productivity were someone else's problem. During the next few months, I replaced the plant manager, production manager, industrial engineering manager, production control manager, plant engineering and process engineering supervisors, and tool room superintendent. This organization quickly realized that Chrysler Manufacturing meant business!

The new plant manager, Rick Rossmann, outlined his strategy to me: ''I organized meetings with local and international union officials to explain in detail how precarious the plant's position was, and what I believed we must do to prevent closure, sale, or, at the very least, major outsourcing of work. We began to work out a detailed plan for the next 12 months. Union officials greeted my assessment and proposals with mixed emotions. Once they became convinced that our goal really was to keep jobs in the plant by improving throughput and improving quality, however, they agreed to take my proposals to the employees.

''I immediately scheduled a Town Hall meeting—the first at any Chrysler facility in the state—for 45 minutes on all three shifts. Everyone was asked to attend—salaried, hourly, and union representatives. This state-of-the-plant message made a sincere but firm appeal for support, cooperation, and participation. I assured employees our intent was not to eliminate jobs and reviewed programs where management wanted their participation. We explained that, although we believed we could get some capital funding in the future, we needed to demonstrate to corporate management that we could and would start a 36-month *self-help* program to make substantial improvements.''

Here were some of Rossmann's agenda items that day.

- *Improve machine uptime and system throughput from current 43% levels.* The uptime and throughput improvement put the plant on a five-day work schedule in 36 months.
- *Reduce scrap to zero from 2.9%.* Scrap after machining at customer plants dropped to 2.7% in 1986 and 2.2% in 1987.
- *Reduce in-house casting scrap from 6.8%.* In-house casting scrap dropped to 5.6% by 1988.
- *Implement quick die change.* Hours required per die change on 500- to 700-ton machines dropped from 7.1 to 2.4 hours; on 800- to 1200-ton machines from 7.6 to 2.5 hours; and on 1600- to 2500-ton machines from 23.3 to 12 hours.

Measurements and indicators are critical in manufacturing. Once we defined what we felt we must track at Kokomo Casting, we began assignments to achieve our goals. Action teams were formed on all three shifts to develop and implement detailed plans. The plant also formed teams sponsored by a production area manager consisting of a job setter, die maker, machine repairman, production operator, and engineer. They concentrated on the process elements influencing total system uptime like hot-metal delivery to the machines, machine startup procedures, automation and die maintenance, and operator training. They improved total casting system uptime from 43% in 1985 to 73% in 1987. Those kinds of improvements will save a plant!

Similar teams with the authority to cut across the organization and recommend process changes attacked the top 10 causes of scrap. As a result, scrap, as a percentage of the total cost, fell to 6.2%, not as dramatic a result as we had hoped because proper die maintenance could not be done due to schedule demands.

Our approach at Kokomo required dramatic changes in flexibility. I wanted major reductions in skilled-trades and production-operation classifications, tremendously improved technology, CIM, computers, and flexible manufacturing systems throughout the plant. I also wanted lasers in there. Our first 10 applications of laser-based processing were in the Kokomo plant for the 604 electronic automatic transaxle. They all worked.

Why? Because I knew this work force was intelligent, and very mechanical. Most pig farmers understand mechanical things and I grew up as a pig and cattle farmer. To do this, you must be able to fix your own pumps, keep your machines running well, and string your own electricity. These people had the right basic aptitudes and they could go to school and get the necessary extra education. I knew we could spike the education in from Purdue, Indiana University, and Ball State—these men and women never would have to leave the factory to learn.

It worked out beautifully. We had a balance of manpower planning, methods changes, and new machines. We put 500 CNC machines into that plant. That is not called "slow walking." They had none when we started. Any manufacturing engineer understands that the first one is a breakthrough, but 500 is a gigantic leap.

Later, there were major product changes required and, if we had the old hard tooling, it would have taken us two to four months to retool. The new computer system we had put in and the CNC equipment there prepared everyone for this transition. Today, most of those product changes are made in two hours to two days. That is massive progress.

Through the Kokomo organization's dedication to continuous improvement and the efforts of the teams, efficiency leaped. Pounds of aluminum cast per direct labor hour invested rose from 95.4 in 1984 to 115.3 in 1987, a 20.9% improvement. The plant turned itself away from the abyss.

This was accomplished in a manufacturing area that, in general, has been declining. In 1980, the number of foundries in North America was approximately 4600. That number in 1991 had been reduced to around 3000. Kokomo was not on the casualty list.

Sharing the Rewards

The original mandate in '80 through '83 was to reduce our stamping plants from six to two. I resisted. The plant on the bubble then was Warren Stamping. It was an inner-city plant, with an inner-city work force, and was built in 1948. It was a plant that, like most manufacturing facilities of that era, was neglected for the past 20 years. Nothing had been done on new press equipment, new die machining, or apprentice programs.

I fought like hell to save it. We ended up closing Mack Stamping, Eight Mile Stamping, and Outer Drive, but not Warren. Eight years later in '87, when Lee Iacocca asked me, "Dick, we're going to award our

Iacocca presents an hourly bonus check at Warren (Michigan) Stamping. The first-ever profit-sharing checks were paid to hourly workers in 1987. The rewards were another important symbol of the historic turnaround at Chrysler. Warren Stamping personnel strongly worked to improve the plant's performance and they were a perfect choice to receive the first check. (Joe Wilssens and Automotive News *photo)*

first-ever hourly profit-sharing checks to the workers. I've asked several other people, but where would you like these to be distributed first?''

I didn't want to go out of state for this. Everyone thought I would vote for an assembly plant, but I said, ''I prefer to go to a stamping plant because how would you like to have your life hanging by a thread for the past five years? That's what these people at Warren have been through. Each day for the past five years, they never knew if their plant would close or stay open.''

Sometimes you can give a plant a chance, and sometimes you can't. In their case, I gave them a new chance each year, and they kept earning a new one, but I could never say to them, ''You guys are here for real.''

By '87, they had really gotten their act together. I was particularly proud of them and knew they had lived through a miserable period. This would be a great reward—not just a monetary one to put in their wallets and take home to the family, but a highly symbolic one. They would have their picture in the paper with the Chairman distributing the first bonus check ever from Chrysler.

It was the first-ever hourly bonus for a company that had started in 1925, and Warren did get the honors and the national recognition in the press and on TV. Because they had struggled the longest and paid a supreme price, I felt they truly deserved it. They did not close down. They came back!

Chapter 12

JUSTIFYING JUST-IN-TIME

There's an old saying, "You earn as you turn." When I joined Chrysler, our vehicle assembly plants were turning material about 15 times a year. Late in the '80s, we had that up to an average of 60 to 65, with a couple of plants over 100. I foresee the day when an assembly plant will turn its material every workday, or 240 work times a year. Going from 15 to 240, that's slicing a big hunk off the ol' hog's rear end!

If I have my material for 30 days before payment is required, and turn it in a day, I'm using that money free for 29 days. Manufacturing people aren't expected to be particularly bright in economics, but I did well in that subject in college, and I understand how to run factories and build cars and trucks.

Inventory is an asset just like equipment, facilities, and cash. It can represent 50% of a plant's total assets. If reduced to zero, each dollar of inventory—stagnant assets—becomes a dollar of cash that can be used for other purposes. All of this can be accomplished internally without increasing total assets.

All inventory cannot be disposed of or transformed into cash, however. A certain amount is needed for work-in-process. The key questions are: "How much inventory must you have to run the operation efficiently?" and "How much inventory do you have now?"

Stacked Against Success

As I mentioned in Chapter 2, in 1980 Chrysler plants were stacked to the ceilings with inventory waiting to be processed or, too often, inventory that was obsolete or damaged. Old-time foremen learned that the best way to avoid running out of parts was to squirrel them away. If a supplier had a major equipment breakdown or strike, if the trucker ran into a ditch, or if production requirements were suddenly increased, the safety bank would cover their shift requirements. Suppliers learned that they could speed payments from Chrysler by shipping parts early because their purchase orders called for payment as soon as parts were shipped.

These practices resulted in a mountain of inventory on Chrysler's books—potential operating capital generating no revenue. Worse yet, inventory was out of control. Much of it couldn't be found when needed, and when it was finally discovered it was obsolete or damaged, which meant liquidation and a significant loss.

This lack of discipline had a disastrous effect on quality at Chrysler. Informal sorting on the assembly line could maintain a certain level of quality, but it was only as good as the precision of the sort. Moreover, a quality problem on the line could be covered for months while available good parts were culled from inventory to replace bad ones in the day's production. Parts were not used in any particular order. Therefore, it was difficult (if not impossible) to trace a defective part to the lot it was produced from on a particular day from a particular shipment of raw material, which meant we could not isolate and correct the defect.

When inventory control became my responsibility, I assigned George Dellas the problem. He had been with me at General Motors and later at Volkswagen. He was experienced in engineering, production, quality, and materials management.

Before he and his team could tackle Chrysler's scheduling and supply problems, we had to develop tracking mechanisms showing where we were and what progress was being achieved.

We chose two criteria. The first was traditional: count inventory on hand. Such counts, however, can be misleading if there is a significant rise or fall in production or change in model mix. Moreover, about 50% of the inventory on the books is normally in transit, since invoices are cut when parts leave the supplier plant. Therefore, we used a second criterion: inventory turns, the number of times the total inventory of a given plant or division turns into finished products.

The Inventory Alpha-Bet

After agreeing on our tracking measures, we established a priority and timing plan. Rather than take a revolutionary approach that might cause chaos, we established a fast-paced evolutionary improvement, concentrating on a product that would show the fastest return on investment. That product was the 1984 minivan. Only after solving the Windsor Assembly scheduling and supply problems did we move on to other plants.

Dellas attacked the problem by using Economic Order Quantity (EOQ). The first useful parameter of the EOQ is *Alpha*, which represents the operational reserve of inventory kept on hand at all times. When inventory is reduced to *Alpha*, there should be a delivery to bring the inventory back to a predetermined level. The quantity of parts delivered is *Beta* which varies significantly over a given time span. The rate of inventory depletion is *Gamma*. When production reduces on-hand inventory to the *Alpha* level, another delivery of parts arrives. The time between deliveries is called *Delta*.

Dellas explains the inventory alphabet this way. Assume that *Alpha* equals 0, *Beta* equals 1, and *Gamma* is any constant number, and there is no operational reserve on hand. Then the only part in inventory is the one currently being processed. When processing is complete, another

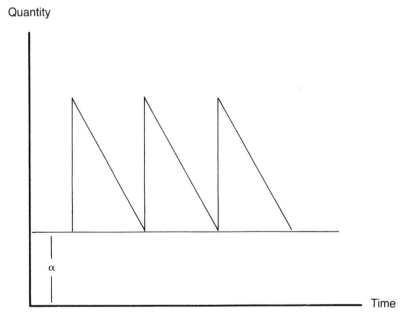

Quantity

α

Time

The Chrysler Just-In-Time system used Economic Order Quantity. Alpha is an operational reserve of inventory kept on hand at all times. When inventory is at Alpha, order new material to bring the inventory up to predetermined, desired levels.

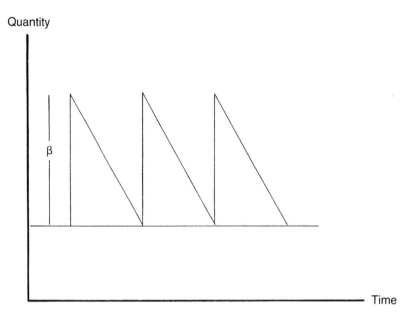

Beta *is the quantity of parts delivered. As shown here, this quantity can vary rather significantly over time.*

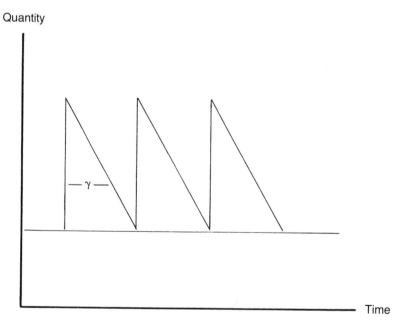

Gamma *is the rate of inventory depletion caused by production.*

Quantity

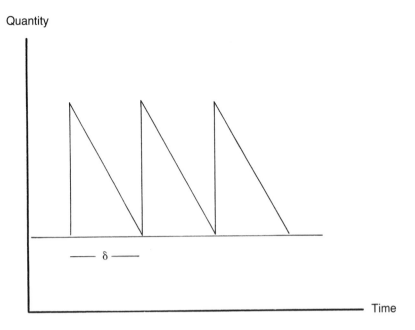

Delta *is the time between deliveries. Note that* Delta *can vary and the variances could come from a number of sources (delivery vehicle breakdown, unscheduled delivery vehicle stops).*

piece (*Beta-1*) arrives at the workstation. If the production ratio (*Gamma*) is constant, the cycle repeats. The Japanese call this Kanban; we call it Just-In-Time or simply: JIT. Whatever its name, it was taught at American universities long before it found its way into Japanese and American manufacturing plants.

Using the EOQ matrix, Dellas and his team set out to revamp Windsor's material-flow system. Their objective was to convert inventory assets into cash assets while stabilizing material supply. When Dellas took the model out to the plants, however, he discovered that none of the EOQ parameters were constant. The rate of production (*Gamma*) varied wildly because of breakdowns, scheduling changes, or changed worker assignments. Vendor deliveries (*Delta*) also varied—trucks break down, drivers opt to push straight through without stopping, or make an unscheduled stop to visit a friend. Material got accidentally left at a freight-consolidation center. The quantity of parts delivered (*Beta*) varied when a supplier shipped too many or too few to a given material release. Operational reserves rose and fell and, at times, were even reduced to zero, causing production downtime.

Quantity

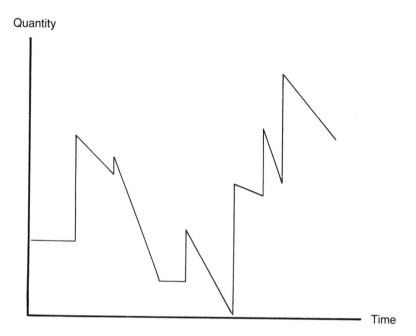

Time

Actual rise and fall of Alpha-*operational reserves. Operational reserves rise and fall and are, at times, even reduced to zero, which causes production to cease.*

Bear in mind that, in this example, we are talking about only one part. The average automobile assembly requires some 4000 parts. The average assembly plant builds roughly 1000 vehicles per day at full production. We had our work cut out for us!

Parts were stacked everywhere at the Windsor plant. Partially built vehicles were parked in any space left vacant. Legions of expediters admonished suppliers to meet contractual commitments. This usually meant, "Send us more of these damned things right away!"

The first step toward part-supply stabilization was in-line sequencing, which schedules vehicles into production sequentially and holds this sequence throughout the assembly process. The production line is laid out without breaks to accomplish this, eliminating building buffer stocks and repair bays. Only continuous build is possible.

In-line sequencing reduced the variability in the production rate (*Gamma*) considerably, making JIT delivery feasible for the first time and giving us control of *Gamma*. It was a start, but we still had no control of sales department orders, which ultimately determined the number of vehicles we would build and the options we had to put in them.

186

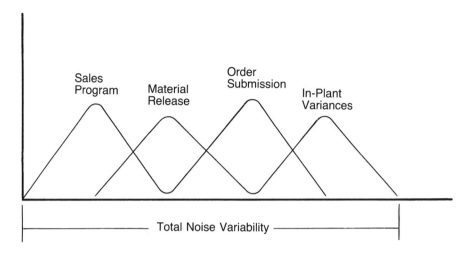

Noise variability is the unintended expenditures of resources because of the variability of sales program, vendor material release, actual order submissions, and in-plant order processing variances. A key in Just-In-Time programs is to relieve noise variability.

Gatelines

To overcome this, we established a 10-day "gateline," which required bringing sales into the picture. We received excellent cooperation from Sales Vice President Tom Pappert. The "gateline" is the first in a sequence of 1800 production operations. The 10-day gateline was a commitment by sales to provide 10 days of firm, buildable orders ahead of the production cycle.

Although the 10-day gateline provided significant relief, we still had to contend with "noise variability"—that is, the fact that the sales program, vendor material release, actual submission of orders, and in-plant order processing were far from stable.

The sales program is an 18-month forecast and build projection based upon economic indicators and field forecasts. An executive committee meets monthly to develop, analyze, and adjust the build program. It takes a macro view, dealing with such items as overtime and total volume per vehicle family. Variability exists for two basic reasons: the marketplace may dictate a build schedule adjustment between regular monthly meetings, and lower level managers who translate macro decisions into the micro-language of computers may unilaterally change the mix within a product family—for instance, alter the ratio of two-door to four-door and the convertible models. It gets tricky.

The vendor material release is developed monthly, based on the latest sales programs and resulting build schedule. It is adjusted weekly to reflect such factors as parts shortages that cause a plant to restrict certain orders and overbuild others to maintain production continuity. Actual sales orders may bear no relationship to the forecast because of increases or decreases in demand in the marketplace, seasonality of demand, or special priorities such as a big fleet order that must be built to a specific deadline.

Spaghetti Order

The manufacturing challenge was to get the sales program, vendor material release, order submission, and order processing in phase. The "spaghetti order" input scenario provided the solution. In analyzing where and how field orders were processed, Dellas found several independent and mutually exclusive departments forecasted, committed to, and attempted to obtain dealer orders. At Chrysler Windsor, these departments could be, for example, U.S. Retail, U.S. Fleet, U.S. Government Sales, Canadian Retail, and Canadian Fleet.

These independent forecasting departments were responsible for obtaining the orders that were the basis for several thousand suppliers to make satisfactory parts and deliver them to each assembly plant in a timely manner for production scheduling and build. A graphic of this order flow resembles spaghetti thrown against a wall, hence the name. Of course, when an order input area failed to make its forecast (up or down), a little horse trading with other areas was needed, and each of these accommodations created variability or "noise" in the total system, adding systemic costs.

Since each assembly plant scheduled its own production, manufacturing centralized these common functions at the staff level. This was the key to stabilizing production; it also was a catalyst for additional materials management improvements. The first step was to create a centralized scheduling department, staffed by transferring personnel over a 12-month period from each plant's scheduling department. Upon completion, we created a new department with a net reduction in total staff. This unit received orders from input areas, feeding them to each assembly plant in the form of a 10-day gateline. In addition, centralized scheduling verified that each order-input department submitted orders exactly to forecasted

Forecast Points

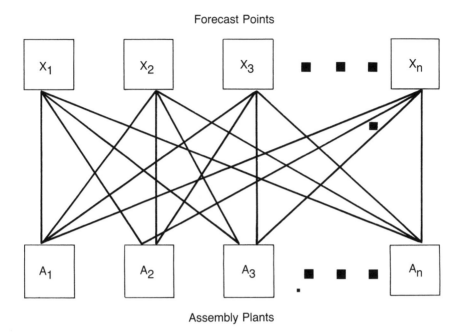

Assembly Plants

Independent forecasting departments generated spaghetti input. It was messy. The input was in the form of projected orders for vehicles. Forecasting points could be sent to a number of different assembly plants.

projections. Centralized scheduling provided the assembly plants with upstream stability of order flow.

The next step was to provide downstream enhancements with the plants themselves. Plants are set up and staffed to build products at a given mix. For instance, an assembly plant may be organized to build 1000 vehicles per day, 50% with air-conditioning, 20% with two-tone paint jobs, and 35% with vinyl roofs. Of course, actual orders may include some, all, or none of these options. In mathematical scheduling, a vehicle with all three options will be built once every 12 units. While the 1000 orders per day will be processed by centralized scheduling at the relevant option rates, the sequence of those orders is random. Thus, the plant will find itself building two or three vehicles in a row with all three options combined, rather than neatly spaced at the rate of one out of 12.

One solution is to overstaff the workstations to accommodate this worst-case scenario. The overstaffed workstations would be extremely busy during certain periods and underutilized during others.

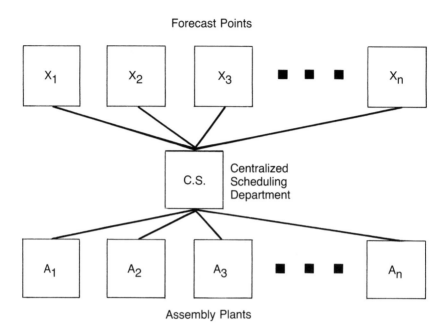

Forecast Points

The creation of a centralized scheduling department relieved the spaghetti input. This unit receives orders from order input areas and feeds these orders to each assembly plant.

Centralized scheduling developed a set of mathematical algorithms that took the random 1000 orders for the day and resequenced them to achieve a smooth work pattern throughout the shift. This eliminated the need to overstaff certain workstations and resulted in lower direct labor hours as well as improved quality and ergonomics.

The *Alpha* or operational reserves number was completely controlled by manufacturing. While we used it to calculate the total quantity of parts issued on the monthly material release to suppliers, the actual *Alpha* number was given to the corporate scheduling department by the plants receiving the parts.

We then implemented our visual management program in each plant. It required that material stocked on the line be no more than 54 inches high, the same height as Chrysler's returnable containers. Now, standing anywhere in the plant, you could see all other areas. By implementing visual management on a department-by-department basis, each plant

Units	Option A 50% Usage	Option B 33⅓% Usage	Option C 25% Usage
1	X	X	X
2			
3	X		
4		X	
5	X		X
6			
7	X	X	
8			
9	X		X
10		X	
11	X		
12			
13	X	X	X

Upstream stability of order flow with a three-option content. This figure depicts three-option content of 50%, 33 1/3%, and 25% installation rates.

could study just how much material it required, compare it to what it had in inventory, estimate needs, and slowly, but consistently, reduce the *Alpha* requirements.

Achieving control of *Beta* (the quantity of parts delivered by suppliers) required manufacturing and purchasing department cooperation. They determined which suppliers most flagrantly overshipped and under-shipped. We found some of our own facilities on the Bad-Boy supplier list. One reason for overshipping was the accounting practice of taking a snapshot of the books at the end of the month. Some suppliers used this incentive to ship everything they could toward the end of the month to make their books look better. One reason for undershipping was the necessity for emergency changeovers caused by schedule changes. In this case, our objective was to stabilize the quantity of parts delivered, our strategy was an educational dialogue with suppliers, and our tactic was feedback on performance and, occasionally, return of overshipped parts at the supplier's expense.

In-line sequencing gave us control of *Gamma* (the rate of inventory depletion caused by production). Control of the fourth parameter, *Delta* (time between deliveries), required the cooperation of manufacturing and

191

logistics. Again it was a matter of identifying flagrant transportation violators and establishing an educational dialogue.

The Transportation Challenge

Chrysler Transport, one of the largest truck fleets in America, run by the Logistics Department, was on the Bad-Boy list. Bob Scroggie, the head of Chrysler Logistics, quickly resolved the problem, however. In fact, he and his colleagues worked intensely with manufacturing to come up with an automotive industry first—the unit train—a dedicated train that goes from Detroit to St. Louis and another traveling daily from Detroit to Newark, Delaware. These unit trains carry large, heavy components such as stampings and engines, and differ significantly from normal rail transportation in delivery speed. They arrive at their destination on the same day they leave home base, whereas normal rail transit takes several days. Most of that extra time is spent when the rail cars are awaiting switching in a yard or siding rather than actually traveling.

Our carriers were instructed in the lessons we learned at Chrysler Transport. All of them were given feedback on performance. If they were unwilling or unable to cooperate, we canceled contracts. It was an attention-getter.

Justified Inventory Transfer?

My JIT philosophy matured at GM's Flint assembly in 1970. I had been in the business about seven years, and, GM didn't use Just-In-Time at that time; it was not a big thing in America in those days.

It wasn't that it was unknown. If you read up on JIT, you'll find that Henry Ford had a JIT system at River Rouge. But everybody walked away from the idea over the next several decades. Then the Japanese reinvented it in the '50s, but we in America never got back into it until the '70s.

I was starting to sniff around and sense that this was important as early as the late '60s. However, I didn't have enough authority then, enough stripes on my shoulder to make it work, and I had some disagreement with my German colleagues at VW because their philosophy on material handling was to rely on safety stock (extra material).

Although my thinking on JIT developed in the late '60s, I didn't get the chance to discuss it as policy until early '79, when I was talking to Lee

Iacocca about what I wanted to do for Chrysler. What do you think Lee knew then about Just-In-Time? Like most people—absolutely nothing! Yet, I made a major point of it then, saying that if he wanted me to work for him, I would want Chrysler to convert to a Just-In-Time system. The only time you have real power is *before* you start a new job.

Then he smiled and said, "Okay, you got it."

Once I had that go ahead, I knew I couldn't accomplish JIT unless I had something in my method of manufacturing that produced *predictability* and *repeatability*. Fred Caffrey and I were tinkering with in-line sequencing as early as 1968 at GM's Flint assembly plant. At VW Westmoreland, as VP of manufacturing, I had put in in-line sequencing, but I couldn't use JIT because it was against VW philosophy at that time. They weren't ready for a gut check, yet, on the cost issue. They will learn.

When I first came to Chrysler, I couldn't put in-line sequencing in right away, but over a five-year period, I did install it step-by-step. I used it first at Windsor for the minivan, the first new product I put in. A plant that had zero JIT went to 70% by dollar value within six months!

In the meantime, I was getting the other plants up to 20–25% JIT as I modified their methods of production scheduling. Ten years later, every assembly plant had a minimum of 70% JIT and at least 70% in-line sequencing. The model plant today in Chrysler—and probably the world—is Jefferson North with 100% in-line sequencing and over 90% JIT. If you want to benchmark an assembly plant, start at Chrysler's Jefferson North.

There are detractors of JIT delivery who say it merely places responsibility for warehousing safety stocks on the vendor. JIT also pressures vendors to locate facilities nearer customers. In the U.S., this forces domestic manufacturers to embrace the Keiretsu system that makes Japanese supply so efficient. Part of Keiretsu's effectiveness lies in the fact that the supplier is located as close to the assembly plant as possible—so close in fact, that some parts, such as fasteners and switches, are delivered directly to the line by bicycle!

If North American suppliers cannot locate nearer to customers, they must find efficiencies in their operations that will enable adjusting to the JIT requirements contracted for in their purchase orders. They will have to employ flexible manufacturing practices and develop a product mix that will enable them to adjust to the assembler's fluctuations in sales volume and variety. They must either develop stable labor relations that will preclude strikes and work disruptions or bear the expense of alternative methods of providing parts to cover such eventualities.

A strike causing work disruption at an assembly facility or an economic recession will affect the volume of parts the vendor must supply. Since JIT delivery, together with its commitment of visual management, is so critical to product quality and efficient materials management, the supplier can expect no relief from the purchase contract except renegotiation to reflect diminished volumes. Most purchase orders, however, allow for sliding prices based on volume.

JIT and the Twinsburg Saga

Are you vulnerable to your suppliers with JIT? Absolutely, but you always have a certain vulnerability, a certain risk, in anything you do. A person has only one heart, for example, and if it suddenly blows, you're done for. These are things we all must live with.

In 1983, a strike at our Twinsburg (Ohio) stamping plant shut down most of Chrysler. The press pounced on this as an example of our vulnerability under JIT. I disagree, both then and now.

We had been moving to in-line sequencing with a heavy focus at our Windsor plant from '80 to '83, and with a lesser emphasis at our other plants, as I've described.

Twinsburg was one of the three stamping plants we had saved, along with Sterling and Warren. Of these, Twinsburg was the most radical by far. Built in 1958, it had 25 strikes in nearly as many years. That's what I call radical!

Deliberately, the very day that Iacocca and I rolled out the first minivan to the public in October of '83 at Windsor Assembly, Twinsburg Stamping went on strike. Because we were on JIT, within one day, we had shortages nearly everywhere. We lost $90 million of variable profit in a single week! Twinsburg's action shut down not only Windsor, but all our other assembly plants. No one needs to tell you that's our bottom line, our source of revenue. This is a situation that all automobile people dread.

Obviously, I had one red-hot Comanche in Iacocca! He and I met with our labor relations vice president, the vice chairman, and Steve Sharf. This key meeting took place right after the "big publicity splash" of the minivan roll-out. It was a tough meeting. Well, I'm a big boy. I played with some big-time football heroes on the playing field and had taken a few hits. There was nobody in that room who could whip me, so I wasn't worried about that. There also wasn't anybody in that room who understood vehicle assembly and manufacturing better than I did. There were different thoughts expressed as to why we were on strike at Twinsburg. It was a most interesting meeting. One of those you never forget.

Was it really JIT's fault? No, I told them, and turning to our chairman, I said, "Let's face it. We're on strike for three reasons. Chrysler always has caved in too easily to these people, and that's why for the last 25 years we've had 25 strikes down there. These guys are pulling a power play on us! They know they have great visibility right now because you're personally embarrassed. You just rolled out the minivan, and now you can't build any more of them because you're out of sheet metal."

He asked, "What are you telling me?"

I answered that, "This is not about in-line sequencing or Just-In-Time. We've got a labor problem there. The local union does not want to allow advancing technology because if they do, they feel it will result in taking people out of that plant. I'll take people out of the cranes, for example, as we convert to pendant controls. They know that. They want dozens of extra people just sitting up there in the sky most of the time, looking down at people on the floor. Another issue is they don't want us to work the rest of a press line when one press goes down. Another is about limits on moving parts from one line to another. Their list of demands goes on and on. They are so restrictive, that, if such demands were granted, we would not be able to effectively manage the plant and its work force.

"This strike is about holding up the progress of technology and flexibility of operations. If you give in to that, you and Chrysler are dead! In that case, you shouldn't have come to work here, and I shouldn't have come to work here. Dammit, there's a time when you must take a stand and show your will, and this is that time!"

This was a classic case in which a local union was totally out of control. Their demands were recognized as outrageous. Management, the international union, the plant employees, and, certainly, employees of the other affected plants, wanted their plant back in operation.

After much urging by me, management held its ground with the local union. When the local union officials realized they had lost the backing of all their union counterparts and the employees, a satisfactory settlement was reached. No restrictive demands were granted and the local union president was defeated in the next election.

I knew those strike leaders didn't have the support of their troops. I know a setup when I see one. I grew up in these factories. I worked day shift, night shift, and weekends—six or seven days a week for seven years. I've been worked over by the best of them. I could see that their leader was a guy who was an over-educated radical, and who thought he controlled Twinsburg and didn't have to deal with Iacocca or Doug Fraser, the UAW president.

Yes, I was mad as hell then, but I didn't care if I got fired. In situations like these, I'm going to do what's right, not what's easiest or popular. I believed wholeheartedly in JIT and the systems we had put in place and was more than willing to fight to preserve them. It's a two-fisted battle.

Today, the Jefferson North Assembly plant is going a major step beyond JIT to SPD, Sequenced Parts Delivery. Where JIT gives you a window of four to eight hours for material, SPD says I want your delivery truck backing up with a car seat just as my eyes first see the car for it coming down the line—now we're splitting hours into minutes. Nobody in the world has a system that efficient but guess who's got the biggest margin of profit all of a sudden of the Big Three? You earn as you turn.

In It for Keeps

From Chrysler's perspective, there is no turning back from JIT materials management. It transformed workplaces that ran managers into workplaces where managers were in control. It's a turn from craziness to sanity. We developed a rolling 10-day delivery schedule for suppliers on JIT that told them exactly what to ship in advance. The plan stabilized their production schedules and allowed them, in turn, to stabilize material requirements from their own suppliers.

The entire process took many years to implement throughout Chrysler. It was worth it. It was why I had such a frank discussion with Lee in 1979. You have to agree on policy issues upfront. We freed over $1.7 billion in cumulative inventory, inventory turnover rates soared beyond our own expectations, premium transportation penalties per vehicle dropped to the lowest in the industry, excess and obsolete material dropped to record levels, part shortages and attendant expediting fell radically, and delivery dates to dealers improved. We proved that this theory about manufacturing materials management can successfully survive the test of reality! You cannot let people bully you or intimidate you into stopping important progress on policy issues. We had justified our Just-In-Time system.

Chapter 13

LESSONS FROM PEERS, OCEANS APART

I got my first taste of German manufacturing practices in 1976, when I became vice president of manufacturing for Volkswagen Manufacturing of America. In my dozen years at General Motors before I joined Volkswagen, I rarely participated in discussions of global market strategy, currency exchange, product homologation (adaptation to foreign laws), or multi-lingual communication. My first trip to VW's Wolfsburg headquarters was, therefore, a shock. These issues were central to the success of the company I had joined, so they had to become central to me.

Duty, Discipline, "German-ness"

Among my new colleagues I found a pronounced *dedication to duty* and other military virtues and practices, and a nationalism inconceivable in the United States because of our melting-pot history. Germans seem able to subordinate their own needs and desires to those of country and company far more easily and naturally than we Americans. German culture is also intensely homogeneous: "German-ness" is the only road to ultimate success and prosperity. This pressure for conformity is oppressive to an American, but it does create harmony and cooperation. I saw this in the less adversarial attitudes of union and management at Volkswagen. The government owns part of the company. Unionization of the work force exists up to the rank of superintendent (that would be unheard of in America). On my visit, I found that 50% of the company board of supervisors were also union members. This is a totally different system from that in the United States.

VW's focus, like that of other German companies, was distinctly global. Germany, which has not been geographically self-sufficient for decades, generates a large portion of its wealth from exports of sophisticated manufactured goods made from the raw materials it imports. Basically, their economy runs on the sale of skill and knowledge, so those qualities rank high in their system of values.

While Americans try to create fairness in the workplace through laws requiring equal opportunity for all races, genders, and creeds, the male-dominated, quasi-militaristic social monolith that is the German workplace prizes industriousness over fairness and precision of execution over individualism.

On a personal level, I found tolerances as tight in human interactions as in our engineering drawings! My German colleagues were polite and correct but rather cool and distant. Titles were preferred over first names. Personal warmth was reserved for nonworking time. I was amazed at how radically the German personality changed when we went from workplace to home, restaurant, or pub.

Their relationship between man and machine is different. I noticed great respect for products and machinery, probably because most material goods must be imported and are more expensive than in the U.S. Germans highly value precision, quality control, and maintenance. VW was engaged in preventive and predictive maintenance before it was even thought of by U.S. manufacturers.

During my time at VW, quality control practices were thorough but old-fashioned. A product would be checked, reworked, and rechecked with an impressive array of gages, calipers, and templates before release. People were tripping over each other doing this work. This didn't bother the Germans. Perhaps this was because, in a socialistic system, one responsibility of an industrial concern is to employ as many people as possible. They will learn. In today's globalization that will not work. Government responsibilities to industry are taken seriously, however. Workers' health care, a burden crippling U.S. manufacturers today, is largely paid by the government in Germany.

Engineers and manufacturing managers enjoy high status in a German organization. Where financial people, product planners, and sales and marketing executives usually are elevated to the top positions in the U.S.,

Volkswagen maintained a meticulous balance. Managing board members represented all disciplines of VW's business. Manufacturing was the equal of engineering, sales, finance, and supply. Even service and parts, often treated like junk dealers in the U.S., had an equal say in important company decisions.

Because of the respect for machinery, equipment, and the tight tolerances of precision execution, the manufacturing engineer is highly regarded, I found. The late Dr. Juergen Ehmer, my colleague in building Volkswagen manufacturing in the U.S., went from this discipline to even more responsible positions within the organization. My close friend and top operations officer at VW de Mexico, the late Wilfried Brenner, was also a manufacturing engineer.

Toni Schmuecker, who was chairman of the board of management during my tenure at VW, initiated me into VW product strategy and global business vision. First of all, he explained, VW attempts to project an image, originally created by the Beetle, of high quality paired with product reliability. After VW acquired Audi and began working with Porsche in the U.S., the company started cultivating a high-tech image, but in the German sense of that term. High technology at VW had little to do with styling and sheet metal, but came from power train and chassis components, steering, braking, fuel systems, seats, and suspension. Germans love power and performance. The third VW strength, Schmuecker explained, was outstanding service, which had the same status as sales in the VW hierarchy.

Schmuecker also taught me the importance of good relations with the financial community. During my time at VW, the top financial officer and vice-chairman was Professor Doktor Friedrich Thomee. ("Professor" is a high honorific in the German language, conferred for life, and used daily in all situations to refer to the person who possesses it.) The title alone gave you the understanding of the power of the financial community.

When VW established a manufacturing base in the U.S., its board of directors planned to have German experts come to the U.S., hire their U.S. counterparts, and supervise them until they were ready for equal status. At a predetermined date, the Americans would take over, and the Germans would go home.

The Germans are detail-oriented and time-conscious. They religiously respect deadlines. Planning is formal, always recorded in writing, and agreed to by everyone who must make the plan work. Once conceived and accepted, a plan is inviolate, and they will fight to the last man to implement it. If there is weakness in their system, it is a lack of flexibility.

So when it was time for the Americans to take over, elaborate documents were prepared outlining our duties and responsibilities in minute detail. Then the formal signing process began, starting with VW of America President Jim McLernon and Dr. Guenter Hartwich, the top VW manufacturing executive and Vorstand (board of management) member, proceeding to Dr. Ehmer and me, then cascading downward to our press shop; tool and die organization; body shop; paint shop; and planning, trim, chassis, maintenance, and quality departments. This exhaustive process was taken dead serious by both the Germans and us, though it made the American staff impatient and nervous. Our culture had not prepared us for such ceremonial formality, but it worked effectively.

We were given only 18 months to establish this U.S. manufacturing base. The Germans are always in a hurry. After dealing with communication, cultural, time zone, unionization, and philosophical differences, we were to hire, train, and deploy a manufacturing organization, finish a plant shell that VW had purchased from Chrysler, and equip and process it to assemble 800 vehicles per day. We also were to build or buy a stamping plant that could support the 800-a-day vehicle build. Our vehicles had to reflect VW standards. Our production costs were to be cut by 10% on the model of VW's Emden, Germany assembly plant. This manufacturing capacity had to be integrated into VW's worldwide operations. The entire project was to launch on time, to VW quality standards, within budget. On April 10, 1978, our first Rabbits rolled off the line. They were on time, met VW quality standards, and met budget plans. The game was on.

The assembly plant in Westmoreland County, Pennsylvania, was America's first large-scale vehicle transplant. No one before or since has done it in a tighter time frame. In addition to our German partners, R.S. ("Dick") Cummins, the plant manager, M.G. ("Marv") McFadden, the general director of personnel, and their staffs worked day and night on three continents to make it happen.

Why the Rabbit Died

As you know, events overtook the Germans' efforts here in the mid- to late-'80s, and their challenge in the subcompact, compact, and intermediate segments of the North American automotive market ceased to be significant. The Japanese were coming!

A factor in this, I feel, was the German industrial organization, which consists of two key groups: a board of management (Vorstand) and board of supervisors (Aufsichstrat). It is much more politicized than our system here. After getting on board, I never really felt we had the full support from all the members of these two groups for the expansion and the original North American product plan. There was nothing much I could do about this, however, except make the best of the situation and execute precisely their launch and manufacturing plan. That part went well. We made all our targets on quality, timing, and budget. We sold the plant out—Rabbits were selling as fast as we could make them.

I agreed to a multi-year contract, feeling that would be sufficient time for the launch and startup phase, and by that time, we would both know each other better. I wasn't worried about the long term but felt there was some added risk working for a foreign-owned company, so a contract was appropriate. It's traditional with European companies, when they hire a foreigner, to do so on a contractual basis at the executive-officer level. At any American company I've worked for, GM and Chrysler in particular, your contract is your next paycheck. If you get paid twice a month, you have a two-week contract, and if you get paid once a month, you have a 30-day contract. Don't forget that.

I knew I was taking a risk and that VW was taking a risk. We hardly knew each other and were suddenly going to be living together 24 hours a day, but it was an excellent learning experience. I soon saw Volkswagen's costs were far too high. If we continued to import our materials from Germany, there was no way we could compete with American builders, let alone the Japanese. Cost is crucial for an entry level vehicle at the subcompact level. Once I saw that many of our parts would come from a high-cost structure, and that we had high labor costs because we had been unionized (not in the original plan), I knew it simply was not going to work as it was originally predicted by VW's planners. However, we enjoyed rebuilding VW to 4% of the U.S. market.

When I left VW, they were still running flat out—they couldn't build one extra car or truck—and that was true for a year or so after that. I told VW management then that I felt their product cycles were far too long. As I've said, at Chrysler, one of the crucial things that was needed was an ongoing stream of fresh products. Volkswagen and other European producers then were on a car cycle twice as long as the Japanese and 50% longer than American companies. A four-year life cycle for a car in Japan, Honda for example, was six years in America and eight or more in Germany. I told them, ''You'll never live with an eight-year cycle for a compact. There are too many entries, and your cost structures must be brought under control because the margin is too thin for the dealer.'' The dealer body is still your lifeline. The VW dealer organization, at that time, was strong, mostly single-franchise, and numbered over 1100. They were professionals.

Another important factor was that VW already had a well-entrenched manufacturing operation in Puebla, Mexico. In Puebla, they had a foundry stamping plant, assembly lines, and a good infrastructure of suppliers. That kind of supplier situation never developed around VW's Pennsylvania assembly plant. The stamping plant was in West Virginia instead of next to the assembly plant. We didn't have a foundry and, therefore, couldn't do our own engine blocks and machining. Suppliers who were crucial to the VW setup never moved to America as they were expected to do.

Now, 15 years later, BMW already has a commitment from 60 German suppliers to move in and around the North and South Carolina area to support them. This is a huge difference in support, policy, and infrastructure. VW Westmoreland was a learning experience for me, as well as for German auto-industry management. The original commitment to manufacture where you sell is still the right one. But as the old saying goes, "Too soon old, too late smart."

Cooperation, Industry, "Japanese-ness"

When I became executive vice president of diversified operations at Chrysler in 1980, I encountered Mitsubishi Motors Corporation and, later, Diamond Star Motors. Chrysler owned Mitsubishi stock since 1971 and participated in joint ventures with the company, some of which involved me intimately.

My involvement with Mitsubishi and Diamond Star was not as direct as it was working within the VW organization, but it was very crucial. When I came to Chrysler in 1980, I had all international sales responsibility and administration. That meant working every day with the Japanese at Mitsubishi. In those days, we were in the process of selling Chrysler Australia (which reported directly to me) to Mitsubishi. Although this process started before I got there, it was my job to finalize the sale for senior management and the board of directors—the conditions under which this transfer would be made and how we would keep Mitsubishi building cars and trucks for us and importing them to America. At that time, Mitsubishi was trying to divorce us because they felt we had the bubonic plague! It was my job to keep romancing them, keep them happy, without losing my credibility.

I had daily discussions with them in 1980. Then, when my duties expanded in '81, I didn't have daily responsibilities with them again until 1983. At that time, it was privately agreed by Lee Iacocca and Dr. Tomio Kubo, chairman of Mitsubishi Motors Corporation, and his president Tojo-san, that they were interested in a potential joint venture manufacturing plant in America.

I went to Japan with a team to meet with Yoichi Nakane, Mitsubishi's top manufacturing person for this special project. We examined and discussed his newest green grass plant (built in 1977) in the Mitsubishi assembly complex—Okazaki. My newest plant was planned while I was still at VW in the '70s and which Chrysler purchased in '83, Sterling Heights Assembly. Thus, we were trying to take the best from each—the latest Japanese assembly-plant thinking and our thinking—and determine how we could put them together.

From '83 to '87, I worked every month with these people developing Diamond Star Motors, and it became a very important prototype for our development of Jefferson North Assembly. Then, from '88 until I left Chrysler, every month I would take or send people to Diamond Star Motors and Nakane would bring people up to review the plant I was planning, Jefferson North. Thus, we worked intimately together for a decade.

The geography, demographics, and cultures of Germany and Japan are very similar. Both countries, overpopulated and poor in natural resources, depend on knowledge and skill to process expensively purchased raw materials into complicated, high-quality, industrial exports. They both inherited a military tradition imbued with the virtues of physical courage, loyalty, self-sacrifice to the fatherland, and duty and honor. Both are monolithic societies that value conformity—"German-ness" or "Japanese-ness"—and industriousness over fairness. Precision of execution has a higher priority than individualism. If you are a woman or a member of a racial, ethnic, or religious minority, you will not get equal consideration or special deference in either country.

As in Germany, the flip side of intolerance and de-emphasis of the individual is cooperation. Japan's unions are company-based and docile. The Japanese worker protests by wearing a black arm band and working harder! Suppliers are considered members of the auto manufacturer's "family." Located close to the assembly plant, they are obsequious in their efforts to please their powerful customer. The Japanese emphasize quality as much—or more—than the Germans.

Manufacturing, viewed as the life blood of the country, enjoys the highest status. The manufacturing engineer's status is equal to that of the design engineer, and the boards of management of Japanese companies are dominated by engineers and manufacturing people.

Japanese planning, based on a high degree of consensus, is as meticulous and time-consuming as the German style. I found a plan is adhered to with the same military precision.

These similarities can teach us a lesson: Countries like these can achieve a high standard of living and world economic power primarily through manufacturing, but excellence in manufacturing seems most probable with a tight, quasi-military organization requiring a high degree of conformity and cooperation. Nationalism, self-sacrifice, devotion to duty, and honor are the bonds that cement individuals into a powerful, productive team.

The sophisticated, high-quality manufacturing sector in Japan depends on a rigorous educational system. Engineers guide a detailed and time-consuming planning process based on consensus, mission, balance, and focus.

Over 50% of the boards of directors of Japanese motor vehicle companies are from the manufacturing or engineering disciplines. This is very different from the American system. One tremendous advantage of this practice is in capital investment decisions. In the U.S., most capital expenditures must promise a relatively quick payoff. The Japanese often do not require a short-term financial justification. If it is the right thing to do—if it brings a quality improvement, a rise in customer satisfaction, or even an ergonomic advantage to employees—they do it. How many American corporate board members would be persuaded to invest by arguments of Muri (eliminate overstrain), Mura (eliminate irregular movement), or Muda (eliminate unnecessary movements)?

Japanese board members with manufacturing operations experience understand technical arguments and the needs of working people. They don't need a detailed story about financial payoff. On the other hand, board members in the U.S., whose experience is usually in economics, law, planning, or marketing, are more comfortable listening to financial and marketing arguments. Most of them never have worked in manufacturing and quite possibly never have walked a plant floor. The Japanese understand the advantage capital investment will bring to their country and companies. Many powerful American colleagues do not.

Dr. Kenneth Court, a Tokyo-based Canadian economist who is the first vice president of Deutsche Bank Capital Markets, Asia, predicted to the

U.S. Congress in May 1992 that he "expects Japan to become the world's Number 1 manufacturing power by the mid-1990s and to surpass the United States as the world's largest economy" shortly after the year 2000. He stated: "It is the result of the unprecedented levels of private sector plant and equipment investment," as well as the growing Japanese commitment to R&D. Japan spends more than 20% of its gross national product on new industrial plants, Court reported. That figure is 10% in the U.S. "Not once in the last 25 years has America invested (in terms of percentage) as much as Japan," he noted.

The Japanese culture has one more advantage: the questions "what," "why," and "how" predominate in their efforts to continually improve. In the U.S., the question "who" is too often asked—"Who is responsible for this?" is occasionally asked so success can be attributed to an individual, but more frequently "who" is blamed for what went wrong. Scapegoating frequently results from the desire to advance a career or protect "turf" in the U.S. It certainly does little to further the company's economic goals.

Stability in every aspect of life contributes to predictability and repeatability in Japan, and these qualities are the hallmarks of manufacturing excellence. The Japanese manager makes less money than his American counterpart, but his job is more stable. He doesn't worry about being fired if the next quarter's profits aren't up to forecast. The system provides stability for vendors, stable and low interest rates (usually), stability in long-term planning, and, most important for a manufacturing company, stability in sales forecasts and thus in the production schedule. There is little of this in the U.S.

Cohesiveness, conformity, and homogeneity create a unity of purpose from the highest to the lowest levels of the society. A Japanese automobile manufacturer is a national institution supported by schools, banks, labor unions, and a government bureaucracy that ensures the smooth functioning of the entire system.

In the U.S., we are busy competing with each other. Antitrust laws, until very recently, made it illegal for auto companies to work together on projects of mutual need or interest, such as air bags, battery technology, or pollution control apparatus. Only recently have we begun to use Japanese and German products and organizations as benchmarks. Imagine how much energy is lost in the U.S. in adversarial relationships between automobile manufacturers and suppliers, between unions and company management, between the automobile industry and the government. What could we accomplish if all this largely wasted energy was redirected?

Because Japan is a country of few resources, the Japanese are compelled to conserve them. They have little space, therefore they have learned to build smaller cars and plants. There is no room for banks of parts, repair bays, or scrap bins. Japanese culture is disciplined and abhors waste.

In the *1990 Harbour Report: A Decade Later*, Jim Harbour states that in 1981, Japanese cars had 240 defects per 100 cars or 2.4 defects per car. In the same year, Ford cars had 670 defects, General Motors had 740, and Chrysler had 810. By model year 1991, Japanese cars had an average of 125 defects per 100 cars, whereas the U.S. Big Three averaged 155, or 1.55 defects per car. Although that improvement is spectacular, it's not enough.

In his 1991 best seller *Euroquake*, Daniel Burstein tells why:

> The world of the year 2000 will look like this: Japan will represent the world's greatest concentration of wealth and technological power. The Asia-Pacific region around it will once again be the fastest-growing part of the world. The German-led Europe will have accomplished a vast economic and geographical expansion in the 1990s and will be enjoying a huge and widely shared prosperity as a result. The Soviet market will finally be ripe for sustaining large-scale successful business ventures. Because of Europe's relationships with the U.S., the former Soviet Union, and Japan, it will have become the most politically influential force in the new global order and will be generating many of the new ideas about the world system. The United States will have become the least economically dynamic of the three major regional markets. Nevertheless, the U.S. will still be a wealthy and powerful nation, despite its fall from grace. A process of American rebirth will be just beginning.[1]

We simply can't wait years for a rebirth in America! We must act now if we are to preserve our global competitiveness and national standard of living. As Red Poling, chairman of Ford Motor Company, said, "Japan is targeting the auto industry around the world. They have 14 million units of capacity." Japan's home market is only 7.6 million units. Guess where they plan to send the other 6.4 million. In 1990, Japan out-invested the U.S. in new plants and equipment by $36 billion! They are aggressively attacking the world market, using manufacturing as a strategic weapon. It's time we did the same.

Benchmark the Best

Most top managers today tend to be number crunchers or planners who never have worked in a factory. That's the big difference between Japanese management, German management, and American management. Most Japanese and German managers are required to work in the factory, while most American leaders-to-be are required to work in other departments than manufacturing. Too many American executives never worked in a factory more than just to get their ticket punched for six months—that doesn't count. That's why we've neglected manufacturing for the last couple of decades. That's why there is such a fever pitch today to fix it.

Because top management knows so little about what manufacturing is all about, they tend to panic now that the heat is on their plants to perform. Some are sending their lieutenants running around the world and measuring who has the best manufacturing model. It's now called "benchmarking" and is the big management thing to do.

My team was benchmarking over the last 15 to 20 years, beginning when I joined VW in 1976 and became internationally involved. I soon was traveling to Japan, Germany, Sweden, Britain, France, Italy, and Mexico. In all these places, I could see just how much we were not doing in America in the middle to late '70s.

At Chrysler, I was sending people to 15 countries. It was a formal program under the four Ms—Manpower, Material, Machinery, and Methods. Every time they came back from Germany, Korea, Australia, Sweden, Japan, etc., they had to give us formal reports. What did you find? How do they develop product? What materials do they use? Do they use pre-coated steel? Galvanized? One side? Two? How do they weld it? All those things!

This was no scattergun approach; it was very formal. That's why, within four years—from '80 to '83—we could have such a massive, quantum jump at Windsor Assembly. We did these reviews in '80, '81, '82, supplementing what I had already acquired in '76 through '80 at VW, and building on what I acquired during my previous dozen years at General Motors.

As a result, I had a library that would choke a goat! From there, it's a matter of taking a position, putting it all together, and then communicating to somebody who would listen. In this case, thank goodness, Lee Iacocca listened and provided excellent leadership.

Where are the Benchmarks?

Today, I would call Chrysler's Jefferson North a benchmark of what you would want in a body shop, and it's definitely the benchmark for a paint shop. It has some areas of general assembly to benchmark, but not

Tips for Business Travelers

My experience with international companies provided me with extensive foreign travel opportunities. Here are things I found helpful.

1. Organize your agenda with your host 90 days prior to the trip.
2. Select your travel team members carefully. Keep the team size small to medium. Two to eight people is the ideal size.
3. Establish each individual's responsibility and their reason for going.
4. Hold daily team meetings on the trip. Update each other and make appropriate adjustments.
5. Provide adequate time for socialization, tours, shopping, and learning about the host country.
6. Develop one "special activity" to unite the travel team and host (for example, Sumo wrestling in Japan or opera in Germany).
7. Demonstrate a disciplined, focused, unified strategy, but in a respectful, calm manner.
8. Be aware of the host country's customs, manners, and styles.
9. Look relaxed and fresh at all times. If you are traveling a long distance, an overnight stop will help avoid jet lag.
10. The purpose of a first trip is to develop a working relationship rather than implementing action from that relationship.
11. Develop, with your team members, a system for appropriate notes from all business sessions. The notes will be essential for follow-up.
12. Don't overdo the local cuisine.
13. Confine your trip to seven to 14 days.
14. Look for product innovations, process innovations, facility utilization methods, world-class suppliers, and people programs.
15. Upon returning home and in a timely fashion, always write a gracious, sincere note of appreciation to your hosts and their associates. Keep it short.

nearly to the degree achieved in the body or paint shops. This was by design: we were trying to move our general assembly automation up from about 2–5% to 10–15%. We knew there were others who have gone to 35–40% automation, but we chose not to do that. If your interest is materials management, you also can benchmark Jefferson North, whether it's in material modules, materials turnover, Just-In-Time, or sequenced-parts-delivery.

Now, you could look at this plant and say, "I would never benchmark there for the work force." Well, not if you are looking for utopia, because the work force there includes predominantly older long-service people with more health problems; they don't move as quickly as younger people can, and they are not as well educated. Nevertheless, Chrysler trained them for the last 12 years and found them to be more than qualified and sufficient to do the job. They are good people.

If you want to see a marvelous power train plant, I feel the Kokomo transmission complex is world class in the areas that were renovated to build the 604 and 606 electronic automatic transmissions. I think the Trenton Engine plant is rapidly becoming a world-class engine facility, and Chrysler's assembly division in general would have to be called flagship plants because they've been well balanced for a long time now in their investments in employee training, modern tooling, and flexible automation. Belvidere, Newark, St. Louis II, Windsor, Graz (Austria), Jefferson North, Sterling Heights, Bramalea, and Dodge City are approaching world class. St. Louis I can be, in the near future.

Or Do What You Always Did

The Germans and Japanese know benchmarking is a cornerstone of world-class performance. It may be as simple (or as complex) as knowing your competitors, but it is vital for survival. An October 1991 poll of members of the American Productivity and Quality Center (Houston) indicated 70% of those surveyed believed manufacturers must benchmark to survive. Seventy-five percent predicted "significantly more" benchmarking efforts.

The process begins by selecting the area to benchmark, identifying companies to study, and collecting data. You must measure against the best in the class. Do not look at only one competitor—no company is best at everything.

The gap between yourself and the best in class may be substantial but don't give up. Take improvements small steps at a time and keep the heat on.

Remember, the data-gathering stage of benchmarking, which is continuous, is a trade-off. No company, particularly a competitor, is likely to provide a plant tour or manufacturing information without seeking something in return. Expect to compare notes and trade information.

Benchmarking pays off big. Whereas some of our competitors struggled for months (even years) to get their new, highly automated plants into operation, our launches came off in record time with incomparable precision. Our JIT material delivery system exceeded the Japanese Kanban that inspired it.

At times, the status quo must be upset. New technology that brings about productivity gains, new techniques that result in lower costs or higher quality, and new strategies that expand the market may threaten established ways of doing things, but they must be investigated, tried, and when successful, put to work. In today's fiercely competitive, quality-conscious world, you cannot do what you always did, get what you always got, and stay in business.

I'm very grateful I had Lee Iacocca's backing over a long period—11 years—to implement the lessons I learned from peers oceans apart. Once I had these ideas strongly endorsed, it helped a near-bankrupt company become today's Cinderella II.

References

1. Burstein, Daniel, *Euroquake*. New York: Simon & Schuster, 1991, pp. 347–348.

Chapter 14

CAN TRAINING BE TAUGHT?

At a time when jobs demand more education and higher skill levels, the United States seems lethargic about retooling our most important factories—our schools. Japan and Germany have longer school days, more of them, and more stringent requirements in such subjects as reading, writing, foreign languages, mathematics, and science.

A Japanese student, for example, attends school an average of 242 days per year while an American student attends an average of 180 days. Add to that the Japanese emphasis on a more basic curriculum, higher standards, better teacher preparation, and a family life that supports study, and you will get a good idea of the quality of product—of people—Americans are competing against. Can practices in the U.S. even remotely compare?

As the monotonous, repetitive labor characteristic of the frontier and primitive manufacturing is replaced with increasingly sophisticated automation, cost and quality pressures are pushing plant leadership down the corporate ladder. Robots, electronics, lasers, and computers proliferate, but we have fewer people sophisticated enough to design, build, operate, maintain, and program them.

The document *21st Century Manufacturing Enterprise Strategy: Infrastructure*, prepared by Lehigh University's Iacocca Institute in 1991, sets forth the importance of education and training to manufacturing today:

In a very real sense, educating and training of the work force are today so important, because for so long they have been considered unimportant. In a classic manufacturing assembly line scenario, specialization was the key factor in employee utility. The work force was attuned to the importance of performing one job expertly. Once the job was learned and the product component or assembly line service accommodated, expertise had been achieved and learning was no longer as important.

The key to employee utility is versatility and willingness to adapt to rapid changes in job description, in skill required, in knowledge to facilitate change, and ability to cope temperamentally with an agile environment. While the skill level of an employee will not necessarily degrade, the skill level required of the future employee will increase. There will be no comfort level achieved by the predictability of performing the same job one did the day before. Quite the opposite, the discomfort that accompanies constant change, unchecked by additional training, will lead to performance degradation and employee turnover. One of the key components leading companies are embracing today is that of addressing functional illiteracy in their work force. Instead of assuming all people with a high school education are the same level and all they need is some additional training, companies are spending time on non-punitive testing and providing education to make their people functionally literate first. This is critical if additional training is to be fully utilized and the fear of change is to be overcome.[1]

Reskilling the Factory

In aging industrial organizations like Chrysler, that are trying to prosper by restructuring and downsizing, seniority systems force a disproportionate number of younger workers to be laid off. As this downsizing progresses, the average age of the work force increases alarmingly. Innovations require retraining these remaining older workers who typically take longer to learn new skills. The retraining cost is borne primarily by the industrial company.

At Chrysler, reskilling begins with a "nickel fund" program based on employee hours worked and set up in agreement with the UAW. For each hour, the company deposits five cents in each of three funds: one for plant-level local training, another for company-wide training, and another for health and safety training. Whether the money is gathered this way or in some other fashion, the cost of retraining makes its way into the product's price.

Japan: Students Stress for Success

Dr. Linda Lewis succinctly isolates many of the features differentiating the Japanese approach to education from the American system. Draw your own conclusions.

- Competition begins early in Japan. Even two-year-olds take a test to enter nursery school, and such tests continue up the education ladder.
- In Japan most students attend "cram schools" or *juku* for extra tutoring to ensure they keep moving up to the best schools.
- Classes run six days a week (including Saturday), year around.
- The only acceptable excuse for staying home is a fever of more than 102° F. For milder illnesses, students are expected to come to school wearing gauze masks over their nose and mouth.
- Teachers are paid fairly well, but work 8 a.m. to 5 p.m. weekdays, 8 a.m. to 3 p.m. Saturdays, plus occasional Sunday meetings and special events.
- Elementary classes run 8:30 a.m. to 3:30 p.m. three days a week, 8:30 a.m. to 2:40 p.m. two days a week, and 8:30 a.m. to noon on Saturday.
- The Japanese expect students to come to school "prepared," meaning they already know the material to be taught. This is the task of the *juku*.
- *Juku* is the term for a costly after-school that all serious junior and senior high students attend—as well as many elementary students. *Juku* prepares students for the next level's entrance exams.
- Even though eight-year-olds may be doing third-grade work in school, they're taught sixth-grade work after school in *juku*.
- By the time they're in high school, Japanese students spend from 8 a.m. to 5 p.m. in school, go to *juku* for three hours on school days—and often most of Saturday, Sunday, and vacation days—then do their night's homework for school. (Adapted from "Japanese Lesson Plan: Compete and Conform," *Detroit News*, March 8, 1992, p. 4B.)

In the past, Chrysler received government help in its new-product-launch training that covered the cost of some instructors, books, training aids, and, infrequently, even classroom rent. The company, however, shouldered the expense of wages. From 1982 to 1992, Chrysler provided upwards of one million employee hours of training prior to every new vehicle launch.

Why? Because I had insisted on it way back in my initial job negotiations. I told Lee Iacocca in 1979, "I won't come with you unless I can focus on high technology and flexible automation and, therefore, I will have to retrain the entire work force. You can't retrain the work force without money—many hours of training and many dollars for each of those hours. I've been in the business long enough to know that financial departments will fight you every step of the way if you are in operations and come asking for money for training. The first things they cut back on are training and maintenance. Unless I have your commitment up front, I am not coming and fighting for those dollars each and every time!" I needed the policy support of the CEO up front.

Because of this insistence on an up-front agreement on training, I came to Chrysler with a commitment that every new product would be accompanied by one million hours of training. In those days, training costs were about $25/hour, so that was $25 million given to us without having to fight through a bureaucracy. I did this because I had a vision that, if that wasn't part of policy, I'd be getting my head slammed around the room several times a year by the number crunchers and even our personnel people. Personnel, you know, thinks it's in charge of training, and the financial people think they are in charge of money. What neither seems to realize is that the place you make or lose money is in manufacturing. Manufacturing can be a money machine. To me, profit and staying in business always come first! And before you turn on those new, high-tech machines, you turn on your people with proper training. Chrysler worldwide invested nearly $500 million in 15 million employee hours of manufacturing training during the '80s. This revolutionary change in business philosophy enabled our people to develop in harmony with the new technology. Balance is crucial when upgrading people and machinery.

Training the Trades

Although U.S. manufacturers have done a respectable job of retraining production operators, they have a long way to go in the critical job of training skilled tradespeople and supervisors. Not a single machine operates without some involvement of a skilled tradesperson. The individuals selected for this work, and their training, determine whether the machine operates when needed and in a manner precise enough to produce high-quality parts at planned production rates. A skilled trades apprenticeship program must be disciplined, thorough, and of sufficient quality to enable graduates to do the tasks required by rapidly changing technology. Long-time automobile executives, like me, and my good friend Heinz Prechter (German-American), have been urging a broad scale U.S. apprenticeship program. It would need to blend work experience and academia.

Upgrading job skills and improving job training also is supported by the National Association of Manufacturers (NAM). Unfortunately, we are beginning the journey to a world-class apprenticeship program as a distinct underdog. Here's why.

- No other industrialized country lacks a federal-state system for administering apprenticeships. The U.S. is truly unique in this regard.
- Each year about 500,000 German companies provide on-the-job training for 1.8 million teenage apprentices—6% of the work force—at a cost of roughly $10 billion. In the U.S., apprentices make up a minuscule 0.3% of workers!
- At Japanese manufacturers, such as Honda, each job classification has a recommended course of study. Employees develop training proposals through a subcommittee advising necessary training and helping develop the employees' ability to accomplish a particular task. Training programs are approved in the light of performance and potential.
- At Chrysler—and I can't imagine that Chrysler is atypical—only 40% of skilled tradespersons complete a formal apprenticeship. What's more, the form of that apprenticeship has not changed in 50 years. Local community colleges teach apprentices generic, traditional, and, at times, obsolete theory. Certifying apprentices for successfully completing contractually defined work processes is often loosely monitored. There are no objective standards to measure skill levels of graduates.

A manufacturing employees' committee polled many skilled trades people across Chrysler. Using the poll, we restructured the skilled trades apprenticeship programs. The new plan proposed the following:

- An update of all course work—adding some subjects, deleting others.

- A first year, held at a manufacturing training center, where trainees receive a combination of theoretical and hands-on lessons.
- A second year in rotation through various plants.
- The third and fourth year served in one plant, completing the apprenticeship.

I believe this approach enhanced Chrysler's competitiveness and can be cloned by any U.S. manufacturing company.

Kokomo Goes To Class

Training paid off big time at Chrysler's Kokomo, Indiana, transmission plant. The 3.2-million-square-foot, 110-acre facility produces 65 different finished transmission assemblies for customers such as Chrysler, Mitsubishi, Iveco (England), Cummins, and Winnebago. This facility provides products for the world.

The introduction of the four-speed electronic automatic transmission was truly different from anything we did in the past. Product design was way ahead of the world competition. The manufacturing philosophy and goals, statistical process control, process design and capability, training and communications, certification programs, and technology applications were totally different and more progressive than previously attempted. The Kokomo philosophy was simple: *the production departments and, in particular, the operators would be totally responsible for product quality. Processes would be controlled through extensive use of statistical methods, and verification/certification programs would be the only monitors used within the quality system.* It was a major advance in employee empowerment.

In 1988 and 1989, training hourly operators and salaried supervision and support staff for the new transmission launch was extensive, 205,000 hours, all of it off the job. It included 10-step problem solving courses, quality awareness workshops, Working Together workshops, design of experiments, failure mode and effect analysis, and technical training on lasers, robots, and machine controllers.

In 1990, to prepare employees for the product and process and for a new culture of teamwork and participation, we invested another 86,000 hours in SPC, design of experiments, skilled trades safety, supervisor and UAW representative safety and health, Chrysler quality, working together workshops, hazardous waste operation and emergency response, supervisory skills, hearing conservation, laser welder safety, and area manager development.

Although the training focused on a new product, process, technology, and cultural approach, it became evident that permanent continued education on and off the job was required if we were to compete in the future. It was also evident—and somewhat frightening—that the American formal education system was not addressing industry's true needs. This shock prompted me and other senior manufacturing management to charge plant managers and their staffs to get actively involved with state and local school systems. Further, this group was asked to help formulate a curriculum that would benefit students and contribute to the greater competitiveness of American industry.

The extensive education and training programs at Kokomo proved themselves at the new product launch. The depth of preparation prior to the new transmission launch was a first for our industry. All machines underwent a 20-hour continuous qualification run-off on the machine vendor's floor and again at the plant after installation. We developed visual aids for each critical dimension and placed them along with SPC charts at the operation.

Color-coded process sheets and operator manuals were issued and used extensively during operator training. Every operator in any way associated with the new product was given a minimum of eight hours of SPC classroom training as well as on-the-job training. SPC is playing a major role in the plant's process control with 275 charts currently in use.

We also developed and implemented a sophisticated goal organization and leadership system. This system provided an objective method for establishing requirements and for assuring a clear understanding of these requirements. It required a regular review with every operating individual at each operating level that promoted teamwork.

The system specifically defined and communicated management's direction and needs to the organization; provided a universal focus in precise detail at all levels of the organization; established benchmarks for quality, cost, volume, and warranty improvements and a simple means of measurement; required individual performance accountability ensuring continuous improvement; was flexible in its measurement system, and was self-perpetuating. Other benefits were the ability to reduce management layers and allow for expanding "spans of control." Implementation was smooth and swift, and the organization grew comfortable with it since expectations and/or performance standards were always clear. We also had very open dialogue between union leadership, management, and the employees.

Tainted Training

I firmly believe job training and education are keys to implementing new technology, whether it be computers, electronics, robots, machine vision, lasers, flexible manufacturing, or a new accounting system. But "training" must be defined. There are "training sessions" that amount to nothing more than gathering people in a room and telling them about the state of the company, new developments that will affect them, and directions the company must take to remain competitive. This is not training. It is merely communicating with the work force. Often it is political lobbying. I would not tolerate that.

Another kind of "training" attempts to teach technical skills. It may occur in a classroom, such as a statistical methods course. It may occur on the factory floor, such as a class in air-conditioning system troubleshooting. Although straightforward and technical, such training assumes that the students will practice the techniques learned when they return to their jobs.

The third type of "training"—the least useful—attempts to change behavior. So does technical training, but here the claims are grandiose: The desired behavioral change will emanate from culture change. Droves of docile corporate employees are herded into sterile classrooms and administered bureaucratically disinfected doses of everything from corporate etiquette to failure-mode effects analysis. Paroled back to their workstations, the trainees are told to put their new skills into immediate practice. Top management then expects the students to instantly transform the corporate workplace into the model promoted by the trainer.

In fact, however, such training often changes nothing but trainees' attitudes toward corporate management. At first, they may believe that corporate culture is changing for the better, but when they return to their desks or workstations to find business as usual, cynicism takes hold. Through sponsoring a never-realized, training-created vision, management loses credibility. Once lost, it can seldom be recovered by the same management team. The lesson here is "protect your credibility at all costs."

Recasting Corporate Culture

Before you begin training for cultural changes, you should remember the dynamics and essence of American corporate culture which *typically* include elements such as:

- We reward fire fighting, with the most dramatic fire fighter getting promoted first.
- We make and adhere to timing commitments as a matter of personal honor.
- We maximize short-term profits.
- We seek quality improvements by increasing the number of times we check an item.
- We make a large quality department responsible for quality levels.
- We prefer short-term fixes and change personnel frequently, discouraging long-term resolution.
- We have a suggestion program in operation, but management ignores the program.
- Management training is charm school—that is, an effort to improve manners to avoid union problems and enhance the corporation's image.
- Trainers have low status. They are, and will stay, outside the management mainstream.
- We do most training during times of low activity such as strikes, product changeover, or downtime.
- Standards are "assumed" and highly subjective.
- We think a certain percentage of defects is inevitable.
- We emphasize schedule and cost over quality.
- We chart and graph only the behavior of hourly and low-level salaried employees.
- We blame some ambiguous individual who cannot be compared with an objective standard for our problems. We stress individual effort.
- We calculate product cost by what it takes to get it to the customer.

The point is that no amount of training can bring about lasting cultural change. The Communist regimes of this century tried to reduce the disparity in status between the highest and lowest social classes. They ignored the fact that man is essentially territorial and abolishing private ownership diminished the means of production. They attempted to diminish individual worth and accomplishment in favor of the collective community, and state.

After 70 years of intensive effort and horrible expense in human lives, these totalitarian methods failed, yet many business organizations still plan to change their culture by organizing expensive mass training.

Certain business practices *can* be changed, and training *can* play a minor role, but cultural change must come from individuals of high status and charisma. The vocabulary of the new culture can be taught, as can its underlying philosophy. Examples can be presented. Desired behaviors can be modeled by the trainer and trainees. All modeling will not cause trainees to change behavior in the desired way because neither trainer nor trainees have sufficient status to stimulate widespread mimicry of their behavior. This must come from top management.

This means managers must know the kind of culture they want. They must practice the new behaviors themselves and require subordinates to do so. Most important, managers must reward the consistent practice of these behaviors until they become habitual. The new habits must be repeated, reinforced, and rewarded over long periods to be sufficiently ingrained to create the new culture. If the manager neither practices nor rewards the behaviors of the new culture, cultural change will not occur. Subordinates do not do what managers say, they do what managers do. They also do what is rewarded.

Chief executive officers and those who report directly to them must, first of all, agree on the nature and objectives of the new culture. They must specify the strategies and behaviors that will make it reality. These behaviors must be important in their employees' annual appraisals.

If the company's officers practice the new culture consistently and openly for, say, one year, and they are tangibly rewarded, most subordinates will mimic them. Only then should you make the rest of the organization aware of what happened at the top and how it should happen throughout the organization. Meetings designed to pass on the message will be awareness only, rather than training sessions. Training happens when a manager or supervisor models the new cultural behavior, encourages it, and rewards those who practice it.

The New Pedagogy

In an April 1987 report, "Can America Compete?" *Business Week* noted:

> Universities are not turning out enough scientists and engineers to meet new demand in leading edge areas of high technology or advanced production systems—nor are they encouraging the study of manufacturing. Behind the brain drain is the flight of top students into the more lucrative finance and legal professions.[2]

Later in November, my article, "Restoring Our Competitive Edge," ran in the same magazine. In it I said the universities are molding the intelligence we need in our businesses. Only by working together—all of us—in our schools, laboratories, and factories will we change what is perceived as a deteriorating manufacturing base.

Many positive changes happened since then, with people now recognizing three fundamental facts:

- If the U.S. is to remain a strong political force, it must be a strong economic force.
- If the U.S. is to be a strong economic force, we must compete through manufacturing.
- For the U.S. to compete through manufacturing, its universities must recruit the brightest students for manufacturing programs and recruit the best teachers to instruct them.

For too long, we have been hypnotized by daily stories about Japanese manufacturing miracles. They are not miracles! The Japanese understand the link between education and industry, as well as the central role that manufacturing plays in an economy. In Japan, there is nothing unusual about the brightest students pursuing careers in manufacturing. Until recently, only a few Americans saw the link between the ivory tower and the factory floor, and their connection to U.S. economic health. Not only was manufacturing not getting the respect it deserved within corporate America, it was at the bottom of the heap in higher education. At Chrysler, I told myself, "I am going to stop complaining and do something. I am going to ask for big changes in university curricula and in the policies of academic leaders."

Chrysler management backed me fully. In the mid-'80s, we saw Chrysler become the Cinderella of the business world by applying the philosophy of scientific manufacturing, new products, and by empowering the people. Lee Iacocca was so committed to the role universities should play in the resurgence of American competitiveness that he spearheaded the effort to establish what became the Iacocca Institute of American Enterprise at Lehigh University in Pennsylvania. The rest of us at Chrysler were just as committed to making America internationally competitive through the proper education of our men and women. Talking about this commitment is easy; fulfilling it is not, for it requires a dramatic change in everyone's thinking. My staff and I visited many universities in the United States and Europe, encouraging them to increase their manufacturing efforts. We explained the importance of manufacturing. We discussed manufacturing issues relating to research. In some cases, we put our money and time where our mouths were.

The results began to appear in 1988, when several schools started or seriously considered new programs to enhance manufacturing education. The first was my own alma mater, Purdue University, whose school of engineering (led by Dean Henry Yang) is consistently ranked among the best in the nation and whose Krannert School of Management (under the leadership of Dean Dennis Weidenaar) enjoys a strong reputation.

Two of Purdue's programs in manufacturing education involve joint efforts with industry. One is the Computer-Integrated Design and Manufacturing Automation Center (CIDMAC) under the jurisdiction of the engineering school. CIDMAC has several industrial partners including Chrysler, and is a part of the Engineering Research Center for Intelligent Manufacturing Systems. Assisted by the National Science Foundation, CIDMAC works on projects that will change the way things are manufactured. Participating faculty and students thoroughly enjoy getting their hands dirty to expand their knowledge. The second program is the Center for the Management of Manufacturing Enterprises (CMME) in the Krannert School of Management. This center has a three-pronged mission: it offers a BS degree in industrial management with a technical minor in manufacturing management; it provides opportunities and incentives for faculty and students to respond to management challenges posed by manufacturing environments, and it provides a network for an ongoing dialogue among Krannert students, faculty, and manufacturing practitioners.

Chrysler was so impressed by the potential success of these programs that it committed $1 million to each one over a period of five years, as well as its funding of programs at many other universities—programs that will help it and industrial America compete in the future. I strongly urge other companies to make a similar commitment.

In June 1992, Northwestern University graduated its first 49 MBAs with Masters of Manufacturing Management (MMM) degrees. These students were educated in both business and engineering. Most important, in a tough job market, they averaged almost three offers each! During the same period, Duke's business school reported almost one in five of its graduates accepted jobs in manufacturing—triple the 1990 figure. The results are showing meaningful progress to support our philosophy.

A classic example is the Leaders For Manufacturing (LFM) program at the Massachusetts Institute of Technology. The program, launched in the spring of 1988, culminates in a single thesis—an original work approved by faculty advisers in the schools of engineering and management—synthesizing and analyzing the student's findings. Students receive one MS degree in management and one MS degree in engineering. The 11

B-Schools Stress Manufacturing

A 1991 survey of the top 25 U.S. business schools conducted by Fujitsu America Inc., (San Jose, California), verified a renewed emphasis on manufacturing on the part of MBA students. "Dramatic changes in manufacturing have occurred on the academic side," says Professor Steven Wheelwright of the University of California-Los Angeles. "The number of schools interested in production or operations is increasing significantly, along with student enrollment and academic staffing."

The study found business schools adding manufacturing courses in response to student interest. Some 83% of the respondents offered a manufacturing curriculum in '91–'92, compared to 43% five years before. Sixty-one percent offered a manufacturing/operations management concentration or major, compared to 48% five years earlier. The number of faculty teaching manufacturing courses increased at 48% of the schools.

Eighty-three percent reported increased student enrollment in manufacturing/operations management. And in 56% of the schools, recruitment of MBAs into manufacturing increased while it dropped in many other fields. Eighty-seven percent of the schools reported more students finding jobs in manufacturing than they did in 1986.

Respondents also saw the following manufacturing trends for the '90s:

- *Joint Global Developments.* Larger companies will acquire and work with smaller specialty shops worldwide to enter and capture niche markets. Engineering know-how will diffuse rapidly across national borders.
- *Flexibility.* Large-volume products will continue giving way to customized products.
- *Advanced Automation.* Large and small factories will automate to satisfy customer requirements.
- *Short-Cycle Production.* Reduced design-to-delivery cycles will allow gearing production to customer demand for less surplus and overhead.
- *Management Style Changes.* Multifunctional teams will reduce bureaucracy and increase worker responsibility.
- *Customized Logistics.* Technology will allow greater coordination and efficiency throughout the logistics chain, from order to delivery.
- *Design for Manufacturing.* Knowledge of manufacturing system capabilities and limitations will continue to be systematized and incorporated into decision making during product design.
- *Quality Management and Control.* Competitiveness will be determined by instituting total quality control management in every step of the organization.[3]

"partner companies"—Alcoa, Boeing, Chrysler, DEC, Kodak, GM, Hewlett-Packard, Johnson & Johnson, Motorola, Polaroid, and United Technologies—provide students with a 6.5-month applied research internship, usually in the second year of the two-year program. Graduates have solid credentials in engineering or science as well as teamwork capability and a strong aptitude for leadership. The leadership from the Dean of Engineering, G.L. "Gerry" Wilson, and Dean Lester Thurow of the Sloan School of Business provided excellent examples of cooperation between academia and industry. I am most proud that my own son, Rick, is a graduate of the 1992 LFM class. He will make an outstanding world manufacturing executive.

Management Makeover

While I was trying to sell the American educational system on manufacturing, my staff and I also were upgrading the educational base within the manufacturing group at Chrysler, though we wished that the schools had trained their graduates in the precision-in-execution skills required by manufacturing *before* they sent them to us.

In 1983, Chrysler manufacturing began to require plant managers to plan a major educational upgrade of their management teams. I received professional support and counsel from Chrysler's long-time vice president of personnel and organization, Glenn White. Local colleges and universities tailored degree programs to Chrysler employee needs. Some courses were even taught in plant conference rooms. Now hundreds of management employees were able to complete bachelor's and master's degree programs. Chrysler's tuition refund program covered the cost of courses relevant to an employee's job.

We also instituted a College Graduate-in-Training (CGIT) program to get new blood into the production process. College graduates, primarily in technology or engineering, were aggressively recruited for plant or division programs. The plant program called for six months of training in various departments, then a two-year stint as a production supervisor. The division program moved graduates around for training in staff as well as plant departments for 18 months, also rounding out the experience with a two-year assignment as a production supervisor. Front-line leadership and experience are absolutely critical for total understanding and manufacturing management.

In 1983, when the Chrysler Institute of Engineering (CIE) was over 50 years old, no employee from a manufacturing department had ever been

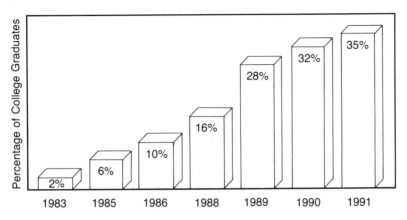

Chrysler's tuition refund program increased each year, helping not only the employees, but the company. The tuition refund program meant that 35% of the company's first-line supervisors have college degrees (in 1991). That figure was 1% in 1980.

admitted to the program! We negotiated our way in. By the time I left Chrysler, 20 manufacturing engineers had graduated from CIE. They are seed-corn for the future. You have to fight for what is right. History comes and history goes, but principle will endure.

By the end of the '80s there were more than 1500 people with bachelor's degrees from 200 universities and colleges around the world in Chrysler's manufacturing ranks. *Talent is where you find it* and we searched the world for the best and brightest. We also had 400 people with master's degrees and 10 with PhDs. Almost 45% of the 6000-plus salaried employees in manufacturing either already had, or were working on, a college degree—most of them in technical areas. I am proud that over 35% of the company's first-line supervisors have or are pursuing college degrees, as compared to less than 1% in 1980. That is what I call "standing tall."

In 1988, *Fortune* magazine reported that 29% of MBAs from the top seven business schools took jobs in manufacturing companies—a rise of 6% from 1987.[4] This interest is also starting to show at other business schools. Dr. Ronald Frank, former dean of the Krannert School of Management at Purdue University, wrote in a letter to *The Wall Street Journal*:

> Your article on the luster-loss of business schools reported that the October 1987 crash caused a decrease in student demand for finan-

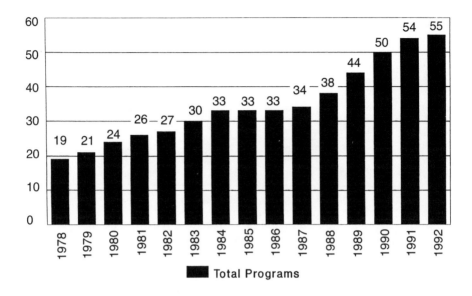

Manufacturing-related programs have shown a steady increase in educational institutions. The number of programs is currently 55, with these courses being taught in 51 educational institutions.

cially oriented MBA programs. What it failed to report is that the demand for MBA programs that focus on technology and manufacturing appears to have increased. This is certainly the case at Purdue University's Krannert Graduate School of Management.[5]

Dr. Frank, presently dean at Emory University, is a strong academic leader for enhancing the manufacturing capabilities of America. Have our young men and women finally realized that, if they want to enjoy the same prosperity as their parents, they must concentrate more on the *value-added sector* of the economy instead of the Wall Street paper chase? There is strong evidence they have. The results are beginning to show in colleges and universities around the country. In 1992, for example, there were 51 educational institutions offering a manufacturing engineering curriculum recognized by ABET, the Accreditation Board for Engineering and Technology.

Educational Strategy

We should not let these victories reduce our intensity. There are fundamental problems to solve when only 70% of American students complete high school, compared to 98% in Japan, and when our graduates acquire far less knowledge away from the educational experience than Japanese students do. Couple this with the decrease in the U.S. college-age population, and disaster could loom on the horizon. For the coming manufacturing millennium, I suggest a long-term educational strategy incorporating the following features.

Teach kids to read. This is true not only for the educational system but for parents as well. Get away from the television on Saturday morning and get your kids interested in books. Literacy is a challenge for the U.S. industrial enterprise—it should not be.

Include school field trips to factories. Let children see what manufacturing is about, as I did when I was their age. There is curiosity there, let's develop it! They must learn to respect and admire the manufacturing floor instead of thinking of it as a place to avoid. Field trips should begin as early as third grade. Vary the type of factory. Don't always go to an automobile plant or local steel mill.

Strengthen the high school curriculum. Emphasize science, mathematics, and technology, including their application to the real world of manufacturing. Local business involvement and pay increases for science and math teachers may be needed.

Get involved at the high school level. Manufacturing companies must get involved with local high schools. In Rockford, Illinois, for example, manufacturers brought computer-aided design to the high schools. A taste of industry high tech whets student appetites. The payback to the company comes in reduced training costs and quicker integration of an employee into the work force. Hands-on experience lets students see if manufacturing is for them.

Encourage children to finish high school. We must discover why 30% of them don't, formulate an action plan, and undertake initiatives to eliminate dropouts.

Develop programs focused on manufacturing in our universities, with cooperation from industry and government. Even though 51 institutions teach manufacturing engineering, we need more. We should *increase* financial incentives and scholarships for students enrolling in these programs.

View universities as a problem-solving source for industry. Some schools are beginning to organize their manufacturing students into teams to tackle real-world problems provided by business (Brigham Young University is a good example). The students work with realistic problems, get the chance to put their new knowledge to work, and must come

Arizona State University Tempe, AZ	Hartford State Technical College Hartford, CT
University of Arkansas—Little Rock Little Rock, AR	University of Houston Houston, TX
Boston University Boston, MA	Indiana University-Purdue University—Fort Wayne
Bradley University Peoria, IL	Fort Wayne, IN Kansas State
Brigham Young University Provo, UT	University—Manhattan Manhattan, KS
California Polytechnic State University	Mankato State University Mankato, MN
San Luis Obispo, CA	University of Massachusetts
California State Polytechnic University—Pomona	Amherst, MA Memphis State University
Pomona, CA	Memphis, TN
Central Connecticut State University	Miami University Oxford, OH
New Britain, CT	Midwestern State University
Central Piedmont Community College	Wichita Falls, TX Murray State University
Charlotte, NC	Murray, KY
Central State University Wilberforce, OH	University of Nebraska—Lincoln/ Omaha, NE
University of Cincinnati Cincinnati, OH	New Hampshire Technical Institute Concord, NH
University of Dayton Dayton, OH	New Jersey Institute of Technology
East Tennessee State University Johnson City, TN	Newark, NJ State University of New
Forsyth Technical Community College	York—Farmingdale Farmingdale, NY
Winston-Salem, NC	Oklahoma State
GMI Engineering & Management Institute	University—Stillwater Stillwater, OK
Flint, MI	Oregon Institute of Technology
Greater North Haven State Technical College	Klamath Falls, OR Oregon State University
North Haven, CT	Corvallis, OR

Manufacturing engineering curriculum is a must if the U.S. can continue to compete in the global marketplace. Listed are the 51 educational institutions—an "honor roll" if you will—teaching manufacturing engineering. The institutions are recognized by the Accreditation Board for Engineering and Technology (ABET).

Owens Technical College
  Perrysburg, OH
	Thames Valley State Technical
	  College
	  Norwich, CT

Pellissippi State Technical
  Community College
  Knoxville, TN
	Utah State University
	  Logan, UT

Pittsburg State University
  Pittsburg, KS
	Waterbury State Technical College
	  Waterbury, CT

University of Rhode Island
  Kingston, RI
	Weber State College
	  Ogden, UT

Ricks College
  Rexburg, ID
	Wentworth Institute of Technology
	  Boston, MA

Rochester Institute of Technology
  Rochester, NY
	Western Carolina University
	  Cullowhee, NC

St. Cloud State University
  St. Cloud, MN
	Western Michigan University
	  Kalamazoo, MI

University of St. Thomas
  St. Paul, MN
	Western Washington University
	  Bellingham, WA

Texas A&M University
  College Station, TX
	Worcester Polytechnic Institute
	  Worcester, MA

Manufacturing engineering curriculum (continued).

up with practical solutions. The corporation gets fresh thinking and answers. It's win/win.

University engineering programs should teach quality. Courses in total quality management (TQM), continuous improvement, or quality control might be given, or instruction might emphasize quality in production-related courses. Engineering students must understand how to prevent defects rather than inspect and detect them.

University engineering programs should teach teamwork. Students should work in teams. Though the educational norm is to give individual grades, teamwork is critical in speed to market, quality, new product development, and productivity.

Universities, industry, and government should increase emphasis and funding on manufacturing R&D. Taxpayers and voters must demand a commitment from Congress and local universities' board of trustees or regents. If you are a stockholder in a corporation, ask the company what investments it is making in funding manufacturing R&D or educational programs at the college level.

Corporate officers should attend research conferences. This is an excellent way to get the latest manufacturing research information to the corporate level. It is not a boondoggle! Select conferences based on their topics, and make an action plan. Purchase the conference proceedings if you cannot attend.

The American reputation of rising to the occasion is legendary. Let's make manufacturing education, training, and research our next national challenge. Training can be taught.

References

1. Nagel, Roger and Dove, Rick. *21st Century Manufacturing Enterprise Strategy: Infrastructure*, Volume 2. Bethlehem, PA: Iacocca Institute, Lehigh University, 1991, p. 29.
2. Jonas, Norman. "Can America Compete?" *Business Week*. April 20, 1987, pp. 44–47.
3. "B-Schools Stress Manufacturing." *Manufacturing Engineering*. January 1992, p. 60.
4. Nulty, Peter. "Where the 1988 MBAs Are Going," *Fortune*. August 29, 1988, pp. 48–51.
5. Frank, Dr. Ronald. "Dearth of Business-School Teachers," Letters to the Editor. *The Wall Street Journal*. August 15, 1988, p. 15.

Chapter 15

PASSION FOR PROGRESS!

On the first day I arrived for work at Chrysler, in my first private meeting with my new boss, Lee Iacocca looked at me, laughed, and said, "You're a man of honor and a man of courage—you showed up! Today, for the first time in our country's history, the prime rate hit 20%! You must have a lot of guts."

Well, I had some ambivalent feelings that day. I made a commitment to the man that I would come aboard, and I stood by that. I knew things were bad for the company, but now they were worsening quicker than anyone could have anticipated. I had no idea the economic plight of our country would balloon the prime rate and make things even more miserable for a cash-starved company like ours. Chrysler was in keen financial distress at that time—this ship was sinking fast with no lifeboats in sight!

So there I was at a high point in my career—pumped up about joining Chrysler—yet, at the same time, it was a low point finding out what a mess I had gotten myself into!

Looking Back

What do I remember best about those Chrysler years? Two of my personal high points came in 1983. First was the very successful launch into production at our Windsor, Ontario, plant of a revolutionary automotive product, the minivan. It was also a revolution in manufacturing for both Chrysler and the industry. In four years, we developed an entirely new philosophy and direction for simultaneously designing and building innovative vehicles. It began early after my arrival and received cooperation from the design and engineering departments. Manufacturing started working much more closely with design and engineering than ever before on new-product development and launch. The minivan was built off the K-car platform but was a totally different vehicle—one that became the crown jewel of Chrysler's success.

In that same year, another high point for me—and everyone in the organization—was when our executive team was able to send our chairman to Washington to pay off the loan guarantee draw-down seven years early with $300 million in interest. That was a huge morale booster! It gave Chrysler total independence—a fresh start. We were no longer linked to the U.S. government. Although we had great appreciation for the loan-guarantee draw-down, we obviously wanted to regain our independence as fast as we could. Now we had done it.

Probably the near-perfect year was 1984 when the auto market was hot and we ran our facilities at near capacity with the result being a staggering $2.4-billion profit! It was enormous and remains the record for Chrysler Corporation from 1925 to this day. Everything was right: The economic environment of the country, our products, our quality, and our people. The whole system was in sync and in balance: products, people, processes, and our program for profitability. It was all working and it felt great! It beat the hell out of the first day that I had arrived—five years earlier.

In 1986, we were at the height of our manufacturing modernization program—every one of us was enormously involved and sprinting full speed. This transition had started, philosophically, in 1980, but I couldn't get it physically moving until 1983. That's when the bulk of our own people, along with the general public, first began realizing what was happening within Chrysler manufacturing—when we rolled out that first minivan at Windsor Assembly. The renaissance had begun and it had become public knowledge.

Things really began accelerating in 1983. We bought the Volkswagen plant, now Sterling Heights Assembly. By '86, we were doing the half-billion dollar Dodge City conversion at the Warren truck assembly complex, along with converting the previously mothballed St. Louis II plant to become our second minivan plant. Our manufacturing revolution was in full bloom; the intensity level was Mach Six! We were running flat out. This pace continued until we finished our massive program and converted every vehicle assembly plant in the U.S. and Canada. I left Chrysler when we were nearing completion of Jefferson North, the first green field assembly plant since Chrysler's 1966 Belvidere assembly plant, and we built it in inner-city Detroit, not in the serenity of somebody's cornfield or briar patch. The new plant is an outstanding replacement for the old. We took care of our own.

To neglect manufacturing for two decades—one new assembly plant in 25 years—and suddenly leap to a Mach Six mentality, modernizing every plant, one after another, was an incredible feat, something the Good Lord doesn't expect humans to long endure. Yet, that was the hand we had been dealt, so we played it with gusto and I, for one, loved every minute of it!

Another key high point for me personally was in 1987 with the acquisition of American Motors. I fought furiously for over two decades to expand the automobile business when that thought ran diametrically opposed to company policy and strategy. Policy and strategy was to acquire other things, not automotive companies. So I was delighted when we acquired an automotive company, expanded our focus on automotive, and received a world-recognizable brand—JEEP.

In 1988, we made a decision as an executive team to bring out a new product every six months, starting with a second-generation minivan in 1990—the crown jewel was to be cared for first. The second edition minivan, the new Jeep, an entirely new trio of family sedans (the LH), a new T-300 full-size pickup, were all products of a decision we made in '88—to have a steady stream of fresh, world-class, new products. Product is the name of the game in the automotive industry.

In 1989 to 1991, I had the privilege to directly oversee the construction of the all-new Chrysler Technology Center (CTC) and the green field Jefferson North Assembly Plant in Detroit. That is a manufacturing executive's lifetime high. To build, grow, expand, and prepare the future—not to close, sell, and mothball operations. The final high point was the honor of being promoted to executive vice president of worldwide manufacturing. The dream of rebuilding Chrysler was on a roll.

These are the high points I remember best.

Throughout my career the drive propelling my actions was to create a sense of mission and establish a sharp focus and urgency on that mission. It was a two-fisted battle in manufacturing that raged more fiercely in me with each passing day. As Lee Iacocca used to tell me: "If I have a Type A personality, Dauch, you're a quadruple-A!''

The Chrysler Technology Center (CTC) brings research, purchasing, design, engineering, and manufacturing planning all under one roof. This is the view from the Product Design area of CTC. (Chrysler photo)

Driven To Be The Best

Those, I feel, are my major accomplishments at Chrysler. These are the things I felt most deeply about, fought the hardest for, took the worst beatings for, and feel the most fulfilled about today.

While championing American manufacturing for 15 years as an automotive officer, I cultivated an international perspective by recommending Chrysler's immediate withdrawal from apartheid-dominated South Africa. I also argued for the retention and expansion of Chrysler de Mexico and Chrysler Canada. Later on, I recommended expanding Beijing Jeep

The chassis rolls of this dynamometer in the Noise, Vibration and Harshness facility at the Chrysler Technology Center are 10 feet in diameter. Above this room is a fully instrumented test chamber that absorbs sounds and echoes. Vehicles are wheeled into the chamber and their tires positioned on the rolls. The rolls spin either forward or backward, simulating various road conditions. (Chrysler photo)

Corporation and business relations with First Automobile Works of China. I strongly pushed for right-hand drive products for export and assisted our sales of Jeep products in Japan through our link with Honda.

I also supported, with personnel and expertise, Chrysler's re-entry into the European market with the minivan assembly plant in Graz, Austria, and broad distribution of North American-built Chrysler products to Europe and the Middle East. This required very close coordination with the vice president of international operations, Michael Hammes, and later Joseph Cappy. I was charged with modernizing a monstrous manufacturing operation that was terribly neglected for two decades. We upgraded equipment, installed new systems, purchased new technology, implemented JIT materials management, rationalized and refocused suppliers, developed close business relations with our dealer body, replaced old facilities, rebuilt union/management relationships, and trained and taught tens of thousands of employees to work as a unified team. Teamwork is power.

In 1980, I successfully pleaded for Chrysler to stay in the truck and electronics businesses when key strategists and staffers were advising the opposite. By 1992, trucks represented 56% of Chrysler's business! Without trucks, we would have had a premature R.I.P. placed on all of Chrysler.

As a manufacturing professional, I led our team to establish the discipline of in-line sequencing and Just-In-Time material management. It was highly unpopular, but the right thing to do. Performance was my mission, not politics.

I directed a massive effort to use SPC and C_p-C_{pk} (6 sigma) capability for operational control to enhance product quality, reduce costs, and empower the employees doing the job. This was controversial, but also the right thing to do.

The rapid rationalization and upgrading of the supplier base and transformation of our quality focus from detection to prevention and proactive cross-functional teamwork were two plays that produced spectacular touchdowns. As Chrysler's chief manufacturing officer, my insistence on a zero-defect mentality was critical to changing the entire corporate culture. I walked the talk.

I nudged my engineering and design colleagues into concurrent engineering and process-driven design. I promoted satellite stamping plants, satellite supplier plants, and supplier R&D centers. My fullback and linebacker tenacity allowed me to fight ferociously through enormous resistance to get the job done right. Coach Mollenkopf would have loved it. I know Lee did.

Worker training, repopulation of apprenticeship trades, educational upgrading of management personnel, integration and diversification of manufacturing management, and regular technology transfer from universities to industry were vital parts of my program.

I involved myself directly in union affairs in an attempt to eliminate the tense, destructive, adversarial tone that dominated Chrysler labor relations for decades. The result: only one significant local strike from 1984 to 1991. That is over 800 million man hours worked—with but one fumble (one strike). I can live with that track record.

My efforts to raise the quality of Chrysler-built vehicles helped produce a 65% improvement from 1980 to 1992 with manufacturing productivity nearly doubling during that period. Our minimum net improve-

In a Nutshell

The Chrysler comeback—what did our decade of dedication accomplish?

- Did Chrysler get saved? Yes! Chrysler is stronger now than ever.
- Did Chrysler pay back its guaranteed loan? Yes! They did it seven years early with a $300 million interest payment.
- Did Chrysler develop its company like Honda? No! Chrysler is a full-line, car and truck manufacturer—distinctive and innovative.
- Did Chrysler save employees' jobs? Yes! Chrysler directly employs nearly 100,000 people.
- Did Chrysler pull back to North America? No! Chrysler is expanding all over the world with a brand-new plant in Graz, Austria; expanded operations in Mexico; an expansion in China, and probably will be announcing some other new plants in the next year or so.
- Is Chrysler making money? Yes! GM isn't. Ford isn't. Neither are five of the nine leading Japanese car companies.
- Did Chrysler's quality improve? Yes! Measurably, from eight fault conditions per hundred vehicles to two, a quantum jump in quality.
- Did Chrysler improve productivity? Yes! Plants that once had 5000–6000 people now produce more product with less than half that many. Productivity doubled.
- Did Chrysler's manufacturing plants improve in safety, flexibility, environmental protection, and in social responsiveness to employees? Yes! The factories compare favorably to any in America. In 1980, the factories were in terrible condition.
- Did Chrysler do this just using their own smarts? No! Chrysler did it by learning a little something from everybody: the Japanese, the Germans, the Swedes, and the competitors across town.
- Did Chrysler diversify its organization with respect to minorities and females? Yes! The manufacturing group led the way.
- Did Chrysler change its materials management approach? Yes! Chrysler's JIT system leads the automotive industry.
- Did Chrysler generate profit? Yes! Chrysler earned $12.5 billion in gross profits and $9 billion in net profits from 1982 to 1990. That is *more* profit than Chrysler earned from 1925 to 1980. The game plan worked.

ment in manufacturing productivity, per year, was $150 million every year for over a decade. This is how Chrysler recovered from the grave. We went to work, together! Chrysler was the domestic low-cost producer from 1983 to 1987 (prior to the purchase of AMC). Chrysler can and should become the low-cost producer again, in the 1990s, now that AMC has been digested and the new products allow volume and market share to grow again.

Chrysler's new products, beginning with the second-generation mini-van in 1990, are now built in totally new or rebuilt factories. They will be supported by totally new material management systems and enlightened, retrained, motivated, and flexible workers.

The privilege of managing the production of nearly 20 million vehicles for Chrysler was a manufacturing pro's dream! My watch encompassed massive restructuring, new ways to develop cars and trucks, improving union and dealer relationships, developing team-oriented supplier relationships, realigning leadership, and converting to process flexibility and high technology—all with the concomitant upgrading of employee skills and retraining. It was a wild, high-energy decade totally committed to saving an American institution—the Chrysler Corporation and its fine employees.

These fundamental changes reinvented much of the company. It started with attitude, teamwork, leadership, energy, and process-driven design. This provided great products like convertibles, minivans, Dakotas, Jeeps, and LH vehicles. It also provided world-class vehicle plants like Windsor, St. Louis II, Sterling Heights, Belvidere, Toluca, Graz, Newark, Bramalea, Dodge City Truck Assembly, and the one I worked the hardest to establish, Jefferson North in Detroit. Chrysler, the business recovery "Cinderella" of the '80s, is now poised to become the "Cinderella II" of the '90s. The "firsts" that were developed during our administration will be around for the next three decades. The ideas will be devoured by foreign competition. I hope the rest of America will do the same.

Looking Ahead

When one looks at what lies ahead for the auto industry, it must be done from a global perspective. That's the way I've trained my mind for the last 25 years. We in the auto industry are producing 45 to 50 million units per year worldwide and are presently having to deal with an over-capacity of between eight and 12 million units. That has a disproportion-

Chrysler's new Jefferson North Assembly plant. In 1986, Dauch promised the people there would be a day for "New Beginnings." At Jefferson North, on January 14, 1992, that day officially arrived when the first Jeep Grand Cherokee rolled off the line. That promise was another commitment kept. A man's honor comes from keeping his word. (Chrysler photo)

ate effect, depending on whether you are in North America, Europe, or the Pacific Basin.

Our major market, North America, has hit lows of 11 million and highs of 16–17 million units per year, depending on whether our economy was running hot or cold. The auto industry is cyclical. As I've said, 1984 was a near-perfect year, we were running flat out, and those conditions do not repeat very often. All of us in the industry could use more of those! We are due soon for a repeat performance.

For Chrysler, probably one of the more difficult periods, and the toughest challenge for everybody to handle, was when the economy started to fall back into a recession, as evidenced by the terrible hit the stock market took in October 1987. This was about three months *after* we purchased AMC. Here we were, having just bought a million units of capacity on top of our own two-plus million, and then by a quirk of fate, we take an economic hit nobody expected.

The stock market dropped over 500 points in one day!

We suddenly had close to 3.5 million units of capacity with only a 1.5 million market share! God, it felt like the first meeting I had with Lee, when the prime rate hit 20%.

Thus, from mid-'88 through mid-'91, we went into a period of tremendous loss of capacity utilization in the industry. For Chrysler, it was even more difficult because of our acquisition of AMC—nobody in either GM or Ford had gone out and bought an extra million units of capacity! Like General Patton in World War II, I had a plan. We laid it out in spades before the year was over. The plan is now nearing completion. The result? Chrysler is presently the only profitable member of the Big Three. Where I come from, results count. Performance is always in style. Politics come and go.

This is characteristic of the kinds of ups and downs this industry has seen. As we look to the future, I see a need for more new vehicle assembly plants. Here again, I'm at odds with most auto executives who are not anxious to build new assembly plants. Look what Chrysler accomplished with its new Jefferson North assembly plant, built in depressed downtown Detroit in 1991. It is already paying off handsomely, and will continue doing so, I feel, for the next 50 years. Indeed, manufacturing is a high stakes, long-term commitment to a profession. It is not for the timid, mental lightweights, or superficial talkers.

More Factories of the Future

Why more capacity? Well, because we need *new* capacity—factories of the future, not old capacity—factories of failure. Look at BMW. They are putting in new capacity in South Carolina. Toyota is building five new assembly plants throughout the world. Fiat and Volkswagen are doing the same. You win a war by working it out, not waiting it out. Yes, some of these moves by automakers are merely shifting capacity around for political and strategic reasons, but most of it is adding new capacity and new capabilities.

In the past decade, we have seen the transplant auto companies expand from roughly 300,000 units of capacity to roughly three million—a 1000% increase—in North American capacity! In the '88-'95 period, we are seeing the same thing happening at a somewhat lesser intensity in Great Britain by the Japanese transplants. Instead of further expansion here in North America, they are concentrating on the British Isles to be able to invade Europe and the Middle East. We also are seeing new assembly plants being added on the island of Japan by Toyota and Nissan.

I don't foresee Chrysler needing any new domestic assembly plants in the next five to eight years—those in the U.S. and Canada are in excellent shape. They may need one in Mexico and maybe one or two off-shore somewhere, but not in the center ring. The assembly capacity is there—it's flexible, focused, expandable, produces efficiently, produces high quality, makes money, and utilizes unique three-shift operating patterns. The system supporting it—stamping and power train—has been pruned and properly focused so it works effectively and flexibly. We planned the products and plants in balance. Thus, all the new products are sourced in North America. We build them, we don't just badge them.

The automotive game plan around the world is to be strategically located for the lowest production costs, highest quality, and right mix of production capabilities, based on an in-depth international economic and political evaluation of where to locate. It's not a case of throwing darts at the map! Many times, the best solution is a joint venture, such as that between Volkswagen and Ford in Setubol, Portugal, to build a new minivan. (I studied that location three years before they made their deal. You have to stay in front of the competition.) We eventually chose Graz, Austria.

Thus, I see this 45 to 50 million annual world volume of cars, trucks, and buses resulting in an underutilization of capacity to the tune of millions of units around the world. We have just gone through a tough cycle of capacity contraction in America between '88 and '91, and now a cycle of underutilization is becoming more severe in Europe than in North America. It also is beginning to be felt, but to a lesser extent, in Japan.

Capacity is shifting as perceived needs change and strategies get modified. Companies such as Chrysler with fresh and exciting products are becoming very strong in market share, capacity utilization, and profitability. Companies such as General Motors have been caught in the middle of a hiatus between products, while others experience the dichotomy of being strong in one region and weak in another. For example, Ford is strong in North America and presently comparatively weak in Europe. There was a weakness in Ford of Europe's product plan.

Keep on Trucking!

Transplants have been making some major adjustments. Honda, running for over a decade at full sail with the wind at its back when passenger cars were hot, has seen the wind shift dramatically. Today, the growth area is trucks—which I define as pickups, minivans, and sport/utility vehicles—and Honda doesn't have any. Honeymoons only last for a while. This is a car *and* truck business.

In 1980, there were people at Chrysler who strongly wanted us to get out of trucks. I advised then-President J. Paul Bergmoser: "There's no damned way I will work for a Chrysler Corporation that makes no trucks!" You have to have the confidence of your convictions. It was a critical issue. Paul is a bright, experienced, energetic man who listened well to his advisors. Paul and Lee made the right decision to stay with trucks.

Thus, Honda today is doing something it never did before, tying in with an affiliate, Isuzu, to get into the sport utility business. Honda also will be extremely focused during the next five years on getting into the minivan business because it's a proven growth segment. By the time they get started, Chrysler should have nearly six million minivans over the curb. The race goes to the fleet.

The U.S. and Canadian auto market is mature with limited growth potential in the years ahead, something like 1–2% per year. The best volume growth you will see elsewhere normally will be in the range of 5–10%, with the greatest potentials in places like China, India, Thailand, Mexico, Eastern Europe, and other locations where the opportunities are tremendous if you can accept the economic, social, and political consequences. My advice to the people in those countries, by the way, is the same as I have followed in my own life: do the best with what you've got; that is, play the hand you were dealt to the best of your abilities. Remember, when you are in a foreign country (market), you are a guest. Therefore, you have to adjust to the conditions in the host nation.

Balance for the '90s

Chrysler is going to be powerful in the decade of the '90s because it has everything in balance. The most important thing is its people. Our people in the decade of the '80s came together as a team—nearly every person on the payroll. Second, we developed an effective new-product development strategy with design, engineering, manufacturing, marketing, and purchasing working together. I see Chrysler getting stronger and stronger, and where it presently does about two million units a year, I see Chrysler having the capability of moving up to annual volumes beyond the three million mark in the '90s. That is how we sized it for continual growth. Our new product avalanche is now hitting the showrooms.

General Motors, the big loser in the last 10 years, will stabilize and, when it does, it will be at a much lower market share than this proud company ever experienced in the past. GM is in the fight of its life and will no longer be the giant among the other players—just another of the big boys.

Back in the late '60s and early '70s, GM wanted to jump into the Swedish social-system approach to manufacturing and I fought that move. "It's going to drive your costs up," I told them. "It will drive your quality the wrong way, and it's not the right thing to do. Yes, it would make you feel good and, if that's what you want, then that's what you should do!" Fortunately, people listened. We did not take that wrong fork in the road.

In 1992, we saw Saab and Volvo close two of their key "social-enterprising" plants. Twenty years ago, all the academics, staffers, and analysts were telling us to social-engineer our plants here. It just shows that you have to be prudent regarding who you listen to and whose example you follow. Experience and intelligence will always win over philosophy and theory.

The future of the auto industry will be a series of giants and mid-size companies. I predict a Big Three for as far as my eyes can see, each company remaining independent, GM included. GM will be resized, reshaped, and will come off Mt. Arrogance. Life is real and they are adjusting.

There were times when many people felt that Chrysler should not remain independent. Never for a second, from my first day there in April of 1980 to this moment, have I ever felt Chrysler could not stand on its own. I fought ferociously along with Bob Lutz at Chrysler to keep our hard earned independence. I was only "in to win," never to lose or tie.

This doesn't mean there won't be joint ventures and alliances, but each of the Big Three should retain their independence. The small companies are rapidly trending toward losing their independence. Witness the loss of independence of fine vehicle brands like Jaguar, Saab, Lamborghini, Lotus, Aston Martin, Maserati, Rolls Royce, etc. Constant speculation surrounds Porsche and smaller Japanese automobile manufacturers. It is a rough World League. Japan's "Big Nine" will likely get reduced. They will not all make it as independents. I believe they will become a "Big Six" by year 2000. "The bloom is off the rose" with them. They are not invincible.

I see the Europeans continuing their migration out of Germany: going south to Spain or Portugal, east to the Czech Republic and the other former Soviet satellites, and to Poland, China, Mexico, the U.S., or Brazil. The Europeans have major adjustments to make, while countering a Japanese invasion from the island of Great Britain. Let the games begin!

I see companies either getting stronger or weaker; none will remain static. Chrysler will get much stronger because the base and new integrated systems are well established with a balance of product, people, and processes. This includes how products and production processes are developed and the right infrastructure is established with suppliers.

End of Dynamic Leadership?

Lee Iacocca's leaving will *not* mean the end of dynamic leadership for Chrysler or the auto industry in general. Lee was a genius in adapting to the hand dealt to him. As he once told me, "The efficient mode of management is dictatorship." He inherited a distressed organization when he became chairman in November of '79, with its terrible record for losing money. It got worse before it got better. From 1980 to 1984, we had to have nearly a military-commando mentality to exist because we were going through abnormal times—technical bankruptcy, the economic equivalent of war, attacks by the media, and loss of confidence by the Wall Street types. But Lee is a man who can adapt to nearly any situation—that's why he is a 46-year survivor in the auto industry. He is a legend who has earned a place in history.

I believe Chrysler's new chairman, Bob Eaton, will be product focused, open and fair to all constituencies and will provide balanced, steady leadership with emphasis on customer satisfaction and service. I think Eaton's approach will also be focused on infrastructure and maintaining a good interface between engineering and manufacturing—the twin towers of American industry.

I see a tremendous amount of dynamic leadership still in the industry. At Chrysler it is Bob Eaton. At Ford it is Alex Trotman. Give GM's Jack Smith a chance. My friend Nakane-san is doing an excellent job at Mitsubishi as are the rising stars at BMW like their product development Vorstand leader, Dr. Wolfgang Reitzle, and manufacturing Vorstand leader Bernd Pischetsrieder. At Volkswagen, it is the new strong willed Chairman Dr. Ferdinand Piëch. Honda's talented Irimajiri-san could resurface. Time will tell. Whether Pacific Basin, North America, or Europe, there will continue to be an ample supply of dynamic automotive leadership.

I have every confidence that the American auto industry has high-quality, dynamic leadership and will successfully adapt and adjust to the '90s. The rest of the world will do the same. The U.S. auto industry proved in the most crucial decade since WW II, the '80s, that America

244

could come back and regain its manufacturing leadership by making the best cars and trucks.

We met Japan, Inc. head on. Today, we can move even more rapidly than we did in those crisis years because the infrastructure and system are now in place; it's developed, balanced, far more mature, and has great momentum.

Sincere Hopes

Many Americans think manufacturing is about as exciting as peeling an orange or as logical to pursue for a career as drinking ditch water when there's nothing else left to quench your thirst. This book should change that perception and convey the emotional highs I derived from extraordinary manufacturing successes, such as the introduction of the nearly perfect minivan to seeing the *new beginnings* of the all new inner-city Jefferson North assembly plant in Detroit. In this book, I revealed the true nature of the manufacturing calling: the discipline required, the full-

---

Gridiron Fundamentals

Manufacturing has a great deal in common with an old-fashioned tackle football game. One lesson football taught me is that the game is won or lost on three critical issues.

The Game Plan. Take full advantage of the strengths of the team, yet be flexible enough to react to the opponent's latest moves. Do you have a game plan? Is it a winner? These are issues manufacturing people must consider daily.

Leadership and Teamwork. On the football field, leadership comes from the coach, team captains, and quarterback, and occasionally a wild-eyed linebacker. Without leadership, the game is lost before the kickoff. Most of us can accomplish feats beyond our normal ability if we have the right leaders.

Skill, Determination, Dedication, Commitment. As Notre Dame football coach Lou Holtz advises new players: "If you are not committed, you are only taking up space and, in football, taking up space means warming the bench."

The globally competitive manufacturing game is the Super Bowl, Rose Bowl, and Olympic gold-medal competition rolled into one. The stakes run from billions in profit or loss to survival or bankruptcy. One man's poison is another man's passion. Manufacturing is my passion.

---

immersion commitment, the essential knowledge, the long days, nights, weekends, years, and even decades that are necessary to total success.

America's most prestigious business bible, *The Wall Street Journal*, told Chrysler to just die with dignity. Instead, we saved 100,000 direct jobs at Chrysler, and 500,000-plus support jobs in North America. That's world league ball. We never confused effort with results: we won the game.

The singular leader throughout all this was Lee Iacocca. Only four of his appointed officers contributed for more than 10 years. I am extremely proud to be one of those four.

I believe that parallels exist between the games of manufacturing and football—the object is to win. The conflict, bonding of teamwork, long and tedious preparation, result in personal satisfaction, fulfillment, even wild joy when it all comes together in the victory of corporate independence, expansion, profitability, and global leadership.

Modern manufacturing is highly complex and will require constant experimentation and evolution, none of which can happen without an adequate level of consistent, up-front investment, followed by precision maintenance. Automation does not run itself.

I hope you agree with me on the importance of our school system in preparing future manufacturing leaders and workers, as well as the role our society plays in fostering a value system that attracts the brightest and best to manufacturing. We desperately need manufacturing education from grammar school through graduate school. We need money and moral support to nurture education to levels still only envisioned. And we need industrial training that never ceases—training that is practical and based on solid educational principles. This is an area where every one of us can contribute. I feel I made a powerful difference. I hope you too are convinced you can make a difference.

Manufacturing must have well trained, well educated, highly motivated people led by enlightened managers, people whose ideas are heard and translated into thousands of little improvements that accumulate every day and eventually result in the perfect products for which we all strive. Such people are empowered.

Most of all, I hope you now know the world is not waiting for us to do what we need to do. We must seize control of our destiny and re-establish global leadership, independence, and pride in American manufacturing. Do we still have within us the spirit that inspired our forebears to transform a wild continent into the leading country on Earth?

World competition is accelerating—it's moving like white lightning! Our foreign competitors spend more time in the classroom and on the job than we do in the United States. They also invest more in manufacturing while we coast along as if nothing was happening, as if nothing changed since our post-World War II boom years when we set the standards for the world. Remember, there is only one way to coast, and that's downhill.

Don't be passive—have passion, whatever your role. Manufacturing needs your support, your participation, and your children's respect. Teach them today that our lives and livelihoods depend on it. *The value-added sectors of the economy call for mining it, growing it, or making it.* I prefer to make it!

If you improve your quality, improve your productivity, improve your flexibility, improve your employee training, improve your profitability, and broaden your base from North America to the world—then I guess you have a track record that will withstand the test of time. Book it! I did with *Passion for Manufacturing*.

Chrysler Facilities

I have referenced many Chrysler facilities in this book. They provide examples in the included discussion and are listed below and on the following pages.

Plant	Function	Comment
1. Ajax Trim	Trim production	Produces soft trim, seat covers, and door trim.
2. Bramalea Assembly	Assembly	Builds the new LH. Plant purchased from American Motors.
3. Canadian Fabrication	Trim production	Produces soft trim, seat covers, and door trim.
4. Detroit Axle	Axle production	Forging, machining, and assembly of axles.
5. Etobicoke Casting	Casting	Produces aluminum and metal castings.
6. Jefferson North	Assembly	Newest plant, opened in 1992. Builds Jeep Grand Cherokee and Grand Wagoneer.
7. Mound Road Engine	Engine production	Six-cylinder and V-8, and V-10 engines production.
8. New Mack Avenue	Assembly	Builds the Dodge Viper.
9. Pillette Road Assembly	Assembly	Builds full size vans and wagons.
10. Sandusky Vinyl Products	Vinyl products	Produces sheet and roll vinyl.
11. Sterling Heights Assembly	Assembly	Purchased from VW. Builds Sundance and Shadow models.
12. Sterling Stamping	Stamping	Conventional presses, transfer presses as well as synchronized stamping lines. Located near Sterling Heights Assembly.
13. Toledo Assembly	Assembly	Purchased in 1987 from American Motors. Builds Jeep Wrangler and Cherokee.
14. Toledo Machining	Machining	Engine, transmission and brake components, and torque converters.
15. Trenton Engine	Engine production	Produces four and six-cylinder engines.
16. Twinsburg Stamping	Stamping	No strikes since 1983 after averaging a strike each year from 1959 to 1983. Produces stampings and subassemblies.
17. Warren Truck/ Dodge City	Assembly	Assembles full-size and mid-size trucks. Will build the new T300 full-size pickup in 1994.

Plant	Function	Comment
18. Warren Stamping	Stamping	Conventional presses, transfer presses, synchronous-press lines. Supports Detroit-area plants.
19. Windsor Assembly	Assembly	First minivan plant. Produces minivans today.
20. Chrysler Technology Center	Design, engineering, procurement supply, manufacturing process, vehicle pilot assembly, vehicle testing, and corporate training.	This facility opened in 1991 and will be completed in 1994. Brings design engineering, supply, and manufacturing together under one roof.
21. Featherstone Road Engineering	Engineering	Leads product development team for the large car platform.
22. Pilot Operations	Vehicle assembly	Advanced production engineering, systems development, and vehicle assembly (pilot).
23. Outer Drive Manufacturing Technical Center	Tool and die	This is a former stamping plant converted to a Manufacturing Technical Center. Soon to be known as Mt. Elliott Tool and Die.
24. Sterling Heights Vehicle Test Center	Testing	Vehicle emission surveillance and driveability evaluation programs.
25. Liberty and Technical Affairs	Research and testing	Identifies new processes, vehicle components, and systems.

Plant	Function	Comment
1. Beaver Dam Products	Chassis production	Packaged power plants; sequenced modular assembly.
2. Belvidere Assembly	Assembly	Never closed, sold, or mothballed. Home of new 1994 PL small car.
3. Indianapolis Foundry	Foundry	Only remaining grey iron foundry in Chrysler.
4. Kenosha Engine	Engine production	Four-cylinder, six-cylinder, and V-8 engines produced.
5. Kokomo Casting	Casting	Produces aluminum die castings. Training and worker attitude turned this plant around.
6. Kokomo Transmission	Transmission production	Produces automatic transmissions and transaxles.
7. New Castle Machining and Forge	Machining and forging	Produces chassis and suspension components. Training and worker attitude turned this plant around.
8. Newark Assembly	Assembly	Original K-car production done at this plant. Will be second plant for LH production.
9. St. Louis I	Assembly	Original home of the LeBaron convertible production (1982). Presently idle.
10. St. Louis II	Assembly	MOA put this plant back in operation. Plant builds long-wheel-base minivans.

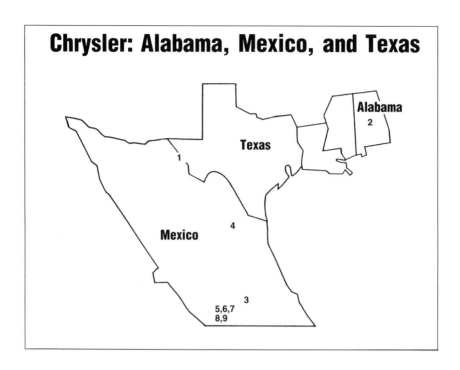

Chrysler: Alabama, Mexico, and Texas

Plant	Function	Comment
1. El Paso-Juarez	Wire harness	Wire harness components and assembly.
2. Huntsville	Electronic components	Builds radios, electronic systems, and controls.
3. Lago Alberto Assembly	Assembly	Pickup trucks and sports utility vehicles for the U.S., Mexico, and other markets.
4. Saltillo Engine	Engine production	Produces four-cylinder engines.
5. Toluca Car Assembly	Assembly	Automobile assembly for the U.S., Mexico, and other markets.
6. Toluca Conversion	Assembly	Conversion facility for convertibles.
7. Toluca Crossmember	Crossmember production	Produces parts for several car and truck models.
8. Toluca Engine	Engine production	Produces six- and eight-cylinder engines.
9. Toluca Transmission	Transmission production	Produces transmissions for front-wheel-drive cars.

GLOSSARY

CONSCIOUSNESS OF MANUFACTURING

During my manufacturing career, I found that providing definitions of terms allowed staff and me to better communicate with the plant workers, other corporate departments, and among ourselves.

Listed on the following pages are some of the terms manufacturing professionals should be using in their day-to-day functions. The terms present a consciousness of manufacturing. This list will also further define terms used in the pages of *Passion for Manufacturing*.

ABET. See: Accreditation Board for Engineering and Technology.

Acceleration. An employee learning period during which the number of units to be assembled for a new product is gradually increased until reaching its scheduled production line rate.

Accreditation Board for Engineering and Technology. Group responsible for monitoring, evaluating, and certifying the quality of engineering and engineering-related education in colleges and universities in the United States. ABET develops accreditation policies and criteria and conducts programs of evaluation.

Accumulator(s). Facility(s) in the assembly process in which units are collected to ensure a uniform flow and adequate volume at the proper mix through the next process.

Actual Effective Point. A specific point in time which identifies a change in material or process, usually noted by a VIN and/or date.

Advance Manufacturing Operations. Corporate organization to perform all manufacturing planning as it relates to staffing, product, process, tooling, facilities, investment, and method of operation.

Advance Shipping Notice. Written communication of material shipped from supplier.

AGV. See: Automated guided vehicle.

APEI. See: Assembly Plant End Items.

Approved Parts Pilot. Pilot phase prior to start of production.

Assembly plant end items. Counting of individual parts received in an assembly plant to build a finished vehicle. Production parts only are counted.

Aufsichstrat. German term for Board of Supervisors. Typically made up of 50% management members and 50% union members.

Automated guided vehicle. Material handling method for productivity improvement. An automated guided vehicle is a programmed carrier which transports goods from point to point.

Automatic tip dressing. A system of weld tip dressing during production at regular intervals. A mechanical method for improving productivity and lowering cost by improving machine welder performance and quality.

Automation. An apparatus, process, or system operating automatically with little or no human intervention.

Back-To-Basics. Training program reviewing the fundamentals of a technology or academic subject to improve employee understanding and performance.

Base coat. Primary color on a vehicle prior to receiving a high-gloss finish.

Benchmarking. A system of rating your own practices, processes, and products against the best, on a worldwide basis. Benchmarking can include products in other industries.

Bill of material. A listing of raw materials, subassemblies, and parts that make up a parent assembly.

Black box. An assembly produced by an outside vendor to OEM's specifications.

Block painting. Method by which a sequence of product is painted the same color to improve quality and productivity and to reduce material usage and expense; also reduces volatile organic compound (VOC) emissions.

Body-in-white. A vehicle body before paint is applied. It is the complete structure of welded and bolted sheet metal as it comes out of the body shop.

BOM. See: Bill of material.

BSR. See: Buzz, Squeak, Rattle.

Built-up for export. Products fully assembled for export from the country of origin.

Business plan. Documented plan that states corporate objectives and the proposed means to achieve those objectives.

Buzz, Squeak, Rattle. Noise-based quality concern in the automobile business. Primary contributor to customer dissatisfaction.

C1. See: Complete pilot phase 1.

CAD. See: Computer-aided design.

CAE. See: Computer-aided engineering.

CAM. See: Computer-aided manufacturing.

Capacity. Quantity capable of being produced.

Capacity planning volumes. Maximum facility production on a straight time and overtime basis for finished products; peak demand requirements for inside/outside supplied parts.

Capital plan. Dollar investments required to support new product/ facility actions as part of the business plan.

Cardboard free. Elimination of the use of cardboard as a means to store or ship material. Cardboard free environments improve quality and plant cleanliness.

Carry over. Repeat of products between model years.

Casting. The pouring of molten metal into a mold.

Changeover. Time between two model years' production periods or time necessary to launch a new product.

CIM. See: Computer-integrated manufacturing.

Clear coat. Application of high-gloss finish on top of the primary color of the product.

Clustering. Refers to the timing and sequencing of product launches. Two or more launches in a measured time frame.

CMM. See: Coordinate measuring machine.

CNC. See: Computer numerical control.

Collapsible containers. Containers made of materials that fold together. Their use requires less factory space and facilitates return of empty containers.

Complete pilot phase 1. Final phase of pilot programs in the automobile business occurring approximately 22 weeks before volume production. A complete unit build is needed at C1. C1 may occur at both pilot operations and the assembly plant.

Complexity. The number of parts and variety of parts required to build a vehicle; differences in processing or work content for two or more vehicles in the same plant. Often referred to as the number of ways or permutations available to build a given product.

Composite. A material created by combining two or more materials to specific characteristics and properties. The materials combined are usually a reinforcing element—such as fabric, fibers, or filaments—and a compatible resin binder (or matrix).

Computer-aided design. The use of computers in designing products. The term "Computer-aided design," or CAD, is frequently linked with CAM (computer-aided manufacturing), which indicates the typical use of CAD as a front-end for the design of manufactured products.

Computer-aided engineering. The practice of using the computer to assist in engineering design, development, calculations, testing, and experimentation.

Computer-aided manufacturing. CAM is the translation of a design into information which an automated assembly machine or numerically controlled machine can use as input.

Computer-integrated manufacturing. A system providing computer assistance to all business functions within a manufacturing enterprise from product design to product shipment.

Computer numerical control. A numerical control system with a dedicated stored-program performing some (or all) of the basic NC functions. These functions control programs stored in the computers.

Concurrent engineering. The integration of design, manufacturing, and support processes. Concurrent engineering typically provides early manufacturing input into the design process.

Containers. Method by which material is shipped, received, or handled in bulk quantity; normally returnable and not disposable.

Containment. Vehicles held prior to shipment to measure quality. Normally occurs at the start of a model year.

Coordinate measuring machine. A machine capable of measuring three-dimensional geometry and making many different measurements in a short period of time. CMMs provide digital readout of the position of a movable machine member for display, computer calculations of geometric measurement routines, or computer-controlled positioning of the machine member.

Cost of non-conformance. Expense for not meeting quality requirements. This includes rework, sort, scrap, and repair.

Cost of quality. Activities necessary to achieve quality results (meet requirements).

C_p; Process capability. Capability index that compares process variation to design specifications as a measurement of SPC.

C_{pk}; Process Capability Index. Capability index that compares both process variation and process location to design specifications as a measurement of SPC.

CPV. See: Capacity planning volumes.

Critical line shortages. The lack of parts at the point of assembly which results in a manufacturing operation being missed or interrupted.

Curves. Refers to graphics or charts that represent volumes attained during production acceleration.

Customer satisfaction index. Measurement of field service warranty based on feedback from customers or product defects.

Defect-free. Pertains to parts or products that meet quality requirements.

Devil is in the detail. An old-time piece of philosophy with great implications for manufacturing quality. Positive performance requires knowing the details of a plan, proposal, program, etc.

Dimensional. A statement of accuracy related to a part's dimensions as required by a print.

Dip coating. A method of applying paint by fully immersing a product in a tank of liquid coating materials, then withdrawing it, and allowing it to drain and dry.

Dok-Lok. Safety mechanism by which a tractor/trailer is secured in position for unloading at a dock.

Doors-off assembly. Assembly of an automobile with doors removed from the vehicle after the paint process. Under "doors-off assembly," the doors of the vehicle are placed on the vehicle as a final assembly step, thus increasing worker access to the vehicle body as it moves down the assembly line.

Downtime. Any period of time during which products are not produced; a time necessary for conversion of a facility due to new tooling, equipment, process and/or product; may also be caused by slow product sales or emergencies.

E and O. See: Excess and Obsolete.

E-Coat. Electrophoretic deposition of primary coating to inhibit rust and corrosion.

Electrostatic spraying. A paint application system in which paint droplets or powder particles are charged electrically so they will attract to a grounded workpiece. Improves deposition efficiency and wrap-around result.

Employee involvement. Management philosophy and follow-up programs designed to bring the employee into the decision-making process.

Enablers. Written means of accomplishing a desired result.

Engineering action letter. Written notification (usually a letter or memo) of a pending change.

Ergonomics. The work atmosphere, tools, training, climate, attitude, or overall environment contributing to an employee performing at peak efficiency and comfort.

Excess and Obsolete. Parts which are not used from one model year or product to the next.

Factory Information System. Computerized feedback of the efficiency and operation of tooling and equipment.

Failure Mode and Effects Analysis. Study (analysis) of detail variables to identify potential for failure.

Feasibility. Verification of the manufacturability of a product within process capabilities and that the product will meet desired quality and efficiency objectives.

50/20 Program. Verification of all equipment used in manufacturing to ensure vendor conformance to requirements; 50 hours on all robots and 20 hours on all machinery and equipment; continuous run time.

First time through. Measurement to determine quality of operations performed correctly on the first occasion.

FIS. See: Factory Information System.

Fit and finish. Visual assessment of quality on a finished vehicle. Assessment is based on measurements of aligning parts and the finish coat of the product.

Flat-tops. Floor-mounted conveyors moving products during manufacturing process.

Flexible manufacturing system. One machine or multiple machines integrated by an automated material handling system whose operation is managed by a computerized control system. A flexible manufacturing system can be configured by computer control to manufacture various products. The term might also be used for assembly systems capable of building more than one product model.

FMEA. See: Failure Mode and Effects Analysis.

FMS. See: Flexible manufacturing system.

Foreign trade zone. A designated area in the United States in which goods from foreign countries can be received, duty-free, for alteration, processing, or warehousing, and then shipped out again.

Gateline. A system by which vehicles are scheduled for production.

Graphics. Engineering-aided descriptions pictorially indicating the relationship of specific parts or subassemblies. Graphics provide operational aids to assembly instruction.

High-voltage electrostatic. Spray equipment in the paint shop using more than 80,000 volts of electrostatic charge on a product to get better transfer efficiency.

Homologation. Modification of products to allow marketing in a country outside of the country where the product is built.

ILS. See: In-line sequencing.

Inch-line. Refers to sheet metal panels showing exact dimensions and specifications. Verification of surface relationship between mating panels (scribed panels).

Initial sample and inspection report. Dimensional inspection results based on a sample of the first batch of a product.

Initial sample laboratory report. Climatic and functional inspection results based on a sample of the first batch of a product.

In-line sequencing. A continuous build, assembly method. Under this method, a product is held in its assembly sequence until full assembly is completed. Buffer stock and repair bays in the assembly process are eliminated.

Interim parts process. A manufacturing process not fully meeting production process conformance and requirements.

Inverted power and free conveyors. Automated conveyor method to move products during a manufacturing process.

JIT See: Just-In-Time.

Job #1. The first finished product produced.

Just-In-Time. A system by which materials are received to coincide with their need and use in the production process; a method by which inventory and carrying costs of material are reduced.

Kirksite. A temporary tool used only for a low-production quantity of specific parts.

Lab approval. A part tested in a laboratory for compliance to design specifications.

Laser optic machine vision. Automated gaging and inspection system using a laser beam and machine vision technology.

Launch. A date to indicate start of production of a new operation or process, line rate change, shift pattern, or product mix change.

Launch windows. Time period in which the start of production can be scheduled.

LBOM. See: Line Balance Optimization Model.

Levelators. Mechanism by which tractor/trailers are raised or lowered to the unloading dock height to facilitate product unloading.

Liberty. Advance manufacturing process, product, and facility development.

Line Balance Optimization Model. Optimum manufacturing schedule based on all facility, product, and manning limitations.

LOA. See: Loss of authorization.

Long-range plan. A sequence of events for new or modified products planned in a five-year (or longer) period.

Loss of authorization. Straight time quantity of production which is lost during a specified period.

Low voltage electrostatic. Spray equipment in the paint shop that uses between 30-60,000 volts of electrostatic charge on the product to get better transfer efficiency.

Machinery. Equipment for producing an object or obtaining some other desired result. Machinery can be computer-controlled or be a high-technology "role player" such as a laser, a robot, or a transfer press.

Major/Minor. The magnitude of a launch. Launch magnitude usually depends on the number of parts in a product, dollar investment, the number of people involved, the number of facilities, tools, and the potential product market.

Management deviation. An agreed-upon temporary exception to quality requirements.

Management Information System. An information feedback system in which data is recorded and processed for use by management and/or technicians in decision making.

Manpower. Number of people—both skilled and unskilled—needed to accomplish a task. Manpower should be trained and deployed with clearly specified responsibilities and precise direction in the best facilities possible.

Market share. Percentage or volume of sales attained by a company within the market it serves.

Mass relief. Method by which breaks are scheduled for the entire collective work force at one time.

Match metal. A completed body-in-white unit measured to exact design intent.

Materials. The elements or substances to be further developed into a final product. May include: steel, aluminum, rubber, cloth, glass, plastics, etc. Materials might also be data that could be worked into a more finished form. Materials should be scientifically evaluated for defect-free input and defect-free output.

Maxims. A general truth or fundamental within a corporation. Operating guidelines that facilitate the desired results.

Methods. The specified way things get done. Means of providing cost efficient, time sensitive, quality-driven solutions to basic problems.

MIS. Management Information System.

Mix. Variation of different products scheduled to production.

MOA. See: Modern Operating Agreement.

Modern Operating Agreement. A cooperative and participative agreement between management and union. A Modern Operating Agreement provides management with more flexibility in work rules and workers with more input through team concepts as well as increased pay for knowledge as the employee increases job skills.

Modular. Complete subassemblies that require no further labor content prior to installation in a vehicle assembly process.

Modular framing station. Equipment that frames a singular product.

Months in-service. Length of time after a product has been used for its intended purpose by the customer.

Multiplex wiring. Multiple-purpose electrical harnesses.

Occupational Safety and Health Administration. A U.S. government agency created by the Occupational Safety and Health Act of 1970. OSHA sets standards and creates regulations to provide for worker safety and health.

Odd box. Outside design and development of an assembly to a customer-company's quality requirements.

Operating performance. Programs of measurement of planned safety, quality, and production objectives; daily, weekly, monthly, annually.

Operation description sheets. A written, detailed procedure for each operation of production.

OSHA. See: Occupational Safety and Health Administration.

Overspeed. A planned production factor at which conveyor line speed is set to ensure the scheduled daily build rate.

P1; Phase 1. The first phase of piloting a new vehicle through body-in-white; done at Pilot Operations Plant.

P2; Phase 2. The second phase of piloting a new vehicle through paint and major ornamentation and interior parts that fit/mate to sheet metal; done at pilot operations.

P-Approvals. The approval of a part with a minor exception in dimensional specifications but is sufficient for pilot project application.

Performance feedback system. Computerized information gathering to measure plant and quality results. Performance Feedback Systems use computer terminals throughout the factory to report on manufacturing progress and to troubleshoot.

Perimeter unloading. Facility design whereby material deliveries and unloading can be done near the usage location.

Permutations. The variety of ways a vehicle can be assembled; a compounding of build variations; applicable to color, options, trim, power train, and chassis.

Phosphate system. Application of zinc/phosphate material coating applied to completed body-in-white to increase the adhesion of E-Coat and subsequent paint processes.

PLC. See: Programmable logic controller.

Power and free conveyors. A conveyor system using a series of chain sections and trolleys to transport parts or subassemblies. In this system, a chain powers (or moves) a free-standing trolley from below. The trolley typically has four wheels.

PQI. See: Product Quality Improvement.

Pre-production and launch. A manufacturing expense category pertaining to a new model year; considers variables such as preparation, training, and execution of a launch.

Pre-volume production. Final phase of piloting a new vehicle prior to launch, normally occurs at six weeks before volume production.

Price of non-conformance. Expense for not meeting quality requirements, including: rework, sort, scrap, and repair.

Proactive. Decisions made during planning to prevent problems.

Process driven design. The basic understanding of current and future manufacturing feasibility that serves as a foundation for future product decisions. Process driven design requires design and manufacturing engineers to work together to develop the product. Concurrent engineering.

Productivity. Output realized for monies, time, and resources expended.

Product Quality Improvement. At Chrysler, a joint management and union program by which product quality was improved.

Programmable logic controller. A solid-state industrial control system with a memory set to operate in a specific manner to store instructions implementing functions such as I/O control logic, counting, and data manipulation.

PVP. See: Pre-volume production.

QIP. See: Quality improvement process.

Quality. First and foremost corporate objective; defined as meeting customer requirements or defect-free products.

Quality improvement process. A mindset or culture on the part of the employees and management to improve quality performance of a company.

Radiant zone. The method and area in an oven for curing a painted product.

Reactive decision. A decision made after a problem is identified. This management style is concerned with correction rather than prevention.

Reliability standards. Measurement of quality based on customer perception of how the product works over a given period of time. Usually based on customer satisfaction surveys.

Retrofit. Modification of a machine originally operated by manual or tracer control to one that operates through automation, typically numerical control.

Rework. Corrective action involving re-processing a part or assembly to meet quality standards.

Robogate. Machinery that frames or initially welds together a vehicle. Robogate is often applied to an indexing of gates for more than one body style.

Robot. A programmable multifunction manipulator designed to move materials, parts, tools, or specialized devices through variable programmed motions for performance of a variety of tasks.

Safety lock-out. Features on equipment to prevent personal injury.

Schedule. Production plan.

Scroll. A document outlining in detail all material, staffing, and process variables in an assembly system.

Sequenced Parts Delivery. Method of improving material delivery. Material arrives exactly when needed.

Self-help. Internal measures enacted to improve safety, quality, and efficiency. Self-help usually involves little or no help (but support) from corporate officials. Self-help concepts are usually developed in a local work unit with a ''grass roots'' approach.

SIMFLEX. See: Simplified Flexible Manufacturing System.

Simplified Flexible Manufacturing System. At Chrysler, machinery that was easily adaptable to perform more than one manufacturing operation.

Soft tool. Materials (parts) produced from tools which are not approved for production.

SPC. See: Statistical process control.

Special means. Parts not considered sufficient in quality or volume to support production. May also refer to cost per piece (or part) that is higher than the normal production price.

SRPC. See: Supplier Request for Product Change.

Standards. Written or published requirements.

Start of production. Refers to the timing of launching a new product/model.

Statistical process control. Quality assurance method using performance data to help identify the fundamental product and process faults that lead to the production of defective materials. Statistical process control helps to formulate corrective actions and prevent defective materials. Statistical process control uses both basic probability laws and statistical methods in developing models for the behavior of the variations witnessed in the quality of manufactured goods as they are produced.

Stereolithography. A rapid prototyping device used to create three-dimensional plastic parts from CAE/CAD data. Stereolithography rapid prototyping combines four technologies: lasers, optical scanning, photopolymer chemistry, and computer software.

Straight time. Normal production hours/day.

Subassembly. Two or more parts combined into one larger assembly. This larger assembly may then be considered a component part of a larger product on the final product itself.

Supplier quality assurance. Measurement and verification of outside vendor supplied parts and process.

Supplier Request for Product Change. Written request for a change in part material or in the dimension on a print.

Synthetic coolant. A coolant containing no petroleum oil. As the name implies, a coolant cools parts as they are machined, flushes particles from the arc gap, and forms a barrier between the electrode and workpiece.

System fill. Refers to the methods by which a production system is loaded (filled) with product.

Tag relief. Individual or operational resting during production that requires employment of additional manpower as replacements to continue operational performance of the system during the individual's break time.

Target pricing. A cost estimation method whereby the vendor and the manufacturer determine cost categories and the profit margin, estimate the cost plus profit, and contract to work together on this basis. Payments begin early and continue through the process. There is usually a financial incentive built into the contract if the project is completed in the agreed-upon time or ahead of time, or below projected cost. Competitive bidding is usually precluded under target pricing.

Targets. Goals; objectives.

TCF. See: Trim, Chassis and Final.

Temporary tools. Tools not considered of sufficient quality and volume to support full production. Tools that will need to be replaced.

Town-Hall meetings. Method of communication. The meeting brings together the various shifts of employees to meet with management.

Training. Educational programs to direct the professional growth of company employees.

Transfer press. A metal forming press with an integral mechanism for transfer and control of the workpiece with several operations.

Trim, Chassis and Final. Refers to predominant portion of vehicle assembly process; after body framing and paint.

Truncate. Rationalization involved in the reduction of suppliers, production parts, tooling and/or equipment.

VIN. Vehicle Identification Number.

Visual management. The practice of storing material only to a height that allows both workers and management to see across the plant floor. Improves work environment.

VOC. See: Volatile organic compounds.

Volatile organic compounds. Organic compounds participating in atmospheric photochemical reactions as designated by the Environmental Protection Agency.

Vorstand. German term for Board of Management. It is the equivalent to the Executive Committee, consisting of the CEO and key vice presidents or company officers.

WBVP. See: Weeks Before Volume Production.

Weeks Before Volume Production. Time span before production deadline.

Weld electrode frequency. The number of times weld tips must be replaced to meet quality requirements.

INDEX